You Were Never in

CHICAGO

D0963021

CHICAGO VISIONS AND REVISIONS

Edited by Carlo Rotella, Bill Savage,
Carl Smith, and Robert B. Stepto

You Were Never in CHICAGO

NEIL STEINBERG

The University of Chicago Press * CHICAGO AND LONDON

The University of Chicago Press, Chicago 60637
The University of Chicago Press, Ltd., London
© 2013 by Neil Steinberg
All rights reserved. Published 2013.
Paperback edition 2013
Printed in the United States of America

22 21 20 19 18 17 16 15 14 13   4 5 6 7 8

ISBN-13: 978-0-226-77205-9 (cloth)
ISBN-13: 978-0-226-10415-7 (paperback)
ISBN-13: 978-0-226-92427-4 (e-book)
DOI: 10.7208/chicago/9780226924274.001.0001

Library of Congress Cataloging-in-Publication Data

Steinberg, Neil.
    You were never in Chicago / Neil Steinberg.
        pages. cm. — (Chicago visions and revisions)
    ISBN-13: 978-0-226-77205-9 (cloth : alk. paper)
    ISBN-10: 0-226-77205-5 (cloth : alk. paper)
    ISBN-13: 978-0-226-92427-4 (e-book)
    ISBN-10: 0-226-92427-0 (e-book)   1. Steinberg, Neil.   2. Chicago (Ill.)—
Miscellanea.   I. Title.   II. Series: Chicago visions + revisions
    PS3569.T37548Z46 2013
    818'.5403—dc23
    [B]

                                                            2012019395

FOR EDIE

Because being here is much
and because all this that's here
so fleetingly
seems to require us and
strangely concerns us—
us, the most fleeting of all.

RAINER MARIA RILKE

CONTENTS

1

Manus manum lavat

A BATON TWIRLS, ITS white rubber tips blurring with speed. The dimpled chrome shaft catches sunlight, flashes, sparkling as it is tossed high into the air, pauses, falls, is caught, spun, flipped around the back, then smoothly grabbed and sent spinning up again.

The baton twirler is not part of a marching band, not on some suburban high school football field, but walking down the center of Broadway on a beautiful summer afternoon in Chicago at the start of a new century. Music throbs; the crowd jamming the sidewalk waves and cheers.

This is the last Sunday in June and the last day we are living in the city of Chicago for the foreseeable future. Maybe forever. Tomorrow the big red truck from Midwest Movers will come and burly men will muscle everything we own down into the street and out to the suburbs.

"If I didn't take my wife's lead," I sheepishly explain to friends who ask how we can leave the city, "I'd still be a single guy living in a one-bedroom apartment in Oak Park."

Today she takes my lead. Though there is much to be done, many possessions still lurking deep within closets, stragglers from the herd, waiting to be flushed from their hiding places and penned in brown cardboard boxes, my wife agrees to take a break for a few minutes and walk over to the thirty-first annual Gay Pride Parade. One last look as residents living a block off the route. To soak in the color and excitement we are abandoning by moving away. Of course we'll be back to watch the parade again, I tell myself, certainly we'll be back, though as tourists, visitors in for a few hours from suburbia.

The festive throng is enormous, filling the space between building and curb. Muscular men, their shirts stripped off, displaying tribal tattoos of Tibetan mandalas, Greek phrases, bands of thorns, "HIV +." Women in cutoffs and bikini tops. Kids with painted faces and balloons tied to their strollers.

We wander the street. Our own boys, three and four, have been deposited at their grandparents' house, to get them out of the way during the chaos of the move. Heading up Broadway, we approach the four-story brick Nettelhorst Elementary School, the main reason we're leaving.

"Why not just send them to kindergarten?" I had implored my wife. "Give it a try. How bad could it be?" Edie replied by calmly pulling the stats: by second grade, 92 percent of the Nettelhorst kids have reading scores below state average. That's how bad.

Music whumps from passing floats. Honorees in convertibles roll slowly by, beaming and waving. The year before, I took our older son Ross, then three, to the parade, by accident. I was heading to the hardware store to buy a plunger and brought him along for company, forgetting that a quarter million people had gathered at the end of our block.

Undeterred—and not realizing that the hardware store would be closed for the parade—I swept him up in my arms and we pushed forward, joining the onlookers. Ross gazed around at the mustachioed leather boys, the bodybuilders in tiny Speedo bathing suits, the harlequins on stilts, the flamboyant drag queens wobbling under giant feathered Mardi Gras headpieces, the bannered vintage convertibles with that year's crop of dignitaries perched atop back seats, where they could be better seen by the crowd. His eyes widened, he pointed a quivering finger and said, "Daddy, those men . . . they're not wearing seatbelts! It isn't safe!"

I loved that. My son was so worked up by the fact that people riding in cars weren't wearing seatbelts—the life-or-death importance of which had been drummed into him—he wouldn't let the matter drop until we reported the emergency to a cop holding back the onlookers, who shot us a single glance of puzzled annoyance before returning to his duties.

The rest of the spectacle didn't strike Ross as unusual.

The Chicago Pride Parade began in 1970 as a protest march to commemorate the first anniversary of the riot of gay patrons at New York's

Stonewall Inn. Marching in the parade in its early years was a radical, risky act, a bold declaration of "We're here too!" A flaunting in the street of something many feared to tell their friends, coworkers, even their families. You could lose your job.

No more. Thirty years later automobile manufacturers have floats. Banks have floats. The Chicago Transit Authority has a float, with employees playing in a band, mimicking the *Partridge Family* TV show. Former mayor Jane Byrne became the first major politician to march in the parade in 1983 and others followed, including Richard M. Daley, the first sitting mayor in the parade, which eventually approached the level of the St. Patrick's Day Parade as a political requirement. One-time gubernatorial candidate Dawn Clark Netsch appears every year, in a convertible decorated with a banner declaring, "I'M NOT RUNNING FOR ANYTHING."

And Cook County treasurer Maria Pappas, twirling a baton.

Catching sight of her brings me unexpected joy. There she is, tall, trim, dark-haired, fetching in a spaghetti-strap tank top, twirling away. I feel a burst of raw happiness so unusual that I instantly begin to pick it apart and analyze it.

Her baton is not news. The former majorette has twirled in seven out of the last eight pride parades. I've seen Pappas do it before. But for some reason, her act never struck me the way it does now.

Maybe because of the lovely summer day. Maybe because of nostalgia— we're leaving the city and decamping to the suburbs tomorrow. Not just to the suburbs, but to Northbrook, a particularly suburban suburb, with neither the moneyed grace of Wilmette or Winnetka, nor the blue-collar pride of Niles or Des Plaines. A neutered nowhere, arrived at through a tactical retreat inspired by the crummy city schools and, to be honest, the city itself. The boys need to go through three locked doors—our second floor apartment door plus two heavy outer security doors—to reach the street, to descend to the muddy, dog-piss-murdered patch of grass between the sidewalk and the curb, there to play for a few closely watched minutes beneath the hulking, black-barked, hacked-up trees outside our place on Pine Grove Avenue, sidestepping bottle caps, petrified dog turds, and broken glass. They can't go alone. They have to get an adult to go with them. So the boys tend not to bother going outside; it's easier just to ride their Big Wheels around the dining room table. Around and around and around. Like rats in a cage. Is that any way to grow up?

Pappas represents, to me, a glimpse of the vanished idiosyncratic glory of the city, the colorful past which always seems to be disappearing over the horizon, if not utterly lost already. The carnation-wearers, the bamboo-cane leaners, the nudge-and-winkers, the organ-grinders, the First Ward Ball revelers, in grand procession headed by Bathhouse John Coughlin, proudly leading his "harlots and hopheads, his coneroos and fancy-men, his dips and hipsters and heavy-hipted madams" to use Nelson Algren's piquant description, "coneroo" being slang for a con man.

That city, that world, is gone—or so the common wisdom goes—replaced by the dull, packaged, homogenized present, our tepid moment of compromised mediocrity. The funny thing is, people always feel that way—pick whatever era in history seems most exciting, most distinctive, real and alive, then examine that period closely; you will find that Chicagoans of the time were also nostalgic, also troubled by what they considered society's decline, also confronting a problematic present while mourning some imagined superior past. Take 1927—a giddy whirl of bathtub gin and tommy guns and flappers in sheer silk dresses doing the Charleston. Chicagoans back then were aghast at their city's criminality.

"We are known abroad as a crude, ill governed city. We are known for our ugliness," Chicago treasurer Charles S. Peterson bemoaned in December 1927, when forming a committee to bring another world's fair to Chicago—1933's Century of Progress—in an attempt to dilute the city's gangland reputation by recapturing the lost promise and excitement of the 1893 Columbian Exposition, a grab at the fading memory of innocent joys: the White City, the Ferris Wheel, and Cracker Jack.

Leap back to the 1893 world's fair, however, and Chicagoans, while certainly basking in the glow of their renewal, also despaired whether the city would prove worthy of all the attention. They worried about disease, about being up to the task of hosting multitudes, and they steeled their resolve by remembering the city's courageous, unified, and tireless response to the Great Chicago Fire. "Our first duty, gentlemen of the City Council of Chicago, is to keep the city in a healthy condition, so that when the world comes here it will not enter upon a charnel house," said mayor Carter Harrison Sr., in his inaugural address on April 17, 1893, a month before the fair opened, calling it, "the most trying period of Chicago's history, except when the besom of destruction passed over it at its mighty conflagration."

Yet at the time of the Great Fire, in October 1871, Chicagoans saw not only heroism, but also a sinful city scourged. "Fleeing before it was a crowd of blear-eyed, drunken and diseased wretches, male and female, half naked, ghastly, with painted cheeks, cursing and uttering ribald jests as they drifted along," the editor of the *Chicago Tribune* wrote to the editor of the *Cincinnati Commercial*, describing the fire. For strength, beleaguered Chicagoans recalled the difficulties of the city's founding. "The rain that helped put out the flames created pools of mud, reminding survivors of the city's swampy foundation," wrote historian Ross Miller.

But at the city's swampy foundation . . .

Charles Fenno Hoffman approached Chicago on a frigid New Year's Eve 1833, five months after Chicago had incorporated as a town, at a meeting where twelve residents voted yes and one voted no. The night before Hoffman's arrival was spent twenty miles away, east along the lakefront in "a rude cabin built of stems of the scrub pine, standing behind a sandy swell about 200 yards from shore."

The twenty-seven-year-old New Yorker lay huddled in a buffalo skin, with his saddle for a pillow, listening to experienced Chicago hands trade stories of the money to be made, of the "meanness, rapacity, and highway robbery (in cheating, stealing, and forcibly taking away) from the Indians." Hoffman felt "indignation and disgust" at the practices described, but also a certain regret.

"I should like to have been at Chicago a year ago," he told his cabin mates.

You get the picture. Hoffman hadn't even gotten to Chicago yet and was already wishing he had arrived sooner—a common sentiment in an era when real estate prices could soar by the hour. There is a tendency to denigrate the present, whatever it is, because we know so much about it, while romanticizing the past, whatever it was, because its less pleasant details grow fuzzier with each passing year, accentuating the cherished highlights even more. This impulse can be particularly acute for newcomers, who missed the great era of the day before yesterday, arriving, as they must, in the confusing, compromised swirl of today, and so can be left with a permanent sense that the party is always ending just as they show up. The party is never now.

But maybe that is not quite true, not quite yet, and here comes Maria Pappas as living proof, marching down the middle of the street. The treasurer of Cook County, a $7 billion a year enterprise, at the time, with 230 employees working like plow horses for this gal, then fifty-one, spinning her baton down Broadway. In a blink, decades pass in my mind, and I am telling my grandchildren about the year 2000, and the quirky leaders we were blessed with back then. They had gumption, like characters in a James Thurber story, the Ohio politicians fanning their soup with their hats and inveighing against any proposal to shift the clocks to Eastern Standard Time as "directly contrary to the will of the Lord God Almighty and that the supporters of the project would burn in hell." Thurber's Columbus city clerk keeps a tuba in his office. Our Cook County treasurer once nested a pair of amorous cockatoos in hers, and now lofts her baton against the perfect summer sky. Them were the days.

Man, I think, she's good. She never drops the baton, not once, not in my sight, anyway, and I watch her as she marches away down the street, doing all sorts of elaborate tricks, under her legs, behind her back, spinning, catching, flinging again. A band plays. The thousands of onlookers clap.

"Later," I write in my column in the *Chicago Sun-Times*:

> I pondered how she could do it. She doesn't care. Astounding. Not that she is indifferent, or doesn't give a damn. But she is proud of herself, the baton queen of Wheeling, West Virginia. She's good at it, and if people want to laugh behind their hands at her, if those too hidebound to imagine doing such a thing themselves want to condemn, well, screw 'em.
>
> That is liberation. Freedom from caring, too much, about what other people think of you. Wanting to be liked, to fit in, is a curse. The curse of the outsider, trying to belong. Which leads back to the irony of the parade; a celebration of difference but, on another level, an orchestrated plea to fit in, to be accepted, to overcome prejudice and wedge themselves into the mainstream by weight of numbers.
>
> Maybe I'm being gulled by a baton, by its wacky appeal. Perhaps Pappas was just another politician, sniffing out votes among the inverts, using her particular gimmick to catch the attention they all crave.
>
> But it didn't seem that way to me. Not that day. Not since. To me, the baton was a nod of solidarity to the besieged community. As if she were saying: Hey, we've all got our stone to bear. I've got this baton-twirling problem myself.

At this point Pappas and I have never met. But she likes being portrayed in the newspaper as the gutsy avatar of genuine Chicago and good-looking to boot. The day after the column runs, she phones and invites my wife and me to dinner. We accept.

* * *

Manus manum lavat—with the v in *lavat* pronounced like a w, "lawat"—is one of the first phrases taught to beginning Latin students, and it means, "One hand washes the other hand." Friends help friends. A better known Latin term for the same concept is *quid pro quo*—"this for that." It isn't on the Chicago city seal, but it might as well be. My meeting the Cook County treasurer, and our relationship over the years, which was to grow more complex and involve jobs sought and advice offered, political campaigns parsed and scandals spun, began in that moment of innocence. There was no calculation, at least not on my part. I was delighted to see her twirling a baton in the Gay Pride Parade and thought it might make an interesting subject for a column. She, a figure of occasional controversy, beset by enemies keen to paint her enthusiasm as a form of insanity, was delighted to see herself bathed in a flattering light, to recognize a friendly face in the crowd—a friendly face with a newspaper column. Pappas invited us to dinner, not at her place, wherever that may be, but at the opulent Astor Street home of her friend, the architect John Regas, a thirteen-room mansion designed in 1922 by David Adler, with an oval central staircase running its four stories. We dined on the rooftop terrace on a soft summer night.

Money tends to awe. It awed in Babylonian times and it awes today. I had never been in a kitchen with twelve-foot ceilings, and gazed at the expanse of cherry cabinets with wonder. Regas later sold the house where we had dinner—he asked $10.5 million and got $9.2 million. By entertaining my wife and me there, by serving us complex red wines and a meal made by her own hands—a proud Greek, Maria whips up a mean Greek salad, a triumph of black olives and cubes of feta cheese—the treasurer arranged for us to savor the fruits of wealth without actually stuffing money in our pockets. I doubt she thought of it that way at the time; I certainly didn't. But such is the case.

Now that we knew each other a little, I would sometimes stop by for coffee at her office in the County Building, which shares an entire block downtown with City Hall. The structure looks like a single edifice, divided down the middle, city to the west, county to the east, but they're actually two identical, mirror-image buildings, constructed at different times. The cornerstone for the County Building was laid in 1906; the cornerstone for City Hall was not set until more than three years later, after the County Building was mostly finished and occupied. Though identical, the County

Building cost 50 percent more to construct than City Hall, a reminder that while Chicago corruption gets the notoriety, the city sits within the even larger, even more corrupt Cook County.

Not that Maria and I talk about this. We swap gossip and compare complaints. She is good friends with David Radler, the Canadian multi-millionaire then running the *Sun-Times* for press lord Conrad Black. Maria is the only person I've ever met who sincerely claimed to be Radler's friend, seemingly oblivious to how improbable that sounds to someone who works for him. At first I don't quite believe her—can she be serious? She *likes* the rapacious little greedhead? The warmest emotion I can manage toward him is a sort of King Midas pity for a man who can survey the wide sweep of this glorious world and only notice the parts that are money. But she does indeed like and respect him, and wants to impress one of his minions with how efficiently her corner of county government operates.

And me? I like having somewhere new to go, someone new to talk to. I do most of the complaining, the typical reporter's whine: the paper doesn't appreciate me, the future of journalism is uncertain. She blithely suggests that I come work for her; there's always room for another county flack, always another county press release to write.

I'm flattered but not tempted. The treasurer runs a tight ship. Men must wear white shirts—blue is not allowed. Workers are discouraged from displaying photographs of their families on their desks. The treasurer's office has cameras. In an attempt to cut down on theft, Pappas has installed them everywhere: high-definition video cameras sweeping the various departments and public areas, flashing images on a giant TV monitor set upon a corner of her desk. People still steal—incredibly, even knowing the cameras are there—but now it's easier to catch them.

Though no thief, I don't want to toil in a white shirt at a bare desk under the watchful eye of those cameras, don't want to appear on that giant TV in her office, don't want to work for the treasurer, don't really want to leave the newspaper. Just having another job opportunity, however unattractive, softens the passing dissatisfactions of the day. Believing the door to be unlocked makes the cell easier to live in.

Besides, I did not struggle to this point in my life in order to write press releases for the Cook County treasurer's office. That's not why I came to Chicago.

2

"God, I am in Chicago"

THE FIRST WHITE RESIDENTS of what would become Chicago came by canoe. They settled at that particular swampy, sandy, and unwelcoming patch of land and not another because three key bodies of water come together—not quite, but very close—right here. The Chicago River, languidly feeding into Lake Michigan at the very southwest point of the Great Lakes system—as obvious a spot for a city as ever there was—and just a short distance away, the Des Plaines River, a tributary of the mighty Mississippi.

These two great water systems approach each other here because a continental divide cuts through the Chicago area. Not the east/west Rocky Mountain Continental Divide, of course, but a different, north/south partition. Ridgeland Avenue in Oak Park is so named because it roughly follows the crest where a drop of water, falling on one side, will go down the Mississippi and into the Gulf of Mexico, eventually, while a drop falling on the other will find its way over Niagara Falls, down the St. Lawrence, and into the North Atlantic.

This proximity made the future site of Chicago a portage—the strip of land where canoes are carried between one waterway and another. That's why Native Americans—the Potawatomi, the Illinois, the Huron—congregated here.

The portage is also why French explorer Louis Jolliet and his priest, Jacques Marquette, came upon the future site of Chicago in 1673, on their way to Green Bay after traveling the Mississippi in the vain hope it would lead to the Pacific Ocean, coming up the Illinois and Des Plaines rivers, then carrying their canoes a mile and half to reach the South Branch of the Chicago River. They returned to stay, wintering in 1674, because Marquette wanted to preach the gospel to the Indians here.

After the arrival of Jolliet and Marquette, Chicago remained a way station for a century. It didn't get its first permanent nonnative resident until Jean Baptiste Point duSable, a settler of Haitian descent, established a trading post at the mouth of the Chicago River in the 1780s, one of a handful who came to trap fur and trade. Between the occasional Indian war and the great European powers still exporting their conflicts to the New World, however, the fledgling United States decided it had to protect such a strategic spot. So in 1803 a wooden stockade was raised—Fort Dearborn—and manned with sixty soldiers, the westernmost extension of American military power. The Indians were married, bought off, or pushed aside, and more residents began arriving, by foot and horseback, canoe and sailing ship.

The event that sparked a hundred years of frantic growth in Chicago had nothing whatsoever to do with the city or its occupants, but occurred more than five hundred miles away: the opening of the Erie Canal in 1825.

The canal was a wonder of the age—a 363-mile artificial waterway, dug by hand, between Albany and Buffalo, New York, connecting the Atlantic Ocean with the Great Lakes for the first time, creating a westward passage that happened to terminate at Chicago, a funnel directing the world's commerce to the doorstep of a frontier outpost and offering a route for raw materials from the interior to flow back east.

The success of the Erie Canal fanned enthusiasm to continue the link, to dig a canal over Marquette's portage so that ships traveling from the east down Lake Michigan to Chicago could continue southwest to the Illinois River into the Mississippi and on to New Orleans (the Des Plaines River was in places more of a stream, and at times nearly dried up, so would not serve for commercial purposes).

To finance the Illinois & Michigan Canal, as it was called, the State of Illinois platted and sold off land in and around Chicago, shifting it from an expanse of wilderness populated mostly by Indians to a grid of rectangular lots bought by farmers and investors. Sale of the land—and the prospect of canal-borne commerce—led to frenzied land speculation, drawing even more people. Bubbles grew and popped. After Charles Fenno Hoffman had a chance to look around Chicago in January 1834, he estimated that four-fifths of the city had arrived since spring. Hot on his heels was William B. Ogden, a young New York lawyer sent in 1835 by his brother-in-law, Charles Butler, to oversee the sale of property he had bought, sight unseen. Ogden found himself knee-deep in a marsh.

"You have been guilty of the grossest folly," Ogden wrote home to Butler, who had spent $100,000 on 182 acres that a year before had sold for $20,000. "There is no such value in the land and won't be for a generation."

But despair turned out to be premature. Ogden drained the property, sold a third of it for the price that had been paid for the whole tract, and decided to stick around. He was elected Chicago's first mayor in 1837, shortly after the town was incorporated as a city, beating John Kinzie, 480 votes to 217.

Ogden personally ensured Chicago's future greatness by creating the Galena & Chicago Union Railroad. Chicago merchants initially balked at the idea of a railroad—local farmers brought their crops into town on wagons, spending money at hotels, taverns, and shops, and the worry was, with a railroad, they'd stay on the farm, send their produce by train, and their business would be lost. The businessmen refused to let a station be built within city limits. "As late as 1847 measures were being put through the legislature for the laying of plank roads, and every effort was made to evade 'the iron horse' as long as possible," wrote historian Mabel McIlvaine. (To mitigate the shortsightedness of the business community, it should be pointed out that farmers coming to town were not a faint presence, but inundated Chicago, filling generally vacant lots like "the camp of an army beleaguering" the city. It took true foresight to see a boon greater than that.)

Failing to find enough support in Chicago, Ogden raised money among the farmers themselves, traveling from farm to farm along the train route, soliciting investments, convincing them that a railroad would not only ease the bringing of goods to market but would increase the value of their property. In October 1848 the first train—a locomotive and two cars—was sent five miles down the first set of tracks out of Chicago, originating at Kinzie Street and heading due west. It returned with a load of wheat.

The goal of the railroad construction was Galena, a town 170 miles to the west of Chicago, because it had a thriving lead mine (*galena* is Latin for "lead ore"). Galena might have become the premier city in Illinois. But it was connected to the Mississippi by the Galena River and, mesmerized by its river access, Galena was even more resistant than Chicago to the newfangled steam-belching mode of transportation. Its businessmen invested only half the amount in Ogden's railroad as Chicago's did, though the two cities were of comparable size.

Galena got a second chance, and blew it. In 1851, Congress approved a land grant for construction of the Illinois Central Railroad, which was to go through Galena. But the city needed to cede land for a station, and the town fathers refused, unwilling to allow a railway bridge across the Galena River, to the horror of more far-sighted citizens. "Gentlemen, you have sounded your death knell," mine owner Hezekiah Gear said. "Grass will grow in your streets; you have ruined your town." The Illinois Central instead cut through Dubuque, Iowa, fifteen miles to the northwest.

Hezekiah Gear was right. The California gold rush lured miners away from Galena, and richer deposits of lead were discovered further west. Farming proved to be as profitable as lead mining. Ambitious citizens flocked to Chicago. Galena, which had 14,000 residents in 1845, making it as populous as Chicago, by 1893 was "almost abandoned" at the exact moment that Chicago was basking in world attention with its great Columbian Exposition. It became a town "left to decay and ruin." Today Galena has a population of 3,400 and an economy based on local tourism and fruity wine. To this day, the nearest bridge across the Mississippi is fifteen miles away, in East Dubuque, and Dubuque has sixteen times the population of Galena.

By 1852—a year that saw Chicago's population increase by 60 percent—Chicago was directly connected to New York City by rail. In 1857, a hundred trains a day arrived at or departed from Chicago. Because of how railroads were established, most trains reaching Chicago were required to stop—few passed straight through, since virtually no railroad company had operations both east and west of the city. Since train routes terminated here, trains tended to shunt goods and people into the city, if only to transfer to ships or other rail lines, a steam-age version of the canoe portage. By 1860, eleven different trunk rail lines branched out of Chicago to the points of the compass.

Contrast this to St. Louis, which, even more than Galena, should have become the foremost Midwest metropolis. St. Louis, founded in 1764, had a seventy-year jump on Chicago—it was a thriving city of 10,000 souls in 1820 when Chicago was still a smattering of rough cabins containing "four or five families" huddled around a rebuilt fort. St. Louis sits at the juncture of the Mississippi and Missouri rivers, directly connected to New

Orleans by water. Its port does not freeze in the winter, unlike Chicago's. Few imagined that the "Rome of the West" could be overshadowed by the swampy upstart to the north. "Did I then foresee what Chicago would be in later life?" Gustave Koerner wrote in his memoirs in the 1890s. "St. Louis, in comparison to Chicago, was in 1836, a stately, magnificent city."

That magnificence was largely thanks to steamboats, which at first fueled the growth of St. Louis, then became the city's undoing. Powerful steamboat interests successfully stalled competition from trains, lobbying the Missouri legislature, which dragged its feet about funding railroad construction.

The steamboat companies also resorted to lawsuits and violence. One of Abraham Lincoln's most important cases as a lawyer was in 1856, when the steamboat *Effie Afton* rammed a pier of the Rock Island Bridge, the first railroad bridge to cross the Mississippi, setting the bridge on fire and sending it toppling into the river just two weeks after it first opened. The owner of the steamboat, whose pilot was accused of deliberately ramming the bridge, sued the Rock Island Bridge Company for damages, claiming that the bridge supports were a hazard to navigation. Thanks to Lincoln's skill, the judge dismissed the lawsuit.

By the time St. Louis managed to throw a railroad span across the Mississippi—the celebrated Eads Bridge—the year was 1874 and it was too late: Chicago had passed St. Louis in population four years earlier, and St. Louis's economic fate was sealed. A reminder that the arrival of transformative technology is nothing new, and those who cling to the past risk losing their future.

Chicago not only was the hub of watersheds and railroads, but straddled a dividing line between the raw goods of the open West—wheat from Kansas, cattle from Nebraska, lumber from Michigan and Wisconsin—and the markets of the East. It was no accident that Cyrus McCormick, who originally set up production in New York, quickly decided to get closer to his customers, in 1847 building his new Harvesting Machine Factory in Chicago (McCormick's partner for the first year, the omnipresent William B. Ogden).

The Civil War basically shut down Mississippi navigation, making Chicago's rail hub all the more important, and the city became a staging area for cattle on their way to feed the Union Army, giving rise to the city's huge Union stockyards.

What really brought Chicago international attention, ironically, was the fire that leveled much of it in October 1871. "There went a shudder over all cities and a quiver over all lands. There was scarcely a town in the civilized world that did not shake on the brink of this opening chasm," Rev. Charles H. Fowler sermonized on the first anniversary of the fire. "The flames of our homes reddened all skies."

Donations poured in—including, famously, eight thousand books sent by England to restock the Chicago Public Library, the result of an extraordinary public campaign endorsed by Queen Victoria, including donations by Alfred Tennyson, Charles Darwin, Lewis Carroll and almost every prominent British author of the day, all unaware that, before the fire, Chicago didn't have a public library (though it had a fine private one). Britain's donated books were accepted, and a tax-supported library was quickly formed around them, while boosters fanned out to scour the country for investors. Laborers hurried to the city to help in its rebuilding, and after it was rebuilt they kept coming, to man Chicago's growing factories.

Chicagoans naturally focus on the generosity of the world rushing to help after the fire, but there was no shortage of those who saw the conflagration as divine punishment and were eager to put Chicago in the same company as Carthage, Sodom and Gomorrah, and Pompeii. "It is retributive judgment on a city that has shown such devotion in its worship of the Golden calf," Rev. Granville Moody preached in Cincinnati, noting that Chicagoans had recently voted against closing saloons on Sunday. Others blamed too-vigorous growth or even the Civil War—the fire was payback for Sherman's burning of Atlanta. "Chicago did her full share in the destruction of the South," an Indiana newspaper opined. "God adjusts balances. Maybe with Chicago the books are now squared."

Such grumbling was quickly swept away when Chicago did not decline, but grew from the ashes of the fire. People came to Chicago and kept coming, for reasons that changed as the decades unfolded. They no longer came here to trade pelts, but to butcher hogs, make steel, study theology, trade stock. They came here to open bakeries or to sell dry goods. But whatever reason drew them here, those who shared a common homeland, a common language, tended to cling together, and as soon as these ethnic enclaves coalesced, others joined them because their kinfolk were already here—the Irish joining the Irish on the Southwest Side, near the canal they had originally come to dig; the Eastern European Jews joining the Jews on the Near West Side, settling there because it was poor, like they were. The blacks joined other blacks on the South and Far West sides because those were the only places they were allowed to live. Your former countrymen were not only comprehendible and familiar, but they helped you—well, some of them cheated or robbed you, but others might help you find a toehold in the city, that essential first step up.

They came here as a roll of the dice, because excitement and opportunity uncommon in dusty Iowa or chill Minnesota were here for the taking on the streets of Chicago. Or so they thought.

They came here on a lark, tentatively venturing out of their hometowns to debut in the wider world. Eighteen-year-old Charlie Sandburg—he wouldn't start using his given name, Carl, until after he was married— begged a train pass from his father, a railroad blacksmith, for a three-day jaunt, financed by $1.50 earned hauling milk on a horse-drawn wagon in Galesburg, two hundred miles west of Chicago. The budding poet and future newspaperman visited Marshall Field's department store and the offices of the *Chicago Daily News.* He also wanted to see the inside of a Chicago saloon, and did, fending off the halfhearted advances of a hooker by telling her, "You're up the wrong alley, sister. I ain't got but two nickels and they wouldn't do you any good."

They came to Chicago leaving behind everything they had and everyone they knew, to try for something different and possibly better. Joe Oliver was the cornet king of New Orleans, but he still had to work as a butler in a white household during the day to make ends meet. He had heard that Jelly Roll Morton was doing well up north, so moved to Chicago in 1919, established himself as a bandleader, then sent a telegram to his protégé, Louis Armstrong, inviting him to play second cornet with the King Oliver Creole Jazz Band at Lincoln Gardens.

"Sorry boys," Armstrong told the members of his Tuxedo Brass Band, ceremonially shaking each one's hand. "I've got to go." Armstrong was earning $1.50 a night in New Orleans; in Chicago he'd be earning $52.50 a week, plus tips.

They came for complicated reasons—Armstrong not only had a good job offer in Chicago, but a wife in New Orleans named Daisy, a disturbed prostitute who had the habit of coming after him with a straight razor, and that was another reason to go.

People came to Chicago by happenstance, on their way somewhere else. In the 1930s, transcontinental travelers changed trains here—the city remained a place where train lines end, and in that sense Union Station is misnamed, because it is not a station, but a terminal. Trains do not pass *through* Union Station, they stop there, and passengers with time on their hands often ventured out into the city. Stars would head over to the Pump Room for lunch, and to brief Irv Kupcinet, the city's top newspaper gossip columnist, about their latest projects and adventures.

In the 1940s, half a million soldiers were processed through Fort Sheridan, north of the city. In 1955, immediately upon taking office, Richard J. Daley bullied the airlines into paying for O'Hare International Airport, which officially opened that fall, an incredible six months after Daley's inauguration, debuting as the largest airfield in the United States. It wasn't even technically in Chicago, though the city owned the property, and Daley set about pressing the suburbs around O'Hare to let Chicago annex the airport, as well as Higgins Road out to meet it, by promising not to demand even more land if they immediately cooperated (they did), then bulldozing the Northwest—later called the Kennedy—Expressway out to O'Hare, bisecting a number of Chicago neighborhoods in the process. By the early 1960s it was the busiest airport in the world.

Abe Peck did not fly into Chicago. He arrived in 1967 while living "the hippie cliché—five guys in a VW bus." They were heading to the Summer of Love in California, driving from New York, where Peck had just escaped the Army —bad eyesight—and stopped to check out the scene in Chicago for a few days. Peck marveled at how wide the Dan Ryan Expressway was compared to the highways that threaded through his home back in the Bronx. They stayed less than a week, crashing with some freaks he met at a poster store on Wells Street, then Peck and his buddies pushed on to San Francisco.

Me, I arrived in the middle of September 1978—also aged eighteen, but in perhaps the least poetic way imaginable, along I-90, 340 miles west from Berea, Ohio, a suburb of Cleveland, riding in the back of a silver and maroon 1975 Dodge Dart Special Edition, my nuclear physicist father at the wheel, my mother in the passenger seat, my little brother Sam fidgeting beside me. I was delivered to Northwestern University's Evanston campus, a much coddled, well-loved suburban egg, to complete my lengthy hatching as part of the Class of 1982. We dragged my steamer trunk through the curbside carnival of welcome, into room 210 of the Northwestern Apartments, a vast seven-story, six-hundred-person coed freshman rookery on Orrington Avenue. Being first on the scene, I had the pick of the apartment's four beds in two bedrooms, and after carefully evaluating the merits of each bed's location, I took for myself what I considered the best spot, tucked into a little alcove in the front bedroom, affording a bit of privacy. The walls were painted an industrial aqua.

My family said their farewells and exited, stage left, with a sigh of relief on both sides, and stage right entered my three roommates, who immediately became my surrogate family, my allies. Nightly we trooped as a unit up Sheridan Road for the start-of-school frat parties. College, we noted happily, seemed to be about beer.

On the first day of class, a scattering of freshmen sat in Fisk Hall—home of the Medill School of Journalism, a three-story, dark red brick building built in 1899, with high, arched windows and glass wavy from age. We went around the circle, briefly explaining why we wanted to go into newspapering. There were several references to Woodward and Bernstein, the *Washington Post* reporters who six years earlier had broken the Watergate scandal and became heroes to many aspiring journalists. I didn't mention them. Instead I cited as my inspiration two humorous memoirs—Hunter S. Thompson's *Fear and Loathing in Las Vegas* and James Thurber's "Memoirs of a Drudge."

Though not aware of it then—I was just trying to be irreverent, funny—those were revealing choices. Both works depict not the good that journalism can do for others, not the impact that reporting has on the world, but the impact that reporting has on the reporter. I wasn't trying to change anything, wasn't trying to help anybody or illuminate hidden truths, but was simply looking to have fun and experience life, to aggrandize, challenge, and improve myself, and so I had quit my hometown and come here.

You would think that hailing from Ohio—Chicago's neighbor but for Indiana—would hardly qualify me as an outsider at all. Not compared to the waves of immigrants who washed over the city, feeding its explosive growth, catapulting it from a frontier outpost to one of the nation's top ten cities in its first thirty years of existence, then taking only thirty more to become the nation's second-largest city, nosing ahead of Philadelphia.

But as I was to discover, being from Ohio was in a sense more isolating than coming from across the globe might have been. Chicago has a Chinatown and a Greektown, the remnants of a Little Italy and a Little Lithuania. There are Pakistanis and Indians on Devon Avenue, Swedes in Andersonville, and Hispanics in Pilsen, which was originally settled by Czechoslovakians (hence its name echoing the Bohemian town that gave the world pilsner beer). There is no Ohiotown, however, no Buckeye bond to bring us together. We may draw out the letter "A," as I realized after my roommates began laughing at me when I complained about their living habits ("What were you, raised in a barn?" I'd demand, and they'd hoot "*baaarn*?!" in reply). But merely being from Ohio wasn't enough for us to recognize each other and help each other.

I might have shored up my new nest by joining a fraternity. Frat members occupy the apex of social life at Northwestern, and later help each other navigate through their careers. I summarily rejected that route as beneath me; I'd visit their frat houses and drink their grain alcohol punch dipped out of plastic garbage cans, but pledging was not an option. A reminder that while outsiders like to emphasize the hurt of being kept out, they also have a tendency, when given the chance to become an insider somewhere, of declining to join, the unstated logic being: you can't reject me if I never try to belong.

Though I don't think fear of rejection was the full reason. Frats also offended my solitary, independent nature. The fact that I was attending Northwestern inspired in me not pride or loyalty, but a certain disdain, a hanging back. The Northwestern campus is lovely and park-like, with stately trees surrounding ornate limestone or red brick academic buildings (diverting our gaze, as one must, from the newer, poured-concrete monstrosities) plus a slice of beach and lakeside promenade. The school welcomes and embraces you, educates you and grants you the rare gift of instant membership in a tight-knit community—the college you attend serves throughout your life as a kind of secondary homeland. But I didn't feel affection for NU. *Rare gift?* I scoffed. *More like an expensive luxury.* I never owned purple clothing, never attended a Wildcats football game, never bought a class ring or a yearbook, never even purchased a Northwestern T-shirt until the week of commencement. Maybe I already knew that as close as the bond can be, after four years you graduate and they throw you out. Then you're just another unemployed guy—worse, an unemployed guy with no idea what to do next and a useless silver spoon tarnishing in the corner of his mouth. At least I was.

* * *

Before you can come to Chicago, Chicago must come to you.

Alfred Adler had broken away from Sigmund Freud—the two Viennese doctors worked together for nearly a decade before World War I, creating the field of psychoanalysis, but Freud wanted followers who would support his theories, centered on conflicts of the interior mind and the libido, while Adler's ideas focused on the importance of family and social connections. They couldn't even agree on what kind of patient their profession should direct itself toward: Freud preferred rich people in private consulting rooms, while Adler looked to the working class. Most of psychology sided with Freud, for obvious reasons—rich people pay better—and Adler, a socialist, struggled to find supporters. He gave a speech in Chicago and was enthusiastically received, later telling his acolyte Rudolf Dreikurs that Chicago seemed open to their brand of populist psychology and perhaps Dreikurs should consider lending his skills to the budding Adlerian group there.

Then Adler died suddenly in Scotland in 1937, leaving his followers bereft and worried about his legacy. That same year Dreikurs, a proper Austrian, bald and bespectacled, fled the gathering storm of Nazism in Vienna. He went first to Brazil, where he got an Adlerian group up and running, and then, trying to carry out his fallen mentor's wishes, Dreikurs went to New York and boarded a train for Chicago, brooding over warnings he had received that he shouldn't even *mention* Adler once he got to Chicago, not if he hoped to get patient referrals from hospitals. America was loud and hectic, and they put sweet sauce on their ham, which was just wrong. Still, the attitude in Chicago had to be better than it was in New York, Dreikurs told himself, as the train rumbled through the immensity of this strange new country. It could hardly be worse.

Henry Williams had left South Carolina and joined the great black migration north, seeking work in Chicago. He found it, on the night shift at the Post Office's Englewood station. Williams lived at 61st and Vernon, but frequently returned home. "He would travel back home in the summertime to visit, and we'd stand there for hours waiting for the train to come in," his nephew, the Rev. Jesse Jackson wrote. "After his stay, we went with him to the station and it was so sad when the train would pull off . . . how we desperately wanted to accompany him . . . bound for Chicago."

When he was fifteen, Jackson finally got his wish and was put on the train to visit his uncle, fortified by his mother's ham sandwiches, hard-boiled eggs, potato pie, and a jug of lemonade. He rode the train to Atlanta, then transferred to the Hummingbird, which took him through Nashville and finally to the city he had longed to see.

"God," he thought, arriving at the 63rd Street Station, "I am in Chicago."

In 1963, a high school history teacher named George C. Schneider applied for a John Hay Fellows program, funded by the Ford Foundation that gave educators a chance to recharge their batteries and deepen their understanding of their subjects. Schneider, who had served in the US Army during World War II, was one of three teachers from the state of Ohio selected. He might have been sent to a dozen different schools across the country, including Columbia, but the Hay Fellowship assigned Schneider to spend his sabbatical year at Northwestern. Schneider arrived with his wife and infant daughter, and would dip down into the city for events like the big auto show at McCormick Place, which impressed him by running a shuttle bus back and forth to the far-flung parking lots—he had never seen anything like that before.

Theodore Dreiser was an eighteen-year-old freshman at the University of Indiana in Terre Haute in 1889, when Chicago, precisely 180 miles due north, began calling to him through a newspaper column, Eugene Field's Sharps and Flats. "Nothing else that I had read so far—books, plays, poems, histories—gave me quite the same feeling for constructive thought; for the subject of his daily notes, poems and aphorisms was Chicago and America," Dreiser later wrote.

> For to me Chicago at this time had a peculiarly literary or artistic atmosphere. It is given to some cities, as to some lands, to suggest romance, and to me Chicago did that daily and hourly. It sang, or seemed to. . . . Chicago was so young, so blithe. . . . Here was a city which had no traditions but which was making them, and this was the very thing which everyone seemed to understand and rejoice in. Chicago was like no other city in the world—so said they all; Chicago would outstrip every other American city, New York included, and be the first of all American if not all European or world cities. This dream many hundreds of thousands of its citizens held dear. Chicago would be first in wealth, first in beauty, first in art achievement.

That boosterism, that forward-straining, triumphant view of endless possibility peaked with the World's Columbian Exposition of 1893, whose temporary glory—you had to visit now or miss your chance forever—drew millions of people from the Midwest and beyond to visit Chicago who never would have come otherwise. It showed them a classical fantasy metropolis—the "White City"—that was far more appealing than the smoky, gritty, often impoverished "Gray City" beyond it. It is no coincidence that the two books written by Chicagoans and published in Chicago in 1900 that have endured for more than a century, L. Frank Baum's *The Wonderful Wizard of Oz* and Dreiser's *Sister Carrie*, while differing in details, both share the same basic plot: an innocent but resourceful country girl comes to a glorious big city where she encounters evil while struggling to fulfill her dreams.

The future looked limitless, particularly if you made the common error of using the past as a template for what is to come—such as the city's enormous growth in the last half of the nineteenth century as a barometer to what would happen in the twentieth. "Chicago is now facing the momentous fact that fifty years hence, when the children of today are at the height of their power and influence, this city will be larger than London: that is, larger than any existing city," Daniel Burnham and Edward Bennett wrote in their 1909 *Plan of Chicago*, citing one estimate that by 1952 Chicago would have more than 13 million residents if conditions continue "in the future exactly as in the past." As it turned out, the population of Chicago did peak in 1950, but at only 3.6 million.

For Chicago, that dream of continual progress died—along with so many dreams of perfecting society—after the slaughter of World War I, when the staggering gang violence brought about by Prohibition gave Chicago its most enduring representative: Al Capone. In the span of a decade, Chicago went from aspiring to become the premier city in the country, if not the world, at least in its own view, to being hailed worldwide as the most crime-ridden. Movies spread that reputation. Chicago was the home of Capone and his tough-talking, tommy-gun-toting surrogates, killers like Edward G. Robinson in *Little Caesar*. "Mother of mercy, is this the end of Rico?"

The movie gangster image stayed strong for half a century—it lingers still, basketball star Michael Jordan providing only temporary relief, an image that seems to intensify the further you go from Chicago. "Ti aspetti la città di Al Capone," is the opening sentence of Italian journalist Marco d'Eramo's 2004 book about Chicago, *Il maiale e il grattacielo* [*The Pig and the Skyscraper*]: "You expect the city of Al Capone."

Well, some do. Asked if he was looking forward to the 2012 NATO summit in Chicago, Russian president Vladimir Putin replied, "Al Capone lived there." But mob murder was never the entirety of the city's reputation. If you were black in the early decades of the twentieth century, gangsters were insignificant compared to other considerations. Chicago was the city of jobs, of dignity, of the great *Chicago Defender*—that famous voice for the voiceless, thundering weekly against lynching, against Jim Crow, against the miserable, degraded life for blacks in the South. The *Defender* would be passed from hand to hand—sometimes in secret, since many Southern towns banned its possession—worn away to a tattered rag of newsprint, and it inspired hundreds of thousands who took the train north. "I bought a *Chicago Defender* and after reading it and seeing the golden opportunity I have decided to leave this place at once," a black Tennessee railroad worker wrote in 1917. John H. Johnson also made the trek, brought by his mother, who accompanied the young man north because there was no school for him to attend in Arkansas City, Arkansas—Johnson repeated the eighth grade just to have somewhere to go. She told her neighbors they were merely visiting the 1933 Century of Progress fair, so if they failed to make it in Chicago, they could return without the shame of failure.

They did make it—Johnson became a multimillionaire by founding the magazines *Ebony* and *Jet*. To this day Johnson, incredibly, is the first and only black man to own a high-rise office building in downtown Chicago— eleven stories at 820 South Michigan. After his daughter sold the building in 2010, there were none, and given the way skyscrapers are now financed, there may never be another.

* * *

In the years immediately after the Second World War, Chicago was no longer a budding Paris, no longer a garish and bloody bootlegger's dream, but a "dreary, worn out city," a provincial cow town, the stomping ground of yahoos and ruddy conventioneers, a self-deluded also-ran. It certainly seemed that way to one visitor from one large metropolis. A. J. Liebling's famous three-part essay, "Second City," published in the *New Yorker* in January 1952 and later as a book, is a masterpiece of modulated contempt. Chicago has spotty garbage collection, bad-tasting tap water, no skyline to speak of—and that's only on the first page. Chicago is "a theater backdrop with a city painted on it," its downtown Loop "is like Times Square and Radio City set down in the middle of a vast Canarsie."

The condemnation stung, particularly since Liebling was factually correct—garbage collection, for instance, *was* bad in Chicago, bad enough that mayor Martin Kennelly had paused to discuss it in his inaugural address the previous April, saying, "The problem of garbage disposal is one of the most difficult we have to contend with."

Still, Chicagoans leapt to defend their city, whose spirit and allure, they felt, transcended its deficiencies, and Liebling gleefully reprinted a few of their complaints in the book version of his critique, chuckling over misspelling, rubbing salt in the wound he had inflicted, noting that while temporary visitors such as himself were "almost all favorable" to his backhand, the "people who were still there"—*still*, as if living in Chicago were a phase eventually outgrown—took a puzzling umbrage at seeing their home maligned.

Liebling, who lived in Chicago for almost a year, off and on, research- ing his report, deflected the attacks with lordly disdain, particularly those charging that he "was a flitting viewer, writing about the place after a visit of a few weeks, days, or hours (according to the degree of indignation of the writer)." "The extreme example of this form of criticism I have preserved in a postcard from a lady named Swift," Liebling wrote. "It bears the simple legend: 'You were never in Chicago.'"

That criticism—you weren't in Chicago long enough for you or your opinion to matter, or else you weren't brought up in the right spot to be considered a true Chicagoan—is the dagger brought out again and again, when convenient, to dispatch any uncomfortable person, observation, or argument. Mayor Richard M. Daley would narrow his eyes, finding himself in an unwelcome face-to-face confrontation, and coldly inquire where his accuser lived—the implication being, "You're not from here, asking *that*."

Rahm Emanuel was born in Chicago, elected to Congress from Danny Rostenkowski's old Fifth District, owns a house on the North Side, and helped raise money for the younger Daley, that platinum bar for measur- ing true Chicagoness, when Daley was first elected mayor in 1989. Yet his opponents were still able to call him an outsider with straight faces during his first mayoral campaign in 2011. Did not Emanuel grow up in Wilmette? Had he not attended fancy-pants New Trier High School there? Did he not leave town for eighteen months to work in Washington? On this basis his connection to Chicago was revoked—for a time—not only in the court of public opinion, but by a court of law.

This is the provincialism Liebling had ridiculed sixty years earlier, typical for a city that once conducted a study to prove its pedestrians walk faster than those in New York. The villagers who yearn to consider themselves sophisticated residents of a cosmopolitan city, yet sniff each new arrival for the stench of unknown lands. Who endlessly debate whether Chicago can be considered a "world class" city, whatever that means, not realizing that to ask the question is to answer it. Parisians sure don't waste much time pondering that one.

In quasi-scientific analyses trying to rank cities as "global," whether Chicago belongs in the elite depends on where you cut off the list—if there are just three, then the global cities are generally New York, London, and Tokyo; if you take the top ten, then Chicago can squeak onto the list— no. 7, for instance, on the 2012 A. T. Kearney Global Cities Index, between Los Angeles and Seoul.

But those trying to cook the numbers to prove Chicago's merit mathematically are missing the point, as eloquently expressed by the great *Chicago Daily News* editor Henry Justin Smith: "The city has been studied, loved, hated, praised and denounced out of all proportion to its statistical position among the cities of the world."

* * *

Abe Peck came back because he was broke. The Summer of Love in San Francisco had fizzled into a stone bummer, and he knew a few people in Chicago from his trip out west. Peck moved here and found a job as a textbook salesman. The job came with a company car, a brown Chevy. Because he had the car, and was still intoxicated by the excitement of the times, he drove some friends he'd met at that Wells Street poster shop, called Headland, to the march on the Pentagon in October 1967. Soon after he returned, he wasn't a book salesman anymore, thanks to the 1,500 unexplainable miles he had put on his company car. So he became a writer for the *Seed*, the counter-culture newspaper produced by the guys at the poster shop.

By the steamy midsummer, Peck was the *Seed*'s editor, going under the nom de guerre "Abraham Yippie," huddling with Abbie Hoffman and Jerry Rubin at the newspaper's unairconditioned North LaSalle Street office, struggling to see who would guide the protests at the upcoming 1968 Democratic National Convention, arguing about what they hoped to accomplish and how they should go about trying to accomplish it. They worked for months with Richard J. Daley's bureaucracy, requesting permits to protest and to sleep in the park, and had the city not stonewalled them, had it let the radicals use Lincoln Park, the entire fiasco might have been averted. Daley drew the disaster upon himself. As relations soured and time grew short, Peck began writing statements warning the *Seed*'s national readership what to expect if they came to the city to oppose nomination of the warmonger Hubert Humphrey, to inform them that this would be no celebration of good karma.

"The word is out," Peck/Yippie wrote. "Many people are into confrontation. The Man is into confrontation. . . . Chicago may host a Festival of Blood. . . . There are many reasons to disrupt the Death Gala. If you feel compelled to cavort, then this is action city. There is no reason to wear flowers for masks. . . . As individuals, we may join in trying to stop Hubert the Hump. As a group, our advice is—Don't come to Chicago if you expect a five-day Festival of Life, music and love."

The protest and turmoil that followed would transform the Liebling view of Chicago—as a nest of self-deluded yokels pointlessly killing time in an aspiring but laughably deficient midwestern backwater—into something far more dynamic and significant, scary to some, appealing to others.

After 1968, Chicago was the riots in Grant Park and on Michigan Avenue in front of the Conrad Hilton. It was ragged hippies chanting, "The whole world is watching!" while being clobbered by pigs in baby-blue helmets. Chicago was the porcine, many-chinned mug of Richard J. Daley, red with rage. That, and the trial of the Chicago Seven, accused of conspiring to cause the unrest, helped Chicago shed its reputation as the home of Al Capone's organized crime descendents and their seedy strip clubs and clip joints, at least temporarily. Now it was ground zero for what was considered a youth revolt, the struggle to stop the Vietnam War. Being epicenter of the rebellion was to some just as romantic as being the seat of literature had been half a century before. "Won't you please come to Chicago?" Graham Nash sang in 1970. "We can change the world."

The sulfurous smell left over from the social explosion of the 1960s still hung in the air in the late 1970s. The important battles had been fought and the wounded carried off the fields; now my generation was let loose, scavengers combing the churned-up, blood-soaked battlegrounds for brass uniform buttons and spent musket balls. The nation we were inheriting had inexplicably shrunk. Nixon, so despised that it almost amounted to a kind of love, was finally gone, the Greek tragedy at last concluded, leaving an empty stage, soon to be trod upon by a diminished breed of men such as the preachy homunculus Jimmy Carter, an improvement over Gerald Ford but not by much. The 1960s were over. Swell party, sorry you missed it.

Abe Peck turned away from revolution, quit the *Seed*, and with the help of contacts got himself a job on a real publication, *Rolling Stone*.

A few days before I left for college, my father and I sat on our green and brown plaid burlap-covered ranch oak sofa—the fashion at the time—in front of our Sony color television, modern because it had a push button for each station, watching an ABC special about the tenth anniversary of the riots at the 1968 Democratic National Convention, jangling black and white images of batons and helmets and flaring lights.

"You wouldn't do anything like that?" my father half stated, half asked, slyly probing, "Protest in the street?"

"Dad," I said measuring my words carefully, with a teenager's gravity. "If I were there, at that time, I like to think that nothing in the world would stop me from sitting down in that street and being beaten by those cops."

I was Northwestern-bound—the heavy purple felt pennant was thumb-tacked on my bedroom wall. My father was born in the Bronx, but had shipped out as a radio operator and seen the world, ending up at NASA's sprawling Lewis Research Center in Cleveland, analyzing subatomic particles and weather patterns. I was his son, so never considered staying in Berea, Ohio, the self-proclaimed "Grindstone Capital of the World," not for a second. Maybe a pang of wistfulness toward those who could stay, toward my friend Jim, inheriting his dad's business and island summer-house. But that wasn't for me; the allure of home was overwhelmed by a kind of disgust—a girl in my high school class got married the day of our prom, so that her wedding dress could be put to double duty as a prom gown. The sight of that white dress at the dance jarred and horrified me, the responsibilities of adult life crashing the high school party.

Cleveland offered nothing. The city had only one tall building—the Terminal Tower, a beaux-arts skyscraper that looked like the box the Statue of Liberty came in. I felt affection for the place, its goofy mayors and sprawling industrial Flats. But staying just wasn't an option—I delivered the Berea *News Sun* for seven years, and wanted to be a writer, but it never crossed my mind to try to write for the *News Sun*. Why aim so low?

Cleveland is midway between Chicago and New York, and I felt the pull of both larger cities, and applied to two elite universities—Northwestern and Columbia, with Ohio State University as a fall-back, since my mother, father, older sister Debbie, plus two aunts and an uncle had all gone there. Good enough for *them*, maybe. But Ohio State represented failure to me, the rough bunker dug in the backyard in case disaster struck.

My father grew up in New York City, so to me New York was my grandmother's apartment building on Barnes Avenue in the Bronx, its dim corridor with black and white square tiles on the floor and an elevator with a diamond-shaped window with chicken wire embedded in it. New York was dense, lumpy wine cookies in a round tin high atop a heavy mahogany buffet and old Jewish ladies on the Pelham Parkway. It was plywood barriers at construction sites covered in graffiti. At the time, New York was seen as an especially dangerous city, a city on the ropes. New York had flirted with meltdown ("FORD TO CITY: DROP DEAD" the famous *New York Daily News* headline read). It was the city of *Taxi Driver.* We would travel there from Berea, visit my grandmother in the Bronx and hurry back to Ohio, having never set foot in Manhattan. I suspected that Morningside Heights, Columbia's home, was just a fancy way of saying "Harlem."

In short: I was afraid of New York.

Chicago, on the other hand, was the Palmer House Hotel. My father had taken me to the city to attend a conference, and we stayed there. Chicago was the Palmer House's gorgeous Wedgwood lobby ceiling, the nearby Blackhawk restaurant, with its famous spinning salad. "Here at zee Black-hawk, we spin zee salad not wance, not twah-ice, but sree times!" a tuxedoed waiter exalted, while my sister and I laughed into each other's shoulders. Chicago was the *Daily News*, Mike Royko, and the Sears Tower.

Yes, Chicago is a big city, like New York, but Evanston, the suburb where Northwestern's main campus is located, is just outside it, immediately to the north, a safe berth from where I could dip my toe into city life without drowning. Such was my teenage reasoning; I had never seen either campus, and neither my parents nor I considered visiting. People didn't do that then, at least not people in Berea, Ohio.

I had gotten the idea of Northwestern from my favorite teacher in high school, George Schneider, a soft-spoken man who wore cardigan sweaters and rectangular glasses, his black hair slicked back like H. L. Mencken's. He taught Honors United States History, leaning against a lectern, hands lightly folded in front of him, quietly talking. He had served in the army, and brought in his old World War II battle maps—large, folded affairs with wide arrows and muted colors of mustard yellow and powder blue and red gone to rose, saved from newspapers—and pinned them up in the classroom. Mr. Schneider respected us and made us think. We loved him. He had gone to Northwestern for a year, then returned home to Cleveland. He always meant to go back to visit Chicago, which he vividly described, from NU's pretty lakeside campus to the ancient treasures on display at the University of Chicago's glorious Oriental Institute. But he never returned.

A planned trip was scuttled because of the riots following Martin Luther King's assassination; so a sense of yearning colored his memories of the place. Mr. Schneider having gone to Northwestern meant something to me.

Or so I told myself. I don't want to claim too much credit for noble motives. The bedrock truth is that Northwestern had an undergraduate journalism program while Columbia didn't, and Northwestern granted early admission while Columbia didn't, but if they offered it, you had to accept immediately or lose the chance. Northwestern had sent me a flattering form letter, based on my SAT scores, inviting me to a meeting in Cleveland where the glories of NU and its famed Medill School of Journalism were ballyhooed. Two days after I stopped hoping I'd get accepted, the letter arrived, offering a full tuition scholarship plus a guaranteed work-study job to help cover my living expenses. By the time Columbia told me I was in, I had already committed myself to Northwestern. On such fine print our destinies pivot.

A comfortable path to the city, without doubt, the son of a scientist, buoyed by memories of swank hotels and fancy restaurants, a chubby boy arriving in a moderately nice car to go to a moderately good school for reasons of moderate, undirected teenage literary aspiration. Not as compelling a story as, say, that of a gaunt morphine addict shuffling down Division Street, or the hardscrabble upbringing of a dock foreman's kid being chased by the toughs on the next block, and many insist the bourgeois stain never washes off.

But while college might be the painless route, it is also a crowded one—some ten thousand young men and women come to Chicago each year as incoming freshmen at Northwestern, the University of Chicago, DePaul, Loyola, the Illinois Institute of Technology, and the University of Illinois at Chicago. They may all have a snug spot in an expensive school, but that is all they have, and the meter is running.

Hundreds more come here to get advanced degrees—Maria Pappas came to Chicago to get her PhD in psychology at Loyola.

Well ... the truth, as always, is more complicated than that. Pappas grew up in a Greek-speaking household in Warwood, West Virginia, a town of two thousand not far from Wheeling, where she played clarinet, twirled baton, and went by the more rural name of "Mary Ann." She got a degree in sociology from West Liberty State College and a masters degree in counseling from West Virginia State University and began working on her doctorate, focusing on Adlerian psychology. It was at an Adlerian summer school in West Liberty that she met Rudolf Dreikurs. He had done his own impressive work—Dreikurs developed a theory that children misbehave because they don't feel sufficiently connected to a group, which sounds about right. He looked at the bright young woman in front of him and said: "What are you doing in West Virginia? You should be in Chicago." The city where, in 1952, Dreikurs founded the Adler Institute, which was always in need of students.

Thus encouraged, in the spring of 1972, Pappas tucked her half-finished doctoral thesis under her arm and went to Chicago to sit at the feet of Dreikurs who, at age seventy-five, promptly died, three days after she arrived in the city. Mentorless and unsure what to do next, she walked into the graduate office at Loyola University and asked if she could finish her doctorate there, one of the rare doctoral candidates to apply to a college in person. Loyola accepted her.

3

"A tolerance for rubes"

THERE ARE ONLY TWO ways to get to Chicago. You either are born here or you arrive. Those born here have a natural claim, the automatic owner-ship that emerging into the world upon a certain spot has granted people, at least in their own view, since time began.

But those who come here also have claim to the city, eventually, and some even become its icons if they stick around long enough. Studs Terkel was born in New York City, Nelson Algren in Detroit. Carl Sandburg, as I mentioned, grew up in Galesburg. Al Capone was born in Brooklyn, as was the superstar who temporarily replaced him as the city's representative, Michael Jordan. Some try to find a bit of foreshadowing in Oprah Winfrey being born in Kosciusko, Mississippi, a town named for the Polish hero of the American Revolution, as if that predicted her eventual arrival at the city with—all together now!—*the largest Polish population outside of Warsaw.* But it isn't as if everyone born in Kosciusko ends up here.

Indeed, Chicago never seemed to quite stick to Jordan and Winfrey, despite their years in the city, perhaps because their feet so seldom hit the street, perhaps because they amassed the sort of wealth and fame that transcends any specific geographic location. God is supposedly everywhere and is often thought of as being in a certain place at a certain time, but nobody would say, "God lives in Chicago." Ditto for Jordan and Winfrey—particularly Jordan, since he made his home in suburban Highland Park.

Perhaps that is hypocritical of me to say, living in Northbrook as I do.

Then again, newcomers are generally scorned, even by their fellow new-comers. Thus African Americans arriving early in the Great Migration, who tended to be from states such as Georgia, Kentucky, and Missouri, looked down their noses at more recent arrivals from Alabama, Mississippi, Arkansas, and Louisiana, for their Deep South country ways. The *Defender* would lecture them on how to behave in the city. Jews from Eastern Europe not only had to face hostility from gentiles, but also from other Jews who had arrived a few boats earlier, particularly those from Germany, who were well established and better off, considered themselves more culturally advanced, not to mention less conspicuous, and were embarrassed by the clatter of their unwashed Yiddish-speaking brethren, a Teutonic smug-ness that history was to wring out of them, ruthlessly. Chicago's Standard Club has the dubious distinction of being a Jewish organization that once discriminated against Jews.

Why this universal resistance? Resources—housing, jobs, spouses—are scarce and you don't want to share them, which you might feel compelled to do if you acknowledged your kinship with less fortunate new arrivals. Plus the basic human need to feel superior to someone else. Not to forget fear—German Jews and Bronzeville blacks had found their place in the city, tried to mold themselves to it as best they could, to develop some protective camouflage against the hostility they faced, and thus worried that the harder-to-miss newcomers would draw unwanted attention. Plus embarrassment—you are primed to recognize the supposed flaws of your freshly arrived brethren because until recently you displayed those same flaws yourself, and are ready to reward yourself for your improvement with a fortifying contempt for those unfamiliar with something you struggled to learn. All those jokes aimed at greenhorns offered a welcome opportunity for people who showed up last month to laugh at those who stepped off the boat yesterday.

The newcomers often returned the favor, viewing the provincials they found in Chicago with puzzlement and hostility. "I am in a strange land, and among strange people, and a strange language, for I can not get these darned Yankees to speak Norwegian," Christian Jevne wrote home to his parents in 1864. "I therefore have to jabber English all day long."

Though frequently inconvenienced, those who come from other places are also aided by their foreignness. As much as being from somewhere else can hold you back, at least initially, it can also help. You experience a place afresh because it is new to you. While lifelong residents prefer to believe that arriving after infancy disqualifies a person from ever grasping Chicago—many police officers insist a superintendent brought from outside the force can never understand the demands of their jobs—the truth is often the exact opposite: coming from somewhere else can be the key to both clearly perceiving a situation and having the freedom to express that perception. Lack of connections allows newcomers to speak openly about the way things actually are—self interest doesn't hold them back—which of course longtime residents resent, not because the newcomers misunderstand, but because they understand all too well. "People used to ask me afterward if I had not spent my life in Chicago," Upton Sinclair wrote in his autobiography, "and I answered that if I had done so, I could never have written *The Jungle*. I would have taken for granted things that now hit me a sudden blow."

Sinclair spent just seven weeks in Chicago in the fall of 1904 "among the wage slaves of the Beef Trust," researching his novel about the meatpacking industry. Not very long, but long enough to lay the foundation for a book that would have Americans gagging on their morning sausage for a century to come. Gathering your material and then blowing town to make sense of it is a common Chicago literary experience. Saul Bellow stressed that he wrote his breakout novel, *The Adventures of Augie March*, while residing in Rome and Paris and London and New York—almost anywhere *but* here. "Not a single word of the book was composed in Chicago," he recalled, adding that dwelling in a distant city "forced you into yourself in a special way."

Additionally, coming from someplace else, not having always been in Chicago, a person can be primed to embrace the city, perhaps more than those who grew up here. While lifelong residency does build passionate devotion, there is a mirror tendency not to fully appreciate things you have been familiar with your entire life. Nobody loves breathing.

If Chicago seems especially leery of newcomers, remember how fast the city grew. It wasn't due to residents multiplying like rabbits, but to outsiders pouring in—in 1900, 70 percent of Chicagoans were either foreign-born or the children of foreigners. The biggest immigrant group was not Irish or Polish, contrary to impressions, but the German-speaking community. They were a very vocal part of Chicago right up through 1917, when their fierce support of the old country brought equally strident reprisals after America entered World War I. Public schools dropped German from the curriculum, *sauerkraut* was transformed into "liberty cabbage," and the city council scrubbed the map clean of most German references, losing such street names as Berlin, Cologne, Frankfort, and Rhine, not to mention Bismarck Place, which became Canton, Eleanor, Charleston, Coyne, and Ancona—though Goethe Street survived a push to make it Boxwood Street, narrowly, as did Schiller and Mozart streets, by merit of artistry surpassing any connection to the spike-helmeted Hun. "As far as I know they did nothing offensive to America," one defender noted in 1919. "Their work belongs to all lands."

Chicago's German community was just getting its sea legs again, finding the pride and confidence needed to join the German American Bund, *Sieg Heil* each other, and parade around public parks in Nazi uniform when World War II broke out, inspiring an ethnic taciturnity that continues to this day, with the exception of Oktoberfest, which brings flashes of *gemutlichkeit* at a few taverns and restaurants in Lincoln Square.

You didn't need a foreign war to make you suspect outsiders. The arrival of a stranger is always an implicit threat—for much of human history, the people showing up are invaders here to kill you and take what you have. The idea that newcomers are here to join you, to build your city and become part of it, to make you stronger and better, is a modern concept, a new dish that a lot of people still can't bring themselves to stomach. Many Chicagoans can seamlessly shift from dabbing away a tear at the irrational bigotry their beloved grandparents faced when they arrived from the old country to sneering at these completely unacceptable *illegal immigrants* using up our *scarce resources* when they should be packed into boxcars and sent back where they belong, without ever feeling the slightest shiver of irony. *Different situations entirely.*

* * *

Wherever newcomers hail from, the city enters their understanding through landmarks and streets, buildings and neighborhoods, a cast of soon-to-be familiar players assembling, a map slowly taking shape in the brain. You figure out Wrigley Field and you figure out the Daley Plaza, then eventually realize that Clark Street runs by both, though you can live here your entire life and not know they are about five miles apart—a mile being an esoteric unit in a city measured by blocks, el stops, wards, parishes, and the time it takes to get somewhere. "Beverly is twenty minutes from the Loop, if there's no traffic," a resident proudly claims, ignoring the fact that there's always traffic. A new arrival soon realizes that Wrigley Field and the Wrigley Building are different places, that 94 and 294 are different highways, and though the road signs claim they're heading east and west they're really going north and south, generally.

Though we were students at an elite school, Medill nevertheless gave us a practical education, as if it were teaching journeymen carpenters to plane boards and frame houses. We were sent outside to describe the red brick facade of Fisk Hall. We were taught to change a typewriter ribbon. Misspelling a name in an assignment drew an automatic F, no matter how good the rest of the article might be. This struck us as immensely unfair. We were indignant to see our hard work drain away on a single blunder. Students argued, not realizing that this rule reflects precisely how professionals think—one mistake does indeed tend to wreck your work, if only by providing the bludgeon for someone who disagrees with your undisputed facts to club you with. One error is too many. It only takes a little spit to spoil the soup.

Among the first tasks we were given that fall was to go downtown, in that pre-Internet age, to get a certain brochure from the Dirksen Federal Building. It seemed an odd, bothersome assignment, but we went. We had to. I still remember emerging from the subway for the first time, climbing those stairs, the rainy city a tiny square of gray light that opened up to buildings and cars and people. I secured the brochure, though we never referred to it again, and it was only much later, wondering what the point of the assignment had been, that its purpose dawned on me: to make us go downtown and get something, it didn't matter what, to break the ice and prod us into the city to find information we needed. That's what reporters do, or should.

I didn't own a car, so went everywhere by el train—buses weren't an option; I felt they were beneath me. Poor people took buses. The el stations at Davis Street and Foster Avenue are just a few blocks off campus, and we grew familiar with the city in relation to the various el stops—Belmont Avenue was home to the dance clubs such as Tut's and Berlin. Addison Street was Wrigley Field, the contours of the lovely, still lightless little ballpark looming to the right as the train pulled into the station. Chicago and State was the fancy shopping mall, Water Tower Place, with its glass elevators; State and Lake and the next few stops after were the Loop, beyond which interest in the city abruptly evaporated. I never set foot south of Roosevelt Road when I was in college.

In the beginning, you just soak it all in. The Picasso sculpture in Daley Plaza and the Water Tower in the middle of Michigan Avenue. The Sears—now Willis—Tower and the John Hancock Building. You arrange them in your mind like a gin rummy hand, examine what you've got, orient yourself, and try to learn the rules and remember what's what. The Willis Tower is the big boxy one, black metal skin and bronze-colored windows, the tallest building in the Western Hemisphere, and the Hancock has angled sides, exterior structural Xs and a pair of horn-like masts studded with communications equipment. If you confuse the two for the first few years, well, everybody does, and not without reason: the same architect, Bruce Graham, designed them both (he explained Willis Tower's staggered rectangular box design to his colleagues by holding a fistful of loose Camels during lunch at the Chicago Club, showing how each cigarette came to a different height). Not that Chicagoans know this—as famous as the city is for architecture, even the most successful architect is thickly veiled in obscurity compared to whoever happens to be second-string shortstop on the Cubs at the moment. After Frank Lloyd Wright and, maybe, Mies van der Rohe, all is darkness—if pressed, add Helmut Jahn, though people recall Jahn's name without realizing they know it only because his Thompson Center is such a poorly conceived and constructed, salmon-and-blue mound of grotesqueness, a white elephant that needed significant retrofits to address its rash of design flaws.

A train can seem to rattle and rush through the city forever, as porches and painted-over factory windows and chain-link fences and semi-trailers parked in gravel lots slip by, mile after mile. But a passenger on a train tends to focus inward, reading or talking with other passengers, so to grasp just how big Chicago is, it helps to be driving a car—enter the city traveling north on Western Avenue, crossing 119th Street from the small city of Blue Island, and after you pass the Walgreen's at the corner you can drive due north for twenty-four miles and still be on Western and still be in Chicago before it passes into Evanston at Howard Street and becomes Asbury Avenue.

That's big. At 230 square miles, Chicago is a little less than half the area of sprawling Los Angeles, a little more than two-thirds the size of New York City's five boroughs, about equal to Milwaukee and Detroit combined. There are seventeen countries belonging to the United Nations that are smaller than Chicago in area. Though, to avoid the risk of provincialism, I should also point out that there are fifty cities in China larger than

Chicago. Beijing is twenty-five times the size. (Part of this, though, is due to differences in definition—Chicago would be even larger if we had an all-powerful central government that could rename the six-country area around it "Chicago.")

Still, by any measure, Chicago is a big place, and so is not grasped as a whole; rather, the finer details emerge one by one. There is a little art gallery tucked within the Water Tower; men inside the scoreboard at Wrigley Field slide the white-on-forest-green numerals into place. The proper reply to "Meet me at the Billy Goat Tavern" is "Which one?"—there were seven in Chicago last time I counted, though the "real" Billy Goat is on lower Hubbard, just below Michigan Avenue. The Picasso cannot be contemplated without raising the eternal question of what it might represent—a simian hunk of oxidized steel that most think of as an ape or an insect or a seahorse or a woman's profile, though to me it has always plainly been a Spaniard's mockery of our desperate midwestern grasping toward European sophistication. It's as if Picasso said, "You want high art? How about a big rusty baboon's ass for you to admire for the rest of time?" It's a good joke and we fell for it.

Stay long enough, and a kind of deeper anti-knowledge settles in. The colonnaded lakefront football stadium is Soldier Field, not *Soldiers* Field, and pronounce it wrong and someone who has been here three years longer than you will archly correct your mistake. Until you hang around cops and firemen who have lived here all their lives and nevertheless call it Soldiers Field or refer to Co-MIN-sky Park or O'Hara Airport. And nobody is going to correct *them*. Certainly not me. Some invented words— "Chicagoland," for instance—are not vernacular, but the exclusive property of newspapers and advertisers and seldom used in conversation by regular residents. Nobody says they live in Chicagoland. "The Windy City" is a historical term, unless you're fighting against a gale downtown, and are permitted to toss off a joking Windy City reference to another buffeted passerby. Nor does anybody use "the Second City" unless referring to the comedy troupe. Anyone who says, "I come from the Second City" doesn't. (It was always a strange expression, defining Chicago as the place behind New York, and after the early 1980s, it was both strange and inaccurate, once Los Angeles eclipsed Chicago in population. Don't expect "the Third City" to catch on anytime soon.)

The proper way to refer to Chicago is "Chicago," pronounced "Chi-CAH-go." Unless you're a gray-haired newscaster, or a scrappy South-

Sider, or chewing gum, and then it's "Chi-CAW-go" with kind of a nasal grimace on the "CAW."

Being official doesn't make a name proper usage; nobody in Chicago calls the Trump International Hotel and Tower anything but "Trump Tower." The mirrored Anish Kapoor sculpture in Millennium Park is titled *Cloud Gate*, but good luck finding anyone who actually uses that. Chicagoans call it "the Bean" because it looks like a bean.

* * *

Eventually, emotional nuances fill in. You can love Wrigley or you can love Comiskey—I'm of the generation to whom its proper name, US Cellular Field, still sounds odd, commercial and temporary—but you can't love both; it's like being both a Democrat and a Republican. There is a South Side attitude—blue collar, Catholic, belligerent—and a North Side attitude: cosmopolitan, Unitarian, easygoing. Baseball fans in a North Side bar welcome a newcomer, joke with him, buy him a beer. At a South Side bar, they shoot cold, appraising looks at each foreigner passing through the doorway and demand to know where he's from and why he's there, uninvited. The South Side thinks North Siders are queers; the North Side thinks South Siders are brutes.

This of course is the white Chicagoan calculus. There is different math for each subdivision of Hispanics—for Mexicans, Puerto Ricans, Cubans, and such—and for Asians, whether Indians, Pakistanis, Koreans. Tensions roil under the surface that are seldom noticed by the city at large. For instance, consider Chinatown; would that be a Taiwanese Chinatown or a People's Republic Chinatown? You might not care, but people in Chinatown certainly do. For blacks, the South and West Sides are very different places, emotionally. The South Side has the frayed gentility found in parts of Chatham or Pullman—enough to put on airs—and other middle-class black neighborhoods, while the West Side tends to be considered a war zone past the United Center, though that too is an overgeneralization, as certain blocks and neighborhoods have been reclaimed from chaos and decay. The livability of any given spot can depend on the time of day and whether the people there happen to be shooting at each other at the moment or not.

The obvious, though seldom-posed question regarding the North-South division is: why? Why the clannish defensiveness on the South Side, the urbane ease on the North Side? The answer has to be one of affluence. Tolerance is a luxury, and if you breeze into town to get your MBA and buy a condo on the Gold Coast, the appearance of an unfamiliar face down the street isn't the existential threat it can be considered if you're paying off a thirty-year mortgage on a brick bungalow in Mount Greenwood by working on a loading dock, same as your father. The tribal, look-after-your-own mentality is easy to sneer at if you're making a fortune trading bonds and sleeping soundly on the thirty-third floor in River North. If you're divvying up scarcity in Bridgeport, however, automatic hostility and suspicion suddenly make a rough kind of sense. Remember, the reason the Irish were there in the first place is that it was outside the city limits, an exile imposed by the contemptuous Protestant elite. Not the kind of legacy that encourages open-mindedness. It's easy and probably accurate to say that white people who preferred to fight or flee rather than to have a black neighbor were bigots. But in their view they were only trying to avoid losing the only place they ever had and keep from being trapped in a decaying slum. Seeing how many neighborhoods did indeed deteriorate over the years, you can't say there wasn't a hard reality behind that concern, even if it was a self-fulfilling hard reality.

Rich or poor, every neighborhood, every street, has its own particular bylaws and ways. Bill Mauldin was a teenager from Arizona, taking art classes and staying at the Lawson YMCA, when he found himself leaning on the rail on the Michigan Avenue Bridge, listening to ringing bells and wondering what they meant. They mean the bridge is going up, as he quickly discovered. "One of the nice things about Chicago," the famed editorial cartoonist later wrote, "is its tolerance for rubes."

I second that.

* * *

Evanston is not Chicago. Sure, the el runs through it, but the el runs all the way up to Wilmette, and Wilmette, with its red brick streets, thickly treed and densely-mansioned, is definitely not Chicago. The el reaches Wilmette like a power line strung into a formal garden, an out-of-place black wire of necessity, a gritty emissary from the city, like a sooty shop foreman, still in his leather apron and steel-toed boots, perched awkwardly on a pristine velvet credenza in the neat outer office of the company president. The city is waiting to see you.

Which leads to the question of where Chicago is, precisely. Not the borders, those are clear enough. But do they matter? Does being born here make you a Chicagoan? That can't be all of it. If that were enough, then Bobby Fischer, born at Michael Reese Hospital and promptly departing the city forever, was a Chicagoan, even as the hate-twisted chess master passed his final reclusive days in Icelandic exile, while Studs Terkel, born in New York but living decade after decade in his cluttered brick house on Castlewood Terrace, was not.

So being a Chicagoan obviously isn't just a matter of emerging into the world here. And merely working in the city every day doesn't do it—trust me on that one. Having a desk at the *Sun-Times* for the past quarter century, first at 401 N. Wabash and then at 350 N. Orleans, no more made me a Chicagoan in anybody's eyes than tacking a postcard of the Eiffel Tower on my bulletin board would make me French.

So is it sleeping here? That has got to be it, right? It's where you put your head at night that makes you a Chicagoan. That's what constitutes "living here" in most definitions. Your place of residence, where you get your mail. Do you have to both live *and* work here? That was the entire case against Rahm Emanuel—those who currently reside here are Chicagoans, while those who leave, even temporarily, even at the behest of the President of the United States, are not. You stop being a Chicagoan after . . . eighteen months, apparently. But if that were true, if living here right now is the key, then plenty of flight attendants and TV meteorologists perched in Presidential Towers between gigs in San Diego and Pittsburgh are genuine Chicagoans, at least for the moment, while Nelson Algren, passing his bitter last years on Long Island, or Mike Royko, residing in baronial comfort in Winnetka, were not.

Could being a Chicagoan possibly be a self-assessment? You can have the credentials to be a Chicagoan, but if you turn your back on the city, they don't matter. Consider Ernest Hemingway, whose legacy is associated with many places he visited, lived in, wrote about, or loved—Paris, Cuba, Key West, Spain, even Idaho.

Chicago—where he lived for a year and met his first wife, where he began writing professionally and which pops up in his early stories—barely registers on the Hemingway radar. The adjacent suburb of Oak Park, where he was born and raised, scores only a single blip, Hemingway's deathless slur of it being a town of "broad lawns and narrow minds." (No one has found an original source for Hemingway actually saying or writing this, so it may be apocryphal, the way many witty remarks are often falsely ascribed to Mark Twain or Kurt Vonnegut.)

Why? Because Hemingway felt snubbed by his hometown. "Nobody in Oak Park likes me," he plaintively wrote to a biographer. So he didn't like Oak Park in return. Whether he uttered his famous putdown or not, it certainly reflects how he felt. Nor did he like Chicago. Even in his youth, he admitted to "hating it," and in later years, he said he wasn't impressed with Chicago, didn't think he belonged here, and gave the city the same backhand he supposedly gave Oak Park. "I never thought Chicago was a tough place," Hemingway said in 1953—"tough" of course being the highest compliment Hemingway could conceive. Chicago, he said, wasn't even as tough as Kansas City.

Being a Chicagoan is a claim you have to press, a case you must make, and Hemingway, by not making it, lost the right. He had liked the place well enough as a young man in love, but having been born in Oak Park, Hemingway had no intention of lingering so close to home. "Gee this is a terribly good town," he wrote in a 1920 letter while living at 1230 N. State Street. "Instead of hating it the way I used to, I'm getting terribly fond of it. However there isn't going to be any permanent settlege down in it . . . because there are so many more most excellent towns in different places that I'd like to be."

Maybe that's the definition—you're a Chicagoan if, wherever you are at the moment, Chicago is the place you'd like to be. I would argue that Chicago is not simply a matter of where you put your pillow but where you place your heart, wherever you're sleeping now. "This is not Chicago," one resident said, surveying the smoldering ruins of the 1871 fire and tapping his chest. "Chicago is in here."

Being a Chicagoan is not a matter of how long you reside here, but how it affects you. It is a process, an attitude, a state of mind. Of course, living in the suburbs, I would say that, and many Chicago residents vigorously resent the suggestion and insist that it is a false claim upon what is theirs alone, the wearing of a ribbon for a battle you didn't fight in. And there is sense there—either you partake in the full spectrum of Chicago joys and Chicago woes, some of which arrive unexpectedly in the dead of night, or you do not. I accept that.

But like all cosmologies that place the holder smack at the center of the universe, the where-you-sleep standard is not a logical argument but an irrefutable definition, and a shifting one at that. When you look hard at the must-be-born-here, must-live-here argument, it tends to be endlessly reductive. Those endorsing it don't generously grant acceptance to all who meet their initial criterion. Instead there are always caveats, exceptions. There is always a smaller inner circle. When pressed they reveal that just living anywhere within the borders of Chicago proper is not nearly enough. North or South Side isn't enough. The right parish is getting close, but even that isn't always sufficient—heck, living on the right street doesn't always count in the subtle calibration, the endless parsing of who belongs.

"I was here first!" cries Dick, an angry boy squaring off against another angry boy in a James T. Farrell story.

"I live on this street," answers the second boy.

"I lived in this neighborhood longer than you," Dick answers.

There is no Chicagoan so firmly established that another Chicagoan can't question his credentials. It's easy to do: Richard M. Daley? The former mayor? C'mon, how can the *mayor*, how can anyone cocooned in that bubble, with a driver and a platoon of flacks and handlers and guards and assistants and money up the wazoo, ever pretend to be a real Chicagoan? Give me a frickin' break. To presume that Daley experiences the city the way actual Chicagoans do? Puh-leeze! Particularly when he's swanning around the world half the time—to *Paris* for the love of Christ!—and after he bugged out of Bridgeport to move to a *townhouse* and every other weekend he's rushing off to *Michigan* to ride his *mountain bike* around *Grand Beach*. Is that being a Chicagoan? Really? *Really?*

Still, even I recognize that four years of study in Evanston, of dwelling in dorms and rented student rooms on the periphery of the city, the inner suburban ring, did not make me a Chicagoan. At best, it introduced me to the broad outlines of the city.

* * *

To college students, Chicago means entertainment. Evanston was a dry town, home to the Women's Christian Temperance Union (my freshman dorm's t-shirts boasted "We're Behind the WCTU," which was literally true, the two buildings being next to each other). Evanston still had only two real bars, one in the Holiday Inn, the other in the Orrington Hotel. Evanston restaurants would serve you a drink, but the law required that you also buy "a meal," though that meal often turned out to be a plate of french fries.

To us at Northwestern, Chicago was the south side of Howard Street, the northern border of the city, where the student taverns clustered—though I never went to the Howard Street bars, not once, because they seemed to me frat territory, where I didn't belong. Chicago was Rush Street, it was Wrigley Field and the dance clubs around Belmont Avenue. To me, Chicago was the bar in the twelfth-floor lobby of the Ritz-Carlton, where I drank strawberry daiquiris—sophisticated!—with my visiting parents and with girls I was trying to impress. It was the elegant shops at the new, fancy Water Tower Place. My favorite Chicago spots were primarily restaurants. Dianna's Opaa, in Greektown on South Halsted Street, with its lanky, serpent-like owner, Petros Kogiones, performing his host duties that were as important as the food—on the nights he wasn't there, you felt cheated— sliding back his sheet of long black hair to greet his female customers with an overly familiar kiss and their dates with a disarming, arms-flung-wide cry of "cousin!" then conducting his odd 9 p.m. ceremonies, calling up all the engaged couples to be officially blessed by Famous Petros in the name of God, the Greek Orthodox Church, and Dianna's Opaa! We'd all cheer and raise our juice glasses of Roditis high.

Or the Berghoff, with its creamed spinach and historic stand-up bar, the last men-only tavern in the city, which admitted women only after a famous melee in 1969 when seven members of the National Organization for Women, armed with the city's new public accommodation law, stormed the place, demanding bourbon. What I loved was the history—well, that and the beer, and the Thuringer and sauerkraut sandwiches with brown mustard on fresh rye bread. The place was jammed at lunchtime. For years, the Berghoff bar had no stools. That's the way taverns used to be: you bellied up to the bar, quite literally, a tradition preserved to keep out the ladies, who liked to sit down, or so the theory went.

Back then, if you examined the framed photo of the crowded Berghoff bar on the day Prohibition ended, and looked at the elegant light fixtures in the photo, then up at the ceiling, they were the exact same fixtures. Unchanged. Cities surge on, but you want a few places to stay the same, to thwart time, to create the illusion of death cheated, which the Berghoff did for me until the Berghoff family, in a staggering act of karmic self-immolation, stripped the place of its photos, its history, and its name, technically going out of business in an apparent bid to save mere money by no longer employing a union waitstaff. They've since stealthily returned to being the Berghoff again, but I've never gone back, glancing through the garish restaurant windows as I hurry past on Adams Street the way you would look at the overly made-up face of an aged relation in her open casket, someone once beloved who served you pot roast for years and then lost her mind at the end and did something awful.

* * *

In the literary biographies I read as a young man, the famous-writer-to-be meets *New Yorker* editor Harold Ross at a party and his career is on its way.

That was my plan.

I secretly thought I was exceptional, maybe even a genius—a condition common as dirt in twenty-one-year-olds—and assumed someone would recognize my excellence eventually and usher me to my rightful spot on the first step of the stairway to glory. Fate would guide me. That was my career strategy. Newspapers held no special appeal—I had spent the winter of 1981 interning at the *Green Bay Press-Gazette*, crunching across the February subzero snow—so cold it squeaked—to fire stations to collect the details of every emergency call and ambulance run, including false alarms. "Every time an old woman has trouble breathing, we have to put it in the newspaper," I'd complain to my friends back at school. No thank you. Nor did advertising call out to me. I had won an essay contest whose prize was an internship at Meldrum & Fewsmith, one of Cleveland's largest ad agencies, and spent the summer before my senior year trying to think of reasons people should buy Caterpillar forklift trucks even though they cost twice as much as the Japanese competition. Pass.

Technology left me cold—maybe because my father was a nuclear physicist—and I shrugged off the advent of computers as an incremental advancement in writing tools. A computer was a fancy typewriter. I had taken "Introduction to Computer Programming" at Northwestern the fall of my freshman year, haunting the subbasement of Tech, learning Fortran and Cobol, using stacks of IBM punch cards. *Why go through all this to generate a calendar?* I thought to myself. *If I want a calendar, I'll go out and buy one.* Thus did my generation's version of the railroad pull out of the station and chug off without me.

Nor did Chicago particularly matter. I suppose, under the circumstances, I should gin up a false fidelity, but the truth is, when I was twenty-one, the city hardly affected my thinking, other than the fact that it was right there.

What mattered was writing. I wasn't even particularly focused on what I would be writing *about*. Something. All I had to do was keep writing and life would work itself out.

In the spring of my senior year, an editor from *Playboy* came to speak to Abe Peck's magazine writing class. I didn't care much for *Playboy*—photos of corn-fed, airbrushed women too unreal to be erotic and articles on how to buy $10,000 stereo systems. But the magazine was one of the few located in Chicago—it was that or the Elks Club International publication—and an editor was standing in front of me. I went up to him after class. He said I should send my stuff to *Playboy*'s top editor, Don Gold, who agreed to see me. Okay, I thought, *Playboy* it is. If need be, I would deign to work there. The magazine's offices were in the Palmolive Building, an art deco gem located where Lake Shore Drive jogs east to avoid running into Michigan Avenue. At the time, as it had for years, the building sported the distinctive blockish white PLAYBOY logo in lighted nine-foot-tall letters at the top—it was the Playboy Building—and while it was once difficult to imagine the structure without the glowing magazine title, it's now hard to imagine the sign was ever there.

Inside, the *Playboy* offices still had a Pepto-Bismol pink, 1960s decor, some hallways plastered to soften their edges where the walls met the floor and ceiling, as if the magazine staff were groovy red blood cells pumping through some giant stud's far-out body. Framed on the walls were various boob-festooned graphics from years past. I was ushered in to see Gold and spread my portfolio—it was big, black pebbled leather, like something an architect would carry—and showed him my college humor magazine layouts and my work in the *Northwestern Daily* newspaper, where I wrote a column called "Fun."

Gold told me to get lost, in polite fashion. "Try the *Reader*," he said, referring to an edgy free weekly. "Get some experience." I don't believe he actually added, "Give up this crazy dream, go home and marry the girl next door." But in memory he did.

My interview was over in minutes; it felt like seconds. I wasn't being welcomed to my proper place in the clouds. At least not today. I remember standing stunned, in the elevator going down, holding my portfolio at my side, thinking: "This is the Polish cavalry of my ego, meeting the German panzers of reality."

By the time I graduated, I was flailing, sending resumes off to *Plate World* ("The Magazine of Collector's Plates") to newspapers in Kentucky and health care magazines in Pennsylvania. I interviewed at Leo Burnett and traipsed through Loop advertising agencies—every one told me I needed to assemble a "book" of ads, which I almost began to do, until I realized I didn't want to write advertisements.

As it had with the city of St. Louis in the 1850s, a comfortable economic present lulled me into a false sense of security about the future. I still had my Northwestern work/study job. Twelve hours a week at $5.30 an hour in the anthropology department, where I worked as the assistant to a professor who had been studying postpartum depression among women in Pilsen and, conveniently for me, left the university that June to join a research firm. The anthropology department was located in a large Victorian house on Sheridan Road, and I had been employed there for the previous three years. Without an immediate boss, my workday consisted of entering this rambling, grand but somewhat threadbare residence, turning on the light to what was effectively now my private office, firing up a new IBM Correcting Selectric II typewriter and plugging away on my novel, plus assorted job queries and complaining letters to friends.

I was fully prepared for life to unfold in this fashion, for Northwestern University to overlook my tiny, lingering presence, for Dr. Gwen Stern to never return to the anthropology department, as the years unspooled and I crafted my masterpiece. Such was my thinking as I turned twenty-two and graduated from college. That I was abusing the system, taking a salary while doing nothing productive for my employer bothered me not at all. Rules are for people who aren't artists.

That idyll lasted a fortnight. In late June they called me into the an-thropology office. Neil, they said, we like you and you're a nice guy and you've been here forever and you know how to fix the copier. But you're not a student anymore and you don't actually work for anybody and you have to go.

Stunned, I wandered, eventually, over to Fisk Hall, and noticed a 3 × 5 index card thumbtacked to the wall: "Wanted: writers," it read. Hey, that's me! I'm a writer! I phoned the number, for a job with a public relations firm in Los Angeles, which, as they say, is not a proper city at all, but a collection of disparate places—the Pacific Ocean, Hollywood, Beverly Hills, downtown. They flew me out and rented a white Mustang convert-ible for me to tool around town in. The next thing I knew, I was sitting on a sun-dazzled balcony at the Beverly Hills Hilton, fresh from the shower, wrapped in a white terrycloth hotel robe, dipping a corner of toast into egg yolk and thinking, "Okay, I'll live here." I settled in Santa Monica, which isn't even technically part of Los Angeles, renting a bedroom in a house with a lemon tree in the backyard.

The Pacific Ocean was five minutes away, and I enjoyed spending Saturdays sitting on the beach beside the Santa Monica Pier. The highlight of my week was eating sushi on Pico Boulevard after work, a cuisine that in 1982 was still exotic enough to require explanation: "They have good restaurants," I wrote to a friend in Berea, "and I have become particular to Sushi (a Japanese dish, raw fish cakes, actually. Taste much better than they sound)." I bought myself a twenty-year-old sports car, a 1963 Volvo P1800, white, with stumpy little fins—my dream car—in a desperate effort to inject some panache into my ground-floor LA existence.

But I was deeply lonely. I knew nobody. I worked at 1901 Avenue of the Stars, in Century City, a sterile collection of skyscrapers built on the old 20th Century Fox back lot, where there was a restaurant called Heaven, a faux 1950s lunch counter set incongruously within a store selling Japanese consumer kitsch: Hello Kitty merchandise, little plastic Godzillas, Astro Boy lunchboxes.

Almost every day I went to Heaven for lunch, on account of its pretty waitresses, who talked to the customers. One day a waitress set down my club sandwich and said, "You have a smudge, honey," and dipped a napkin in a glass of ice water and rubbed some soot off my forehead. I sat there, frozen, feeling her hand and the cold water on my face, and realized that another human being hadn't touched me for weeks. That was Los Angeles.

I'd like to say that I missed Chicago, but that would also be pandering. It is more accurate to say that I missed living in a world where people knew me, and I missed myself as I had been just the previous spring at Northwestern, turning out columns and papers, running a comedy show on WNUR, Northwestern's radio station, helping to write the college humor magazine, beavering away at my novel, juggling girlfriends, waiting with some degree of confidence for success to sneak up from behind and give me a big hug. I was desperate to get back to a version of *that* life, and couldn't quite understand how I had gotten myself sunk so quickly into *this* one. The starting shot had been fired, my classmates had surged out of the blocks. The clock was ticking, the red second hand sweeping. Success was still looking for me, somewhere else, her hand cupped beside her mouth, calling my name. "Yoo-hoo, *Neee-il!*"

But how would she ever find me here, alone in Los Angeles, doing this?

You either make friends who pull you upward in a city, or you excel at your job and rise through the ranks, and I did neither. I lasted three months in Los Angeles. Hated my job at the Bohle Company, hated writing press releases for twelve-year-old BMX bicycle racers and captions for Epson America, hated cruising around Sunset Boulevard in my P1800 looking for . . . for what? I don't think I really knew. Exactly three months after I arrived, I shrugged and quit my job, probably days ahead of being fired on general principles, for not being a team player and for making caustic asides about companies we were paid good money to not only effectively hype but also to sincerely love in our hearts. Freed of the burden of employment, I headed east, back toward Chicago.

4

"Give her my regards"

CHICAGOANS CREDIT—or if you prefer, blame—the blizzard of 1979 for the election of Jane Byrne. She defeated mayor Michael Bilandic, a bland, soft-spoken man who, though generally competent, had neglected to make sure that city streets were plowed after the big snowstorm and, worse, let the Potemkin village plowing of his own mayoral neighborhood—why look, everything's fine!—fool him into believing streets were clear city-wide. He came off not only as inept, but arrogant and out of touch, and so was drummed out of office by a woman who had never been elected to anything.

The full version, of course, is more complicated. Bilandic became mayor after the death of Richard J. Daley, elevated to the post by the wheezing Chicago Democratic machine because he promised not to run in the 1977 special election. Bilandic was a placeholder, a delaying tactic to give the city's various power brokers and factions time to balance their interests and decide what to do next. But once in office, Bilandic changed his mind, upsetting black and Polish politicians, who, feeling they were being de-nied their long-awaited turn, lined up behind Byrne. She won fourteen of sixteen black wards, helped by the city's decision to try to unsnarl the el lines after the blizzard by expressing trains through the South and West sides. The snow is a shorthand for Bilandic's deficiencies, a kinder, quicker explanation than delving into how the pressure of simultaneously holding office and campaigning got to him and, toward the end, Bilandic became emotional, perhaps even unhinged, such as when he gave a speech comparing himself to the crucified Jesus Christ, to the horror and amusement of his audience.

That's why Bilandic lost. As for why Byrne was in a position to win, the key incident explaining her career had occurred twenty years earlier, in 1959. Her husband, Bill Byrne, was a handsome Marine Corps fighter pilot. The couple lived in Texas, but Jane and their toddler daughter Kathy were back in Chicago, visiting her parents. Bill Byrne flew in to join them and, setting down his Skyraider in heavy fog at the Glenview Naval Air Station, crashed into the cemetery next door and was killed.

A new widow and devout Catholic, Jane Byrne threw herself into the presidential campaign of John F. Kennedy. Which put her into contact with mayor Richard J. Daley. Who was both touched by her tragedy and gradually recognized Byrne as someone who could help him solve a new but growing problem—how to appease complaining feminists—simply by being a female in his overwhelmingly male-dominated Democratic Party machine. This was standard Daley procedure; he believed that appearing to address problems was the same as actually doing something substantive about them. Thus each helped the other. *Manus manum lavat.*

The blizzard might have been what inspired a majority of voting Chicagoans to pitch out their sitting mayor and elect a feisty candidate whose previous job had been commissioner of consumer sales, weights, and measures. But it was the crash that jarred Byrne out of the path of being a Texas military wife and mom and set her on the road to having her name on a ballot in Chicago and becoming its mayor by the greatest landslide in Chicago history: 82 percent of the vote, her first, last, and only electoral victory.

Without an actual plane crash, however, it can be difficult to look back on your own life and put your finger on the moment where you started becoming the thing you were going to be.

Having blown an entire year following college—after leaving Los Angeles, I camped out at my parents' house, pretending to be F. Scott Fitzgerald penning *This Side of Paradise* for five months until my dad booted me out—how did I return to Chicago and snag a good union newspaper job at the *Chicago Sun-Times*? By inches, by accident, and without key individuals ever reading a word I'd written.

I came back to Evanston because there were people there who knew me. "Home," wrote Robert Frost, "is the place where, when you have to go there, they have to take you in." My old college roommate, Kier Strejcek, let me stay in his attic for the first few weeks, sleeping under an inverted V of bare silvered insulation while I looked for an apartment and a job. Then I moved in with a pair of girls I knew who had an empty bedroom. As a housewarming gift, my friend Cate Plys—a year younger and about to move back home after graduating—gave me a cardboard box of food she had cleaned out from her cabinets and refrigerator. I weighed 148 pounds, 50 pounds lighter than I had freshman year.

It was a strange time—one of the girls I lived with, Fern, was a model, and would come to breakfast in her underwear. I'm not sure whether, distracted by this, I actually did once jab a tablespoon of oatmeal into my eye by accident, or whether that was just a flip line invented to amuse my friends and slyly brag about my living arrangement—it must have been the latter. Though Fern was very disconcerting—willowy, blonde, with pale blue eyes and a slight bump on the bridge of her nose—she was too petite to be a runway model, so posed for catalogues and bra box photos. With troubles of her own, she would crawl into bed and spoon around me, which I should have just accepted and appreciated but, being twenty-three, instead found off-putting as soon as I realized that was to be the extent of it. "This may be fine for your gay model friends," I testily informed her, "but to me, you climb into my bed, it means something. Don't sign any checks you can't cash." So she stopped.

And I thought I was a genius.

Speaking of checks, my share of the rent was $160 a month, and my parents paid it but kept a running tally of what I owed them. My father had no connections, no well-placed friends, no useful advice. I didn't realize it then, but Northwestern had become my parents now, my clout, my influential uncle. Though an inattentive one. The bulletin board at Fisk Hall served up no second magic index card to send me jetting to another city to try again. Instead I dutifully showed up at the NU job placement office, pawed through the files of job openings, and made phone calls. These connected me with basic entry-level positions at the most marginal companies imaginable—one prospective employer interviewed me in his bare feet amid the jumble of his dirty hodgepodge of a warehouse office. As I sat stiffly on the edge of a broken, stained orange chair, in my suit and tie, portfolio on my lap, gazing at those toes, horrified to my core, the realization began to dawn on me that I had squandered my years at school, that I was now in the slurry, the frozen sloshing trough of nobodies whom nobody had sent, and I had better find a way to climb out quickly before I drowned.

To top it off, the guy with the bare feet didn't offer me a job.

Meanwhile, the mechanical rabbit of my classmates' success was scooting further and further ahead, disappearing around the bend. Fellow NU student Julia Louis-Dreyfus and three of her colleagues from the Practical Theatre Company had been plucked out of the grandly-named forty-two-seat John Lennon Auditorium at the corner of Howard and Custer and catapulted into the fame and riches of the TV show *Saturday Night Live*. She was a year younger than me, and I hadn't known her or the others at school—I only went to their performances—so I couldn't call them up and say, "Hey, take me along!" But they were proof that the climb upward was possible, and also something of a rebuke. While I was splashing around, trying to find any kind of job I could hold onto, some people who had sat with me in class—the people with talent—were becoming stars.

You work what connections you have. I don't remember being savvy enough—or enough of a suck-up—to keep on good terms with my professors out of self-interest, to use later on. But my magazine writing teacher, Abe Peck, was the one professor at Medill I sincerely liked and respected. He was in his late thirties, with a slight New York accent, like my father, wore jeans, a compact, trim man with longish hair.

Unlike many of his Medill colleagues, Abe had not only written in the recent past, but had written for *Rolling Stone*, which represented the union of hipness and good journalism. He had moved from *Rolling Stone* to the *Chicago Daily News* and then the *Sun-Times*, before following a pair of newspaper colleagues to Northwestern, to give himself time to write a book about the underground press in the 1960s.

Peck thought enough of me to ask that I take a look at the book he was writing, a task that at the time I grumbled about, resenting the effort it took and envious of his high-rise apartment, but then rationalized: "He does have contacts—maybe he can help me."

So perhaps I was savvier than I recall. Something prompted me to occasionally present myself at his office, a scruffy unemployed twenty-three-year-old in green fatigue Army surplus pants, eager to give him the update on my struggles, as if we were friends. During one such check-up, he cast me a long, pitying look. "Still trying to get by on the old Neilio-centric Universe Theory, eh?" he chuckled, plucking a piece of paper off his desk. "I've been looking for you. Call this number."

Years later, I asked Abe why he helped me; he did not remember any particular quality of mine. He said while he helped hundreds of his students, and editors with jobs to fill learned to turn to him, he didn't automatically help every student—he had his own reputation to think of—so I must have had something on the ball, enough that he asked me to read his manuscript and could recommend me without fear of embarrassment.

The number was for the *Barrington Courier-Review*. Their "Mr. Weekend," Dave Hoekstra, had left to take a job with the suburban edition of the *Chicago Sun-Times*—after sending his clips to Lon Grahnke, an editor who happened to grow up in Berwyn, just like Dave did—and so the paper needed a new Mr. Weekend. The *Courier-Review* was run by Drew Davis, who knew his suburban weekly was too small to attract talented writers with established careers, so he trolled journalism schools like Medill or Columbia University's graduate program, hoping to get a few years' service out of skilled young reporters just starting out. Davis was a buzz-cut marine captain in the reserves who communicated the fact that he'd prefer me to wear a tie to work by silently reaching over to the neck of my open shirt, grabbing a clump of chest hair between his thumb and forefinger, and yanking it out. He retired a major general.

The pay was $12,000 a year, and the job entailed reviewing movies, writing a column, and creating a weekly page, about both suburban distractions and entertainments in the city. Even as far away as Barrington, a suburb thirty miles to the northwest, Chicago was still the place with the Big Fun.

That's how I learned there was tremendous theater in Chicago, by going to plays for the *Courier-Review*: *In the Belly of the Beast* directed by Robert Falls and starring William L. Petersen as the murderer Jack Henry Abbott, banging his head against filing cabinets in the tiny Wisdom Bridge Theatre. Frank Galati confessing his agonized love in *The Dresser*. And *Hamlet*, another unforgettable Robert Falls production, with Aidan Quinn slowly writing "To be or not to be" in red spray paint on a wall and then turning to the audience, jerking his thumb at the dripping words and saying, "That is the question!" While Broadway in New York was ossifying, Chicago's theater scene had burst into a golden age. Or so we told ourselves.

Being Mr. Weekend was the perfect job for dating, in that my mandate was to continuously attend cultural events, and I didn't have to pay for any of them. I had met a girl just before graduation. Edie Goldberg was a sales clerk at Mindscape Gallery in Evanston, which sold expensive art glass and high-priced pottery, ceramic vases, burl-wood boxes and other finely tooled knickknacks. Edie was my age, ninety pounds dripping wet, with high cheekbones and a mass of curly, pre-Raphaelite strawberry-blonde hair. She was going to school at Northeastern—not the one in Boston, but the one on Bryn Mawr Avenue.

Pretending to browse the gallery, flattered that she was paying close attention to me, unaware that saleswomen there worked on commission, I asked Edie what she was studying. "Philosophy," she said. I asked her if she had read *Nausea* by Jean-Paul Sartre. My older sister owned the paperback and I had read it back in Berea because it was on the shelf, had an intriguing title, and was a short book.

"No," she said.

"Then you're not studying philosophy," I airily pronounced, returning later to lend her my copy and ask her out on a date.

As with Chicago, it was not love at first sight; I have to be frank about that. Not on either side. She saw me as a type: a rich Northwestern kid—and to her, everyone who attended Northwestern was rich—who would buy her a much-needed dinner and then be told to get lost. I saw her as a really good-looking woman who, contrary to the norm and for reasons mysterious, agreed to go out with me.

The first date was dull, at the Keg, a nondescript restaurant in Evanston—really a bar that serves food. The only fact I can dredge up from that night was my surprise at hearing her talk about spending a year working in a kitchen on a kibbutz in Israel. *Hmmm, a kibbutz* . . . I thought . . . *she must be Jewish.* I still didn't know her last name. There might never have been a second date, but it was chilly, so I loaned her a sweater and then had to get it back. The second date was a disaster—she had a migraine headache and sat over cocktails at a table in Leslee's, a basement jazz bar, pressing her fingertips against her temples. "You know, we don't have to go to dinner if you're not feeling well," I told her soothingly, and she surprised me by immediately thanking me and hopping up and leaving, hurrying to the el to connect with a bus for home. My understanding was a pose—I had never heard of migraines, and thought this was the old headache routine and I was being brushed off. That made sense to me. I moved to Los Angeles, let a year go by, and forgot about her completely, until back in Chicago, cleaning out an old phone book, transferring important numbers to a new one, I came upon her number and called.

It was that third date. We hit the bar at the Ritz-Carlton—someplace familiar—for strawberry daiquiris. But the evening dragged. She looked bored; I knew I was. We didn't have anything in common to talk about. This wasn't working. Suddenly inspiration hit. "I know a place," I said, "where we can dance." We drove to 950 Lucky Number, an unpretentious North Side club on Wrightwood, just off Lincoln Avenue, where the DJ played "Bela Lugosi's Dead" by Bauhaus—a pulsing, dripping, clicking sensuous song, nearly ten minutes long. It seemed to go on forever. Dancing to that song changed everything. The next day, at lunchtime, we sat at Cheers, an outdoor café in East Rogers Park, up Sheridan Road from where she lived, and I tried to wrap my head around this sudden shift in the quality of my life.

"So let me get this straight," I told her, comprehension slow to dawn. "I'm going to call you . . ." I pointed at her for emphasis, "and you're going to go out with me"—here I flattened my hand against my chest, as if to make certain she knew exactly who we were talking about. "And we're going to do this again. Is that correct?"

Edie grew up in Bellwood, a modest, blue-collar close-in western suburb. Her father was a partner in a metal tube-bending business. I eventually came to understand that machines were involved. Though to look at Irv Goldberg—a short, powerful, pragmatic guy who'd driven a tank in World War II—you wouldn't be surprised if machines weren't necessary.

She was Irv's daughter, a feisty, no-bull gal. No North Shore grandiosity, no love of pricy stores, no wacked-out astrological beliefs or psycho theories to send me screaming for the door. She had been fourteen when her family moved from Bellwood to Skokie—her new friend's mother smiled at her for not knowing the brand name of the shoes she was wearing.

I was amazed to be dating her, this woman in tight jeans and a black rabbit coat bought at a street fair. Not just entranced by her looks, but by the fact that she was a city girl—she lived on St. Louis Avenue, near Northeastern. I would pick her up at Mindscape, go to her apartment in the city. Occasionally she'd trek out to Barrington, where I lived with two other guys from the paper in a lovely old house with stained-glass windows owned by a college professor who, despite his advanced degrees, thought it was a good idea to rent his home to three men in their early twenties while he took a visiting professorship up in Wisconsin. Edie still shakes her head at how squalid the place became in just one year.

The winter Edie and I started dating, the General Motors Corporation loaned me a new midnight-blue Chevrolet Corvette for a week—publicizing the change in style—and I picked Edie up at the Metra station in the flashy sports car without first telling her I had it. A surprise.

We kissed hello and drove off. There was silence for about ten seconds. I couldn't stand it anymore.

"Well???" I said, grinning, practically bouncing up and down at the wheel.

"Well what?" she said.

"THE CAR!!!" I almost shouted. "Whaddaya think of THE CAR! It's a Corvette! Isn't it *great*?!"

She looked around, genuinely perplexed, as if noticing we were in a different vehicle for the first time. "This?" she said. "You know I don't care about this kind of thing."

That's Edie. She of course had no car. She took public transportation. My California-coddled sports car immediately began to die in its first Chicago winter, and I remember being awed—just *awed*—when she used the city bus system to get us to an auto shop that stocked the hard-to-find battery cables for a 1963 Volvo P1800 that I needed after the cables on mine exploded. I got on a bus with her, for the first time, feeling adventurous, as if on a lark, tickled that permission to travel on buses had suddenly been granted to me by this marvelous woman, a woman who knew things, who had practical solutions at her fingertips. She had a wary, catlike way of walking down the street, always glancing around, gauging her surroundings, especially at night—I used to mockingly imitate her, tiptoeing like a silent movie villain, hands up in front of me, fingers spread, eyes wide and darting about, spinning around, flinching, scanning the skies for peril. "That's not funny," she'd say, unamused. "You have to be aware in the city."

I don't think any new couple with scant financial resources ever had a more luxurious first year of dating. We saw Twyla Tharp dance her "Nine Sinatra Songs" at the Auditorium Theatre and Leonard Bernstein conduct the Vienna Philharmonic at Orchestra Hall and the Neville Brothers play their Cajun music at Fitzgerald's on Roosevelt Road. We went to galas and opening nights, staying downtown at the Congress Hotel and the Ambassador East, which yanked its advertising from the *Courier-Review* when, in my write-up about our breakfast at the Pump Room, I compared their eggs Benedict to an Egg McMuffin, unfavorably.

I kept thinking I'd meet Mike Royko, the syndicated columnist whose street-smart column set a tone for the city, telling tales of arrogant fat cats with connections and powerless nobodies getting the shaft. Edie still laughs at me for this, for standing around the premiere party of *Dreamgirls*, gobbling up peel-and-eat-shrimp from the base of a dripping ice sculpture, scrutinizing every balding, middle-aged man in aviator glasses and whispering to her, "Do you think that's Royko? Do you think that's Royko?"

I'd been in Barrington less than a year when Mike Chapin, the man in the *Courier-Review* hierarchy between me and Drew Davis, accepted a job as editor of the *Wheaton Daily Journal*, an anemic—some editions were just ten pages long—newspaper in the far western suburb. He took me with him, to edit the arts and editorial pages and write a news column. When I told Drew I was quitting, he said I couldn't quit, because he was firing me. I was still twenty-three.

People live their whole lives in the suburbs. I met residents of Wheaton who literally had never been to Chicago, thirty miles away. Or so they insisted, though to me the claim defies belief, like saying you have never read a book or tasted chocolate. It certainly was a separate, insulated world. Wheaton is a Christian community, intensely so at the time, home to the evangelical Wheaton College and fifty-three churches.

Contrary to expectations, I liked that. "At least they believe in something," I'd tell people, when they asked how a Jew could write a column in such a strongly Christian community. They sure made my job easy. The fundamentalists have a philosophy I called "wallpapering the world"—instead of personally rejecting what they don't approve of, eliminating it from their own lives, and concentrating on their own rich theology, they try to stamp out what they don't like everywhere around them, to remove it from life in general so that others will not be confronted with its existence and face choices that only the faithful are qualified to make. This had the effect of making them seem, at least to me, to be more focused on what they don't believe in than on what they do, more concerned with the behavior of everybody else than with their own actions. Wheaton true believers picketed a convenience store for selling the magazine I had tried to work at. They protested in front of the College of DuPage for staging *Sister Mary Ignatius Explains It All for You*, and railed against rock music.

In "The Truth about Rock Ministries," the Peters brothers talked about how heavy-metal music drives teens to suicide, and flashed slide after slide of risqué album covers to a packed audience—Tina Turner's endless legs, spread wide on her *Private Dancer* cover—inspiring me to form another theory: that believers from strict religious upbringings hold protests against things they are secretly fascinated with as a way to experience the illicit thrill of contemplating a taboo while safely purporting to express their condemnation. This was most obvious during a lecture against pornography in a Wheaton College classroom, where a speaker produced a stack of low-quality smut that I'd hesitate to touch, fanning it out on a table and inviting the audience to "see for themselves how bad it is." There was a whoosh as the room rushed up as one to investigate the situation.

I wonder how many developed a taste for porn after that, the latest manifestation of a fine Chicago tradition that could be traced back to evangelical preachers leading their flocks into the Levee red-light district in the 1890s and 1900s to do battle with sin, only to inadvertently introduce them to vice and emerge with one or two fewer faithful. Minna Everleigh, the notorious madam, said that while she appreciated the business, she regretted to see "so many young men coming down here for the first time." Of course it's impossible to determine what actually happened, whether some of the pious were indeed lost to the bars and the brothels they were trying to shut down, or whether that was just an amusing calumny cooked up to mock their efforts. Given the dearth of specific examples, I'd guess the latter. People often mistakenly assign an undeserved gravity to our ancestors—maybe because they're dead—and dry jokes have a way of eventually being read as sincere reportage. But I was in that room at Wheaton College, and saw the students crowding around the table.

Not that Wheaton consisted *solely* of evangelicals. The town had its share of peculiarities. As if to counterbalance Wheaton College, it is also home to the sprawling, gated headquarters of the Theosophical Society, a bizarre nineteenth-century attempt to develop a homegrown Baha'i-like mash of the world's faiths and beliefs, flavored with a heavy dose of swami mysticism, and I toured its main offices, which were stacked with boxes of obscure philosophical tracts by society cofounder Madame Blavatsky. A reminder that despite easy generalization, not every suburb is a Levit-town of identical ticky-tacky houses, that they do tend to have their own particular aspects of uniqueness and excellence—not nearly as many as a city, of course, but charms and quirks nonetheless.

Still, I never considered living in Wheaton, any more than I had considered settling in Berea. Indeed, if I am indeed a Chicagoan, to the degree that I may be, I would attribute it to being rootless in all other places. I was born in Berea but wouldn't stay there, moved to Los Angeles, and promptly left. I worked in Wheaton but couldn't imagine living there—an indication that actually residing in a community must count for something, because I viewed moving to Wheaton as a declarative act akin to being baptized.

Oak Park was as close to Wheaton as I could get. I appreciated Oak Park because, like Evanston, it is bound to the city by rails, both the el and Metra, the commuter system, which was not intentionally designed as parallel-but-superior public transportation for the affluent, but in effect is. Chicago street names continue into Oak Park—Lake Street and Division Street, North Avenue and Chicago Avenue, Washington Boulevard and Roosevelt Road—as opposed to Evanston, which demurely renames the Chicago streets as they cross the border, Damen Avenue becoming Custer, California Avenue becoming Dodge, like a Victorian lady inventing polite terms for parts of the body. You could also get the *Chicago Reader* in Oak Park, and the free alternative weekly was a marker for the city to me—could you get the *Reader*? Part of your Chicago identity was forged by what you read regularly—did you prefer the global perspective of the traditionally Republican *Tribune* or the grittier, city-oriented, Democratic-with-lapses *Sun-Times*? Did you bother with the ethnic papers, the niche publications? Or did you get all your news from television, which is like trying to breathe through a straw? These choices help define you. I live in the suburbs, but almost never read the *Daily Herald*—maybe once a year—because, to me, it's a newspaper for suburbanites. That I *am* a suburbanite doesn't enter into the equation.

Oak Park had a city feel, with its own little downtown pedestrian mall, like State Street's, boasting its own little art deco movie theater, the Lake, which is on Lake Street but, like the whole village, nowhere near a body of water (Oak Park struck me as a landlocked, collegeless Evanston). Oak Park is embroidered not only by the world's highest concentration of Frank Lloyd Wright houses, but also by the architect's home and studio, which highlights the unfairness of Hemingway's alleged line about "narrow minds," since at the exact moment Hemingway was growing up in Oak Park, Wright was revolutionizing architecture a few blocks away. Edgar Rice Burroughs was there too, writing *Tarzan of the Apes*, published when Hemingway was thirteen—which, taken together, true, do not turn Oak Park into Weimar Berlin, but at least raise the question of whether Hemingway condemned the village on its own merits or as a safe surrogate for condemning his parents, whom he despised.

Wright gets all the press, though my favorite houses were a pair of enormous, Alp-like Victorian mansions on the 400 block of North Kenilworth Avenue. I would stroll past, bring visitors by to gape, and wonder how the owners skipping up their front steps—with a certain air of guilt,

I imagined—had managed to find a way to live there. They couldn't both have inherited their splendid berths. What should I do to be like them? I wanted to live in a house like that.

"West is best," my boss told me—a racial code, since Oak Park's eastern edge borders Chicago's West Side ghetto. Oak Park prides itself on being an integrated community, yet its residents tend to cluster racially within it, the implication always being: stay among your own. No pioneer, I rented a one-bedroom apartment a block from Oak Park's western border, Harlem Avenue, in a large courtyard building on Washington Street, near the distinctive hot dog stand Parky's, whose sign is of a hand holding a hot dog, its pinkie arched upward, to show that these are hot dogs for sophisticates.

I was already secretly writing for the *Sun-Times* while on the staff at the *Wheaton Daily Journal*—well, "secretly" is the wrong word, since they printed my byline. Nobody at Wheaton seemed to notice—at least I thought they didn't notice—and I certainly wasn't pointing out my infidelity to them. Or to cite a core tenet of journalism: it's easier to apologize than to get permission. I hoped that if the subject came up they'd admire my spunk, but I couldn't be sure. Ambition is a form of betrayal—you can't give 100 percent to your current master while scanning the horizon for your next. But who could be content at the *Wheaton Daily Journal*? I called it "The Amityville Job," a nod to the movie *The Amityville Horror*, whose advertising tagline was the sepulchral cry, "Get out!"

Perhaps that isn't being fair either—the *Daily Journal*, now defunct, did publish journalism beyond routine reportage on the various qualms of the faithful particular to Wheaton and the zoning spats typical of every small town. A reader phoned me to say that her son, five, had been raped by the janitor at the local Montessori school, and she was shocked when she called the police and nothing happened. "I expected them to show up with their sirens blaring," she said. Just dropping that story into a regular column seemed too jarring, so I used the crime as the starting point for a weeklong series on child sexual abuse as strong as anything in the Chicago papers. It was the beginning of my real, postschool education, that of interviewing child molesters in prison and gazing at life as it is—or, rather, can be, at its worst. One day I entered the office of assistant DuPage County state's attorney Brian Telander to interview him about the kindergartener. On his desk was a large color photograph, a big 16 × 20—there were children in the brightly colored photo, and at first glance it seemed like a family Christmas portrait from Sears. He saw me looking at the photo, and spun it around so I could see properly—it was a crime scene photograph of a woman who had been murdered and her children murdered and piled on top of her on a bed. The bright red color was blood. I saw that photo, in my mind's eye, at some point every week, if not every day, for years to come, usually when returning home at night through the alley behind my apartment in Oak Park. I can see it now.

* * *

The *Chicago Sun-Times* hired me because I kissed a girl in a bar.

This is the part of the narrative that people usually skip, the dirty little connection where they get their hooks into their future, such as it is. The bestowing of a favor, the cut in front of the line. I started writing for the *Sun-Times*, freelance, in 1984, less than two years out of college. Not out of any talent or worth of my own, individually, not because of the quality of anything I had done in the suburbs, but due, still, to the lingering benign influence of having gone to school at Northwestern in general and having taken Abe Peck's magazine-writing class in particular, which nudged me ahead of all the other minimally competent would-be journalists in the Chicago metro area who would have loved to write for a big daily newspaper.

The bedrock truth is this: while still in school, on the second-to-last day of Abe's class, in a festive, summery mood, he had asked us what we wanted to talk about during our final session of the year. I, wisenheimer boozehound that I was, even then, raised my hand and said that while I didn't care about the topic, I'd prefer the setting to be the bar at the Orrington Hotel.

For some unfathomable reason he agreed. We had class in the bar, and while Abe held a discussion and left after an hour, a classmate and I remained and, our judgment skewed by many Singapore Slings, spent the afternoon making out in a dark corner.

The romance began and ended there—I soon left for Los Angeles; she took a job at a paper in Dallas—but by the time I returned and was trying to plot my escape from Wheaton, she had also returned and was a copy-editor at the *Sun-Times*. I ran into her at an Evanston party and she took pity on me—that afternoon at the Orrington bar must have shifted me from the ranks of slightly known classmates whose fates are of absolutely no interest whatsoever to the smaller elite of men with whom one had shared some kind of intimacy, and thus held in the mildest of proprietary concern, like a second cousin you've met a few times at family gatherings over the years. Someone worth helping.

She gave me the phone number for Valerie Mindel, an editor at the *Sun-Times* in charge of putting out a secondary-education supplement five times a year. The school guide—called, with characteristic newspaper creativity, "School Guide"—was a marginal publication whose entire purpose was to print ads for junior colleges, business schools, technical institutes, and art academies. Convention held that a few stories about education ought to be inserted between the ads. Nobody on the *Sun-Times* staff wanted to write these stories—they were practically advertising—and so Valerie was always on the hunt for writers skilled enough to be able to produce the stuff without requiring lots of time-consuming direction and hand-holding from her, but not so skilled that they refused to stoop to writing for the School Guide.

I called the number. Valerie said she had no assignments. That might have been the end of it, and I might have grown old and bitter in Wheaton, a seed drying out in the crevice of a rock. But just having the phone number of an editor at the *Sun-Times* was a kind of low-grade power, and I passed the number on to another classmate, Mary Kay Magistad. She was working at the *Chicago Evening Post*, an office without a publication, the first (and as it turned out, last) step by a group of investors who were, briefly, considering the possibility of starting a new afternoon Chicago newspaper. That wasn't as daft a notion then as it sounds today. There was a rough sense to the idea; remember, the great *Chicago Daily News*, an afternoon paper, had folded only six years earlier, and an argument could be made at the time that the market might support three newspapers.

My dream was of getting in on the ground floor at the *Post*—present at the creation!—so I of course wanted to keep on good terms with Mary Kay. I gave her the number just to show her that I too was in the loop. Here—I struck out, but maybe this will work for you. To my surprise, it did. When Mary Kay—who would go on to report for years from Southeast Asia, opening up the Beijing bureau for National Public Radio—called, Valerie gave her a story to write. I remember, some time later, listening to Mary Kay describe her new gig at the *Sun-Times* and wondering: *why didn't that work for me?* She breezed through the door I had pushed against in vain. Persistence was still an unfamiliar concept to me, then, but obviously the number that hadn't worked at one point was working fine now.

So I tried again. This time, Valerie not only needed an article, but needed several articles, right away. I remember blurting out something dense like, "Don't you want to see any of my work?" and the answer was no, she didn't. There wasn't time for formalities. I had gone to Medill; that was enough. She assigned me three stories.

That was my Captain Byrne moment, my plane crash, the event that jarred me from whatever track I was on—suburban nobody pointed toward public relations—to writing for the *Sun-Times*. (Not the empyrean, either, but it would do.) I made out with a girl in a bar and called the phone number she gave me, twice. Of that sequence of events, it is the second call, I suppose, that I could take some small pride in, because most people, initially thwarted, never even place the second call.

The importance of dumb luck in life, particularly in career advancement is, I believe, underappreciated. Everybody likes to fancy that they forged themselves, Prometheus-like, out of red-hot struggle and raw talent. And maybe we do, in part. But random chance also plays a big part. I called back on the right day. Maria Pappas was a busy psychologist and lawyer living in Chicago when one of her clients, alderman Rickey Hendon, mentioned to her that she might make a good politician. He was impressed with her smarts and her bigheartedness—she did a lot of pro bono work. But he also knew that Chicago's well-off Greek business community was looking for a candidate to get excited about, and suggested that she might consider running for the Cook County Board of Commissioners. Pappas had never heard of it. "What's the Cook County Board of Commissioners?" she asked. Hendon explained that, basically, it controls the jail and the hospital and the forest preserve, and he was sincere enough to become her first campaign manager. She would pull in the Greek money and the white votes, and Hendon—who is black—would take care of getting the black community on board. There were thirty-five other candidates along with Pappas vying for ten commissioner seats.

Besides her ethnicity drawing automatic support from deep-pocketed Greeks looking to back a compatriot, and her African-American campaign manager drumming for her, Pappas benefited from three other significant boosts that pushed her ahead of the pack, three qualities that helped her yet had nothing whatsoever to do with her talents, abilities, or achievements.

First, her parents had named her Maria, which prompted many voters, she believes, to vote for her because they mistakenly assumed she's Catholic. She's not—she's Greek-Orthodox.

Second, her last name is Pappas, and in the 1970s, the Cubs had a top pitcher named Milt Pappas. Chicagoans assumed they were related, and maybe even that she was his wife—voters asked her about Milt Pappas so frequently that she approached the former ballplayer, hoping he might campaign for her. (He refused. But nobody knew that.)

And third, of the thirty-five candidates running in an election one incumbent called "a crap shoot," Pappas's name was randomly selected to be listed first on the ballot. Studies show that, all things being equal, as they usually are in low-level races like the one for the Cook County Board of Commissioners, where money for advertising is scant and often all the candidates are unknowns, voters will tend to shrug and pick the first name on the ballot. When the ballots were counted, the ten commissioner seats on the Cook County Board were won by seven board incumbents, two seasoned Democratic Party pros, and one newcomer, Maria Pappas.

* * *

Contact made, I got busy, writing as many articles for the *Sun-Times* as I could, trying to find education themes that had the tang of the offbeat, of the strangeness I savored—a professor studying why fish in arctic waters don't freeze solid, a college course for train engineers that put them on a full-sized locomotive parked in the middle of a darkened classroom with a movie of approaching railroad track speeding up or slowing down as they worked the throttle. In some School Guides, I had six bylines.

The key to making the leap from the School Guide to the main paper involved dropping my stories off at the office. We were supposed to mail them in—there was no rush; the guides were not time-sensitive—but I detected a crack in the wall, and to the degree that my success, such as it is, wasn't dumb luck, it was that quality of wedging myself into any narrow gap I found and pouring my energies into the breach. Success in writing—or anything else for that matter—is like giving birth: you have to push.

I should remember my first glimpse of the *Sun-Times* newsroom on the fourth floor of the paper's trapezoidal gray, squat, and charmless building on North Wabash Avenue. It was back in the day when reporters still stubbed out their cigarettes on the tile floor. But since I went on to work there for the next twenty years, until they tore the building down to make room for Trump Tower, the truth is, it all blends together. I did not stare with open-mouthed longing at the romantic clatter of the newsroom, as one is supposed to do. At least I don't think I did. There was a window from the hall to the newsroom, and I do remember gazing through it and seeing Harlan Draeger, a short, balding, middle-aged, comfortable-looking man in glasses, laughing at his desk, eating an apple. He seemed a welcoming figure.

There was no time to stand and yearn. My focus was on locating the features editor, cornering her, and asking the one question that no editor anywhere, a hundred years ago or a hundred years from now, can answer in the negative: "Are you looking for good story ideas?"

Why yes, she said, as a matter of fact she was, and for months after that I peppered her—and then her successor—with story suggestions, with the things I thought were interesting and wanted to write about.

If a small town is lucky to boast one or two central elements—Oak Park is Frank Lloyd Wright, Wheaton is Protestant Christianity in all its pitfalls and glories—a city the size of Chicago can be whatever a writer wants it to be. It's a big enough place; there's enough stuff in it. Thus if you want Chicago to be a city of sports teams, you can spend your life attending games and talking to athletes. It can be a city of theater and plays, or music and concerts, or food and restaurants. God knows there's politics—election and corruption. A bottomless pit of crime, if you prefer, a city of murders and murderers. You can focus on the buildings, on architects—there are only three cities in America with readily identifiable skylines: New York, San Francisco, and Chicago—after that, you need a caption to know whether you are looking at Dallas or Los Angeles, Pittsburgh or Boston.

None of that interested me, particularly. My Chicago was the Chicago that other people weren't writing about. If a story appeared anywhere else, it killed my curiosity. I had the answer and didn't need to go in search of it. Whatever was in the headlines, almost by definition, was of no concern to me, because my involvement would be piling on. The standard reporter's instinct of wanting to leap upon the day's big story was completely absent in me. Maybe part of that was timidity—I didn't want to be part of the scrum. I didn't want to be an echo or a supernumerary. But it was more visceral than that—somebody else's story was a half-eaten sandwich, gummed over and revolting, and I wanted no part of it. I wanted to write about something fresh, something that I had cooked up, something that puzzled me as I went around the city: why don't birds die when they land on the el's electrified third rail? What do bridge tenders do in the winter when the river freezes? Who changes the lightbulbs on the masts atop the John

Hancock Building? What do museum guards think about as they stand there all day? I wanted to see things most people didn't see, write about bars that stayed open all night, ask Nobel Prize winners at the University of Chicago not about the recondite fields of expertise that won them the prize—the standard question—but this: when they got their Nobel Prizes home, where did they put them? On the mantel? On their desks? And do they show them off to dinner guests? Nobody, as far as I could tell, had ever asked Nobel Prize winners that, and it seemed to me the obvious question, the thing that regular people would really like to know.

The first story I wrote for the *Sun-Times* that wasn't in the School Guide was on thrift-shop bakeries. Most foodstuff manufacturers have a thrift shop—a modest store attached to the factory where frugal customers can go to buy squished loaves of bread, day-old rolls, and cupcakes whose squiggles of icing are misapplied. The idea is to make a little revenue from products that can't otherwise be sold. Manufacturers don't generally advertise these establishments—it would annoy their supermarket chain customers if their own suppliers began bragging about underselling them. Many thrift shops weren't listed in the phone book. Executives at Entenmann's Bakery refused to even talk about theirs. So the stores exist in a kind of tacit limbo. They're secret public places, filled mostly with perfectly fine products at bargain prices, since you can't invite customers to patronize a store, even a low-key one, whose stock depends entirely on what gets screwed up at the factory the day before. You need regular inventory.

I had seen these stores and wondered about them. Thrift-shop bakeries were the ideal story for me, a dynamic I would repeat again and again in the decades to come—notice something dim and fuzzy in the corner of my field of vision, grab it, drag it into clear focus, put it under the light and take a good look at it, illuminate readers about something that they either didn't know was there, or knew about, vaguely, but never really thought about before.

To write the story, I visited the big Butternut Bread plant on Garfield Boulevard, and the Kitchens of Sara Lee in Deerfield, to watch chocolate chip cheesecakes march through its 110-foot-long oven and note the deformed cakes being whisked away to the thrift shop. There was a moment that underscored the personal appeal of journalism for me—we had lunch, sirloin steaks on nice china in a boardroom at Sara Lee, just this public relations spokeswoman and myself. It was out-of-the-ordinary for me to eat a steak, period, never mind for free, never mind with an adult lady in a wood-paneled executive office. Knife and fork in hand, I look around, smiled to myself, and thought, "I like this."

The more time you put into a story, the better it will turn out, and I was free to focus my full energies on articles for the *Sun-Times*, having gotten myself fired from the *Wheaton Daily Journal*. The most famous graduate of Wheaton College is Rev. Billy Graham, the charismatic evangelical preacher. He was making one of his occasional visits to Wheaton, and after his speech I had the chance to meet him. We talked about the newspaper and Graham mentioned that he is friends with Helen Copley—owner of the Copley chain of newspapers, of which the *Daily Journal* was the smallest. He had spoken at her husband's funeral, he said, but didn't get the chance to see old Helen as often as he liked. Next time *you* see her, Billy Graham told me, you say hello.

Well, I had never seen Helen Copley. I was never going to see Helen Copley. She was enthroned at the flagship paper out in San Diego and would never visit the Midwest, and even if she did, she'd go to our larger sister paper in Elgin. But in the column—which generally praised Graham, particularly compared to scandalous reverends like Jimmy Swaggart and Jerry Falwell—I began musing about the circumstances that might lead to me to actually someday meet Helen Copley. "I promised that the next time I saw her," I wrote, "perhaps playing pinochle at Bebe Rebozo's with Nixon, the Hunt brothers and Colonel Ky, I would say hello for him."

Bebe Rebozo was Nixon's bagman. The Hunt brothers and Colonel Ky were similarly shady, minor 1960s characters. The whole sentence is a mediocre Hunter S. Thompson pastiche. A mature editor might have razored out that attempt at humor—we still set up pages using hot wax—but there was a hitch: *I* was the editor.

Well, except for Mike Chapin, my boss, who the day after the column ran asked me to take a walk with him along busy Schmale Road and, in as gentle a manner as possible, fired me. Helen Copley never saw the joke or complained about it, as far as I know. It was a prophylactic firing, in case she ever did.

* * *

I was twenty-five years old, cut loose, but not adrift. I had an apartment in Oak Park, where I lived with Edie—she had moved in after pinning my shoulders to the ground with her knees, straddling my chest, and gleefully informing me, "You have a roommate!" and refusing to let me up until I agreed.

Impressed by the cool figure of public defender Joyce Davenport on the *Hill Street Blues* TV show, Edie had gone to the Illinois Institute of Technology's Chicago-Kent College of Law. I teased her about that choice: *Chicago-Kent? That's a law school advertised on the cover of matchbooks!*

Maybe Northwestern rubbed off on me more than I let on.

She could amaze me just by studying. She would be sitting at our folding metal dining room table, reading a book. I'd bring her a cup of tea and a brownie. She'd take a bite out of the brownie. An hour would go by. Two hours. She would still be reading, the brownie still sitting there on a plate, still with one bite out of it. The tension built.

"How do you *do* that?" I finally blurted out.

"Do what?" she said, looking up from her book.

When it came time to take the bar exam, she did as most law students do—spend the night before in a hotel downtown, so there won't be any traffic to fight to get to the test on time. We stayed in the Westin, on Michigan Avenue, and turned in early. About 1 a.m. workers started tearing up the street below our window with jackhammers.

"Call a judge," she called out groggily in the darkened room. "Get an injunction ordering them to stop." I didn't know any judges, so instead I called the police—turned out, the workers had a permit; they do construction work at night, so as not to interrupt daytime traffic on Michigan Avenue. Edie went off to the test, a little less sharp than she had hoped to be. I went to work, but swung by the hotel before lunch, to make sure she had what she wanted—a baked potato, cottage cheese, and peaches; elderly lady comfort food—waiting for her in the room.

After lunch I went to the hotel manager to get our room changed. I don't know why but I whipped out my press card—I guess I really, really wanted Edie not to have to go through the jackhammer business again before the second day of the bar exam. The manager switched us to a room away from the street.

Going to Chicago-Kent didn't seem to harm Edie's employment prospects—she passed the bar exam and snagged a job working as an assistant corporation counsel for the City of Chicago. If you are sitting at an outdoor café and a car jumps the curb and kills you, your heirs will inevitably sue the city, claiming there should have been a guardrail to protect you, whereas common law clearly states that the city is not obligated to protect all persons from all possible hazards everywhere, specifically dusting its hands of the need for guardrails on the public roadways except in areas of proven past peril. Edie's job was to get the case thrown out, or at least the city's name removed from the list of entities being sued.

Collecting unemployment proved impossible—I waited in a long line, spent an hour or two in the grim, fluorescent-lit state unemployment office, with its worn molded plastic chairs, thinking all the while of Kafka, and never went back. Nor could I begin searching for a full-time job again—I had just been through that, a few years earlier. Perhaps the dynamic route, the path of the champion, was not in finding another job. Maybe there was another way. I bought a bright blue ledger book to track my payments and expenses and dubbed myself a freelance writer, which meant writing everything from the scripts for late-night local TV commercials for used car lots and third-tier mortgage companies to articles for *Newsweek* in Japan, from creating brain teasers for *Games* magazine to producing a newsletter for Castle Metals, a steel wholesaler in Franklin Park. I liked working at Castle Metals, liked wandering around the clean, sparsely populated expanse of light-gray offices and talking to people about the intricacies of selling steel by the ton. Quality matters with steel—how fine it is and how easily it can be cut, which translates into how quickly you can push it through your production lines, which determines how fast things can be manufactured, which affects the bottom line. Quality, and how fast you can deliver the goods are the most vital aspects.

In that way, the steel wholesale business was very much like the profession of freelance writing, as I understood it: tell me what you want, tell me how much of it you want, tell me how fast you want it.

Going to Northwestern still helped. To survive as a freelancer, you need lots of projects going all the time, so as one stalls you can work on another and keep the checks coming. I scanned the people section of the alumni magazine to see what my classmates with jobs were up to. There was Elizabeth Brewster, who went to Medill with me, named editor of *Mature Outlook*, a magazine Sears sent to every person over the age of fifty-five who bought insurance from Allstate, which it owned.

"Hey Liz!" I enthused over the telephone. "Hail to purple, hail to white!"—we had, as far as I knew, never met at Northwestern—"Congratulations on the promotion!" Before I got off the line, I had an assignment—write a piece on the head-in-a-vise dull subject of senior housing options: managed care, assisted living, nursing homes. Which I wrote because (a) I needed the money and (b) you never know. In this case, writing about extended-care facilities was karma's test to see if I was worthy. I wrote it and was rewarded. Every article I wrote for the magazine after that was a celebrity profile. Every single one. For the next ten years. *Mature Outlook* flew me to Jamaica to golf with Arnold Palmer, put me on a cruise ship heading toward the Panama Canal, sent me out to Los Angeles so often to talk to aging stars that I was able to use my United frequent-flier miles to get a round-trip ticket from Chicago to Tokyo, where my brother Sam had moved after graduation from Washington University in St. Louis. Older celebrities are far more pleasant to interview than those in the initial fever of fame—the world's attention has waned, the spotlight wandered, the frenzy stilled, and the torture instruments of regular life have been spread before them, so they appreciate any notice they get. Jazz trumpeter Dizzy Gillespie and I enjoyed a quiet dinner together while he shared memories of blowing with Charlie Parker; cartoonist Charles Schulz showed me around his private ice skating rink while we talked about Snoopy; country singer Loretta Lynn hugged me and whispered about southern ghosts; Patricia Neal, still beautiful, met me at the door to her room at the Orrington Hotel, in her nightgown—she had slept late—a floor-length, elaborate affair that looked straight out of a 1930s movie, and I perched nervously on a chair and interviewed the star-crossed actress.

Thus I had plenty of time to write for the *Sun-Times*—there is an irony there. While a *Sun-Times* staffer working a story typically was obligated to rush to a scene, look around, grab a few quotes, and whip out something for the next day's paper, I had leisure to spend days and weeks on a project.

For instance. In 1986, cocaine babies were suddenly a concern. *Newsweek* ran a story on the problem, quoting one Ira Chasnoff, head of the Perinatal Center for Chemical Dependence at Northwestern Memorial Hospital. *That's right here!* I thought—a common path to finding stories: notice a passing reference to something local in the national press and go after it in depth. So I called Chasnoff.

We spent a pleasant hour in his office talking about the difficulties of treating babies damaged in the womb by cocaine. Every organ could be affected. Then he potched his hands together, gave them a rub, and said that he was looking forward to reading my article, giving me my cue to stand up and leave, which I began to do.

But at the door I had a thought, stopped, turned, and asked him a question that, in my mind, made all the difference between being a mediocre reporter and being a less-mediocre reporter. Maybe the question seems obvious to you. But when I tell this story to journalism students, I draw out this moment, to see if any of them has any idea what I asked Dr. Chasnoff. They never do, not even after I give this hint: "Remember, I'm writing a story about cocaine *babies* . . ."

Any guesses? No?

I asked: "Where are the babies?" (Actually, in my memory, I asked, "Where are all the babies? We haven't seen any babies. You could be making this up." But that seems rather cheeky, even for me, and it was probably just "Where are the babies?" or "Can I see the babies?")

Oh, the babies, he said, leading me down to a clinic, where I met little Leanna Dorsett, three months old but weighing only five pounds; she had been one pound thirteen ounces at birth. I held the twitchy, squirming, crying infant. Chasnoff wasn't sure whether her jumpiness was due to withdrawal still, or from prematurity—she was born three months before her due date, which happened to be that very day. Leanna had lost a few fingers by winding her umbilical cord tightly around her hand in the womb, and had a clubfoot and other deformities. They had to analyze her chromosomes to determine her gender. I also met her mother, Delores, a dull-eyed drug addict with seven kids, and started going on Fridays to the clinic with her. Not for terribly long—maybe a month. I brought a photographer for the last session, but Delores didn't show up—I had to phone her and agree to pay the cab fare to get her there.

I remember leaving one session—at Northwestern Hospital in Streeterville—and striding directly into the Neiman Marcus department store on Michigan Avenue to window shop, smiling at myself, even then, the pampered suburbanite trying to shake off his encounter with urban ugliness by rushing into perfumed reality as he understood it.

The story ran on the cover of the Living section, with a photo of Leanna being examined, her huge eyes staring, her face gaunt, and began with Delores freebasing cocaine and going into premature labor on Mother's Day. The story got noticed, though not all the notice was approving. Delores's social worker phoned me, irate. "Don't you realize that this kind of attention is the worst thing for an addict?" she fumed.

"Oh, let me get this straight," I said. "She's thirty years old. She's got seven kids, two of them horribly deformed by cocaine. She's still taking drugs and *I'm* causing her trouble?"

That I actually did say. You have to become a hard-ass in this job, you just do. We're not a social service.

Eventually I was writing as many as five news stories a week for the *Sun-Times*, setting off alarms at the Chicago Newspaper Guild, which filed—or threatened to file, I never did get the straight story—a grievance to management, complaining: You have this scab kid doing a reporter's job. Either hire him full-time or dump him.

Ken Towers, the paper's editor, called me in for an interview. He was later parodied in a novel by Charlie Dickinson, who portrayed him tilted back in his desk chair, tossing a baseball into the air to see how close he could get the ball to the office ceiling without touching it. Towers did love the Cubs, and he had a certain rough, almost canine simplicity—the sort of man who always seems to have just woken up, who needs to rub his face for a few seconds, grabbing his nose, digging the heel of his hand into his eye, before being able to speak a few sentences. While still in high school, Kenny joined the paper as a copy boy at sixteen, rising through the ranks as the editors above him were tossed overboard or quit on principle during the various tempests at the *Sun-Times*. I used to say that Ken Towers was the cabin boy who became captain by hiding in a pickle barrel while all the officers sailing the ship were swept out to sea. It almost goes without saying that he later taught journalism at Northwestern.

The only fact I recall about myself at the interview was that I was sunburned, having just spent two weeks in Haiti researching a story on Haitian voodoo, an idea that I had interested the *Atlantic* in printing. Voodoo struck me as a funky folk Catholicism, strangely sweet and colorful. I had sat in a peristyle while a priest prepared a love charm, constructing an elaborate package of thread and spice and chopped-up needles. He put a spell on Edie, which explains a lot. Self-described "supreme master" Max Beauvoir summoned a servant by clapping his hands together twice, and boasted how Ronald Reagan's woes, such as his being shot, were entirely voodoo's doing. Another practitioner, who had been working in a sugarcane field with a machete when we were introduced, carefully explained how he could cure AIDS with a red candle.

The *Sun-Times* offered me a job. It was not covering City Hall, or reviewing plays, or even being a news reporter—they were starting a weekly section called "The Adviser," telling people how to keep Japanese beetles off their lawns, choose a health club, fight speeding tickets, and solve other prosaic problems. I would be the section's writing staff, along with fellow new hire Patricia Smith, who went on to well-deserved renown as a slam poet.

It wasn't much of a job, from a journalistic point of view—I'd be explaining to people how to use chopsticks or pack for a vacation. But it was a step up from the School Guide, and it paid real money—a princely $33,000 a year. Having freelanced or, if you prefer, been unemployed, for the better part of two years, I took it, after brief deliberation. "I have to give it a try," I told Edie, over the phone from Castle Metals. I was twenty-six years old. I never did write that voodoo story.

5

"Your show of shows"

WHEN PEOPLE ASKED me why my brother Sam was living in Japan, I'd answer, "Because it's as far away from our parents as he could get without leaving the earth's gravitational field."

It was a joke, sort of. They were good parents, in the main. They loved us, in their fashion, and we loved them, as much as we were capable of loving anybody. Growing up on a suburban cul-de-sac in Berea, Ohio, was pleasant, what I remember of it. Of course I have my complaints, but when compared to the nightmarish accusations that some people can hurl at their parents, our childhood was nothing to gripe about.

When it came time to settle down, however, my older sister Debbie chose Texas, I ended up in Chicago, and Sam moved to Tokyo. Debbie and I had nothing to say to each other, but even living half a world apart, my life was oddly in synch with Sam's. I quickly moved from the Adviser to become a night-shift news reporter. Working 7 p.m. to 3 a.m. at the *Sun-Times* meant that I got home to 1125 Washington Street in Oak Park at about the same time Sam was getting back to his apartment at 1–42-11 Katsushika-Ku in the Shinkoiwa section of Tokyo, his watch set fourteen hours later. We tried talking on the phone, but at a dollar a minute it was too stressful and cost too much to say anything meaningful. It was easier to mail microcassette tapes, and we'd tape ourselves while going about our days. For the first year, Sam taught English.

"Mister Fujimora," he'd say, leading a class. "What . . . did . . . you . . . do . . . this . . . weekend?"

"Ah. . . ." replies a hesitant, heavily accented Japanese voice. "This . . . weekend . . . I . . . ah . . . play . . . *mahjong!*"

Being five years older than Sam, I clearly recall when he was born, an ordinary day in the life of a suburban boy about to enter kindergarten in the mid-1960s, sharply illuminated and seared into memory by the flash of the biggest thing ever to happen to him in his life up to that point. It was August, and I was outside at a neighbor's, in the side yard of the Johnson's house—the houses were all new, modest, single-story wood ranches, set at angles to each other around Carteret Court. I was playing on the lush green grass with Ricky Johnson, whose father was a fireman, in a cardboard refrigerator box, which we were making into a fort or a spaceship or some such thing. My older sister came tearing up to us. "Dad wants you home *now!*" Debbie said. "I think you're in trouble."

We ran back together to find our family's sea foam green 1960 Nash Rambler in the driveway, the left rear door flung open—my mother in the backseat, which itself was strange, her belly enormous, her jean jumper wet—her water had broken. At the hospital, they took her inside in a wheelchair, which shocked me. Then we were at our grandmother's house on Rossmoor Road on the East Side of Cleveland, in her little pink kitchen. My grandmother was standing in her nightgown, holding the telephone—my father calling from the hospital. What is it? What is it? I danced around her, wanting to know—a boy, a brother, a baby brother. The memory ends with my father arriving with presents—a plastic sailboat for me, with rigging that tied to little cleats and a hatch that slid and everything. My sister got a glass terrarium with cactuses in it.

A few days later, we were back home. My parents sat me on the couch— sharp angles, no armrests, a dark red nubby fabric with gold threads in it, very 1965—put a square fuchsia satin throw pillow on my lap and carefully set the new baby there. "His fingers are this thin," I later marveled, to my pal Danny Malloy, plucking a single reed of goldenrod out of the pebbles by the swing set in our backyard.

* * *

My father never visited Sam in Japan. "Why would I go to Japan?" he asked, with sincere bafflement. "What is in Japan?" My mother, God bless her, went without him. I went too, using those frequent-flier miles earned writing for *Mature Outlook*, after Sam had been there about a year and a half and had shifted from teaching English to headhunting for a Swiss firm. Japanese mid-level executives at the time tended to adhere to their jobs like barnacles, and if you wanted to add middle management to your company, you had to hire a mercenary to snatch someone from another company, in violation of cherished Japanese norms. Being a foreigner helped to accomplish this, since what you were doing—convincing workers to abandon their place of employment—was antithetical to prime Japanese values of loyalty and steadfastness.

After two years on staff, the *Sun-Times* gave me a three-month unpaid sabbatical to go visit Sam. My inclination was to just leave without any kind of farewell—I was not an expert at navigating interoffice politics, and I had resentments; I felt, like every other reporter, that my light was being hidden under a bushel, and thus didn't care to go around glad-handing the management. But a kindly editor, Mary Dedinsky, told me that I should go say good-bye to Kenny. "You have to," she said. So I nudged myself into his glassed-in office at the end of his day and the beginning of mine and told him that I was leaving for a while, going to Japan to visit my brother.

"Well, I hope you come back," Towers said, "because I always thought you could be our next Sydney J. Harris." Harris had been a beloved syndicated columnist who wrote a ruminative, philosophical, watching-the-cherries-ripen kind of column. It was as much encouragement as I ever got in those early years, and I clung to it. It also surprised me that it would occur to Ken that I might *not* come back, as if he were reading my mind. Perhaps he had more on the ball than I gave him credit for.

* * *

For me, Japan was an odd world studded with small shocks. Some were clever: a little sink built into the back of a toilet tank. That saved room, and when you flushed, a jet of water automatically shot into the basin, allowing you to wash your hands without having to touch a grimy knob afterward. Plus the water you had washed with then drained into the tank, ready for the next flush.

Some were nightmarish. The most recognizable structure in the city, Tokyo Tower, is a copy of the Eiffel Tower, only thirty feet taller and painted orange. Next door is the Zojo-ji Temple, where Sam and I walked through a graveyard for fetuses, with life-size stone baby sculptures, the *mizuko jizō*, some dressed in little pink or blue knitted caps and bibs. Sam translated for me a few notes of deep remorse left by the grieving mothers, or rather, nonmothers, who stuck pinwheels in the ground in honor of their babies who weren't, and of course made donations. Sam explained that the place is something of a scam, run by the monks to make money from the guilt felt by women who had miscarriages or abortions. It's really a memorial, not a graveyard, since the fetuses aren't actually buried there, but I didn't know that at the time, and it was as eerie as could be. When the wind picks up, all those pinwheels flutter and your heart just groans.

Tokyo is quadruple the size of Chicago in area, with more than four times the population. Its residents live in hutches. You entered Sam's studio apartment in the Nakaya Building through a light-green metal door so small that it struck me not as the entrance to a human dwelling, but like the door of a fuse box. I could rise to my toes in the doorway and easily touch my head to the top of the doorframe, and I'm only five foot nine. Standing in the center of his single room I could, by planting one foot on the floor, lean and touch one wall and, without moving the planted foot, shift over and touch the opposite wall. For both of us to sleep on the floor on thin cotton futons, we had to first take his tiny kitchen chair and put it on top of his tiny kitchen table. In the cramped shower bath you could neither sit down nor fully stand up, but only crouch under a fine mist of water before trying to dry off with a towel the size of a dishrag.

And the people there hated him, hated me, hated us. You could measure the dislike scientifically because there was a red dot on train platforms, marking where the doors would open after the train stopped. Since the trains were so crowded that you couldn't always get aboard any given train when it arrived, people would line up behind the red dots. The train system was so finely calibrated that the crack between the doors would stop directly over that dot. Sam and I would be standing behind our red dot, waiting for the next train, when we began to notice that the other lines were four, five, six people deep, but nobody was standing behind our dot, we realized, because nobody wanted to be crammed onto a train next to us. That's how strong the aversion was: they'd rather miss a train and have to wait for the next one than find themselves forced into close proximity to a white person.

"Look over there," one businessman on the subway remarked to another late one evening in Japanese, which my brother spoke with increasing skill.

"See those two funny-looking foul-smelling big-nosed white people?" Sam reacted to this by taking a step forward, fists doubled, harsh tonal Japanese syllables tumbling from his mouth. I had to wrap my arm across his chest—he's five years younger but three inches taller than I am—holding him back while he screamed at some salaryman who, horrified at being detected, clicked instantly from drawling smugness into the shame mode, head bowed, face frozen, staring at the floor, arms rigid at his sides, shoulders hunched, babbling apologies.

"Your life here is hell," I told Sam. "Why don't you to move to Chicago?"

It might have begun and ended there. But I was tired of Oak Park—I had lived a block from Parky's Hot Dogs for five years, two of them with Edie. But I had not proved to be the steadfast companion she had hoped for, and she moved out, taking all her furniture with her. That was one reason I was visiting Sam, to confer, as brothers, and figure out the Situation and what I should do next. Edie being gone made the apartment empty and dreary. The steamer trunk I had dragged into the Northwestern Apartments at the start of freshman year was now, a decade later, the coffee table in my living room. To top it off, the Oak Park village fathers ripped out the village's downtown outdoor pedestrian mall, dismissing it as another failed 1960s social experiment. I liked that mall. When they cut down those stately trees and put Lake Street back in, it seemed an apt moment to quit Oak Park and finally move to the city. That's where single people live.

I looked at apartments downtown—Ontario Place, with balconies overlooking the Sun-Times Building. A quirky one-room loft on Pearson, with a huge industrial window staring at the Hancock. But I had too many books for a one-bedroom high-rise apartment whose walls were mostly glass. And the Pearson place had no lease—it was month-to-month. Loyola owned the building, and they could tear it down from under me at any time. Its current occupant owned a black leather couch and an electric keyboard and that was about it. My pile of possessions would look like furniture stored in a warehouse in this place.

Eventually I found a large old apartment atop a comfortable brick six-flat on Logan Boulevard at Mozart Street, with built-in bookshelves and newly sanded, sun-washed oak floors. Before I signed the lease, I asked Edie to take a look at the apartment and tell me if she thought it was okay—so much for my plunging into the city singles scene. And she did. We never could stay broken up for long, no matter how hard we tried. First, every date

I had with another woman invariably included a moment where I would look at her, narrow my eyes, and coldly think, *I broke up with Edie . . . so I could spend time . . . with you?* Second, fate kept nudging us back together. Once I bought a pair of tickets to see Frank Zappa, the rock guitarist. But nobody would go with me—I don't know if it was Zappa, or me, or some combination of the two. I figured I'd have to sell the second ticket. The day of the show, I was standing in line at the bank in the Carbide and Carbon Building on Michigan Avenue, and heard a cough. It was Edie, standing in line behind me, grinning at the coincidence. I know we're broken up, I said, seizing the moment, but I have this extra ticket and would you . . . sure, she said, she'd be happy to.

The apartment on Logan Boulevard had an extra bedroom for Sam, who surprised me by quitting his job and moving to Chicago. He had grown sick of Tokyo—the noise, the pollution, the crowding, the sheer exhausting *pace* of life there—and since I had a room designated for him and had asked him to come, he came. I was amazed, and delighted; sometimes all you have to do is ask.

* * *

On an overcast afternoon in October I met Sam at the International Terminal of O'Hare airport, a little embarrassed to lead him through the parking lot to the crappy blue two-door Chevy Citation that had belonged to our dead grandmother—by then the P1800 had been sold off as too expensive to keep repairing. The first place I took Sam was Johnny's Grill, a diner at Kedzie and Milwaukee, six blocks from my—now our—apartment, where he had steak and eggs. He couldn't afford beef back in Japan. Johnny's is tiny; the cook scrapes your food off the grill, pivots, and sets it sizzling on the plate in front of you. Then Sam slept the sleep of the jet-lagged in his new home while I went downtown to work at the paper.

The move from the Adviser to the news section was accomplished in the same way I had gone from the School Guide to features. I used to compare my ambition to the Russians' endless quest for a warm water port—you push in one direction, and if thwarted, you push in another. You are given a mandate, and rather than merely do it, you stretch its boundaries, from what you are expected to do toward what you want to do.

In this case, I was supposed to give practical advice about everyday situations. How to winterize your house. How to clean your garage. Straightforward stuff. But one could, if one were so inclined, *expand* the definition of what practical advice meant. For instance, I decided to write an article on abortion clinic listings in the phone book. At the time, the Yellow Pages lumped legitimate clinics that terminated pregnancies together with sham clinics run by Christian zealots who offered no services other than a free pregnancy test, which lured young women into their offices and forced them to wait for the test results, creating an opportunity for the evangelical staff to enthusiastically lecture the captive would-be murderess on the horrors of abortion and the fiery pit that awaits harlots. I had learned of their existence in Wheaton.

To write the story, I paired myself with a woman from Planned Parenthood, who posed as my girlfriend as we visited a couple of the sham clinics and listened placidly to their spiel, not only against abortion, but contraception. One showed us a chart of the failure rates and risks of the various methods. Nothing was safe or guaranteed except, of course, total abstinence accompanied by prayer.

Nobody up the line of command at the *Sun-Times* noticed the story until after it ran—a surprisingly common occurrence at newspapers—under the utterly bland headline, "Abortion counseling can differ."

Scott Powers, the features editor, a slight blond man with round glasses, called me into his office and angrily chewed me out. What was I thinking? Conducting a *ruse*? This sort of thing was exactly why we had been denied a Pulitzer for the Mirage Tavern—a series of stories on a decoy bar the paper opened in 1977 to catch city inspectors shaking down bribes. Photographers hid in the walls and snapped as the cash changed hands, the jukebox turned up to cover the sound of their shutters clicking.

Yeah, I thought, but lacked the fortitude to actually say, but if we hadn't set up the bar, we'd have no classic investigation to be wrongly denied a Pulitzer for doing. Just as, if I hadn't gone around with this Planned Parenthood gal and listened to these fanatics lecture us on the health hazards of condoms, I'd have written another dull article about how to fertilize your lawn and you wouldn't be yelling at me.

Alan Henry, the city editor, also noticed the story. But unlike Powers, he wasn't upset. He lifted his wing, gave a whistle, and I scurried from features over to news to burrow under it, starting, as one did back then, on the night shift.

I could romanticize that job, could depict myself as the Shadow, slipping through the green-tinged underworld of Lower Wacker Drive, warming my hands over oil drum trash fires, covering the unspeakable. And sometimes I did view myself exactly that way, as the Watcher of the Night, the *Angel Nacht*, in my illiterate faux German, wearing fingerless wool gloves, the better to take notes outside in the cold, reporting on suicides and murders and fires. The bloated, blue white face of a corpse that bobbed up in the Chicago River in spring when the ice melted. The great round window of the Rose of Sharon Church, backlit by flame on a subzero night three days before Christmas, the fire hydrants frozen, the West Side landmark burning to the ground, its ceiling collapsing, killing a twenty-seven-year-old fire fighter. The glitter of a dark lump of something small and wet and awful in the harsh light of an alley where a man had just jumped out of a building on Jeweler's Row and hit the sharp edge of a dumpster coming down. The special airlock room at the Cook County Medical Examiner's Office where the decomposed bodies are taken. The endless moment when the orderly reaches for the sheet and slowly draws it back.

Nor were the suburbs excluded. A deranged woman, Laurie Dann, walked into a second-grade classroom in Winnetka and started shooting the children. An Evanston man was crushed to death by a steamroller. An Oak Park lawyer was shot and killed on the el. (Practical tip: if somebody is robbing the train you are riding on, do not stand up and exclaim, "That's not a real gun!")

"Hi, I'm Neil Steinberg from the *Chicago Sun-Times*," I said over the telephone to the lawyer's neighbor. "Not interested," he replied, hanging up. Pesky subscription solicitors! I immediately phoned back. "Hello, I'm Neil Steinberg. I'm a *reporter* from the *Chicago Sun-Times*, and your neighbor was just *murdered* on the el." He gasped and sputtered, while I smiled and thought, "Not so cocky *now*, are we?"

Still, most of the bad stuff happened in the city. At 4 a.m. on a drizzly cold March morning, the Paxton Hotel, a flophouse on LaSalle Street, burned, a terrible, five-alarm fire, with people on the upper floors hanging out the windows, clinging to the ledges, screaming to be saved while those trapped in first-floor apartments waved their arms through the burglar bars. When the fire department arrived, there wasn't even time to run out hoses, at first—all Tower Ladder No. 10 could do was extend its ladder basket and drive along, raking the front of the building, pulling residents out one after another, while firefighters who were rushing to get at the burglar bars with their saws sidestepped the bodies of those who had already jumped and the mattresses they flung out ahead of themselves in a desperate attempt to break their falls. Nineteen people died. At one point, the brown-yellow smoke shifted toward the onlookers standing in the street, utterly blinding us, so thick it set off smoke alarms in nearby buildings. I shot my hand out to a telephone pole, just to have something to hold onto while the world went stinging black. Later that morning, heading into the paper, I stepped into the elevator, and everyone, nicely suited and dressed for their normal work-a-daddy days, turned to gape at me, and I realized that I reeked of smoke. I looked down, hiding my grin.

I wasn't used to being around people and tended to disdain them, wasn't used to being outside in the daytime. The sun dazzled and annoyed me. I liked driving around at 3 a.m. The city is less crowded and more eerie and romantic at night, and needless to add, darker. It's as if all the people have died, and you, alone, prowl through the empty city, unseen and unimpeded. As if you own Chicago and the daytime laws no longer apply. Officially, bars close at 4 a.m. in Chicago, which doesn't give you much time if you work until 3 a.m. But certain places, like the 1944 St. Louis Browns—that was the name of the basement bar, with photographs from the team's lone pennant-winning year—just ignored the law, as well as the one that said places of business couldn't play videotapes of movies for their customers. I'd stop by after work, have a few beers, some Jays barbeque potato chips, watch *Batman* and wait for the sun to come up. The pressmen came there too, still in their ink-smeared folded newspaper hats. The bartender served beers two at a time to the pressmen, reaching into a cooler with both hands and grabbing a can in each hand, cracking both open simultaneously and setting them on the bar in one smooth motion.

They still printed the *Sun-Times* on a row of ten mighty Goss presses in the basement at 401 N. Wabash—you could feel them rumble to life on the fourth floor, and Edie said she could smell the ink on me, even though I rarely had reason to go down to the presses. As I left work each morning at the end of my shift, Wabash Avenue would be jammed with big boxy trucks, collecting the papers to distribute across the city, the scene a pool of bright light and solemn activity in the sleeping darkness, like an outpost on the moon.

When I still lived in Oak Park, I would sometimes get bored of going straight home on the Eisenhower Expressway, and would take Washington Boulevard back, the leisurely route, savoring the semi-danger of driving through the West Side at 3 a.m. One night, bored, I impulsively turned left at Cicero Avenue and drove past the big red Magikist lips sign into

Cicero, Capone's old stomping ground and still a wide-open town of all-night bars. There was a large, 1950s-era sign, not neon, but individual bulbs, spelling out "YOUR SHOW OF SHOWS." Thinking of Sid Caesar, I pulled over and parked.

The place was your usual bar, but very dark, no light at all except for a single bare bulb illuminating a black woman, buck naked, standing on a platform behind the bar, holding onto a pole and performing a weary parody of a shimmying dance. I took a seat directly in front of her and ordered a five-dollar Coke. A woman in a teddy came over and sat down on the stool to my left and introduced herself. She was pretty. "Hi," she said, "I'm Rochelle."

"Hi," I said. "I'm Neil Steinberg. I'm a reporter for the *Sun-Times*." Must have been reflex. She was not deterred. I bought a five-dollar Coke for her too. She leaned in close and sweetly informed me that for thirty-five dollars I could take her into the back room and screw her. I asked her what it's like to be a prostitute, politely seizing upon the implications of her offer while ignoring the offer itself, for a variety of reasons, partially moral scruple. ("There are two things in life a man should never pay for," I liked to grandly pronounce. "One of them is parking.") And partially due to imagining what that back room might actually look like. But primarily because I didn't have thirty-five bucks on me. In fact, ten bucks just about wiped me out. I finished my Coke, thanked Rochelle for the conversation, left, and never went back.

"YOUR SHOW OF SHOWS" is a reminder that not just Cicero but Chicago in the mid-1980s retained the sour tang of the conventioneer clip-joint town that Liebling had sneered at thirty years earlier. There was still a run-down Woolworth's 5 & 10 store on North Michigan Avenue. Parts of the central business district still seemed like a Reginald Marsh painting—seedy stretches of Wells Street along the elevated tracks, shabby little liquor stores, the shell of the old 666 Club standing alone in a parking lot in the South Loop near the "JESUS SAVES" neon cross at the Pacific Garden Mission. The faded 1950s red lacquer ambience of Jimmy Wong's Chinese restaurant on South Wabash. The Woods Theater, incongruously containing a cowboy bar, the Bar RR Ranch, tucked in its basement, and the Greyhound bus station still across the street from the Daley Center. There were no apartment buildings in the Loop, no dorms, no grocery stores, no young professionals walking their dogs or students hanging around. The 60602 zip code, encompassing two dozen square blocks of the Loop, listed seventy-one residents in the 1990 census, and many of those were in one nursing home. After 6 p.m., the saying went, you could fire a cannon down State Street and nobody would be hurt. None of apartment buildings between Michigan Avenue and Navy Pier had been built, nor any further south by the museums. When they first opened a bar in the basement of North Pier Terminal, just west of Navy Pier, I would occasionally stop by after work and park my car on the grass beside it. There was nobody around to care, especially at that hour.

* * *

Covering fires and murders or bumbling into brothels were the exceptions. Many more night shifts were spent at public meetings—though to be honest, the participants at zoning board hearings offer a dimmer view of human nature than murderers and whores do. At least people kill each other out of uncontrolled passion, or naked greed, or gross inebriation, or some other extreme of human emotion or behavior. Prostitutes are invariably drug addicts feeding a habit; they aren't acting out of the finely calibrated selfishness that prompts sober citizens to line up behind a microphone in a well-lighted room at a zoning board meeting. You can't hope to jam a stick in the ground without all its potential neighbors jostling each other to be first to explain exactly how the stick will destroy the quality of their lives; how, while playing, their children will stumble against the stick and be abraded, giving rise to fatal infections, or how the stick will eventually start to lean, undermining property values. At such hearings, the distinction between city and suburbs is effectively nil. In the suburbs, every new structure more complex than a mailbox is portrayed as the emotional equivalent of a pit lined with spikes and covered with a grass mat. In the city it's no better: the prospect of a new high-rise condo downtown draws every resident from every surrounding, nearly identical high-rise constructed within the past ten or fifteen years, people who testify with straight faces that Chicago is full—the city reached its point of maximum human saturation, alas, with the arrival of themselves, and now the addition of even one more person to their neighborhood would, it pains them to report, mark the advent of a nightmarish dystopian world of overload, gridlock, and social breakdown. Oh, and the views from their apartment would be ruined.

But even the zoning board meetings were atypical. With so much news to gather, the average night was spent working the phones, tracking down stories. By 10 p.m. I would be holding a yellow legal pad, slumped on a ratty office chair in front of three small TV sets, tuned to the three local ten o'clock news programs, monitoring them for anything we might have missed. At midnight, I'd be reading the next day's paper, hot off the presses, listening to the crackly static of the photo-desk police scanner, gazing at the white-haired profile of the night copyeditor, wondering if I was looking at myself in forty years. Most nights were highlighted by a juicy double cheeseburger covered in pickles and a couple of beers at the nearby Billy Goat Tavern. That was what most nights were like in the big city.

I spent five years on the night shift—I think the management hope was that eventually I'd get tired of the hours and quit. Because I wasn't the most popular guy in the newsroom. My colleagues looked down on me; I had been tarred as a scab before I was even hired, viewed as a magazine writer taking a newspaper reporter's job. And my bosses, well, I had a habit of blowing off my mouth—I felt that as a journalist it was my moral duty to answer questions. How could I ask other people to talk about their situations if I weren't willing to do so myself? So when Alan Henry was fired, over a trivial error in news judgment, I told *Chicago* magazine that it was the biggest mistake our new editor, the much-loathed, pompous pooh-bah Dennis Britton, ever made. Thus the night shift, and Sundays too. They'd have fired me, if not for the union. I didn't mind working Sundays—it gave me Fridays off, and forced me out into the city—I think I've been to services at every church on the South Side, marveling at how parishioners would turn in the pews to shake my hand and smile warmly, welcoming me, genuinely delighted that I was there. That's not the typical reception at synagogues.

The true beauty of being a newspaper reporter is that you are constantly being sent places that you would never imagine going to, and compelled to delve into topics that you heretofore never thought about. You must become an expert in the span of a few hours and present your findings the next day to a public that will immediately seize upon any error you might make, no matter how slight, and wave it over their heads, shouting and laughing, mocking and complaining. It inspires a certain exactitude.

6

"I'll get you a judge"

SAM AND I LIVED together for six months on Logan Boulevard, on the third floor, eye-level to the green canopy of breeze-tossed trees. Chicago's downtown is ringed with miles of wide, park-like boulevards—the original intention was to bring nature into the dusty city, and provide a place for the wealthy to drive their horses and carriages. Thus Logan is lined with century-old mansions, facing a double strip of grass with stately maples and oaks that flank either side of the main thoroughfare. Sam and I would throw a football there. Or we'd open the windows, let the spring air in, and sit on the window seat, playing chess. Eventually I splurged on a fancy chess table for us, after first visiting a certain table several times at the furniture department on the eighth floor at Marshall Field's, pondering the excess. One day I found myself stealthily moving my chess table behind a screen, so no potential rival would see it, be similarly smitten, and perhaps snatch away my beloved. At that moment I realized how silly this was and finally swallowed hard and bought the thing. It was so beautiful, with walnut drop leaves and inlaid patterns and a drawer for the pieces, that I refused to let Field's deliver it, worrying they might scratch the wood, preferring to carry it out of the State Street store over my head, gently finessing ourselves, man and table, through the revolving door.

My brother found a job almost immediately. Unlike me with my two years of freelancing, Sam isn't the kind to stay unemployed long. He went to work at the Kyowa Bank, a Japanese establishment where his coworkers were at first amused by his Japanese language skills, the way you'd smile at a dog in a bow tie.

I tried fixing Sam up with one of Edie's friends—Edie and I were back together again. The prospect was Laura: pert, pretty, blue-eyed, blonde-haired, Jewish. We had a bland Hanukkah dinner together, the four of us. But Sam wasn't interested. He was still thinking about his girlfriend back in Japan, Yuri Hiraki. In the spring, he informed me she was coming to visit.

"That must mean it's serious," I said, slipping easily into my role, reading the dutiful older brother lines. "You don't have a girl come from Japan for a date and then send her back."

He didn't. Together, we met Yuri at the airport. She arrived wearing a leather Mickey Mouse baseball jacket and bearing gifts—sake cups—meticulously wrapped in lush paper and gold elastic. She stayed. It was a big apartment, but not quite big enough for both a couple in love and a single nighttime reporter. Very quickly they moved into the apartment Edie lived in over on Melrose, and—now that I had properly proposed gazing, not into her eyes, too anxious for that, but at the brass multicolored peacock atop the NBC Tower as we walked downtown—Edie moved back in with me. A few weeks later Sam and I were sipping beers at the bar at the Victorian House, an odd tavern located in an old house on Belmont Avenue. "I'm marrying Yuri," he told me, casually, conversationally, the way you might say, "The Cubs look good this year." I should not have been surprised, but I was. I'm not sure whether my reply was an attempt to alert him to possible pitfalls in life or just to absolve myself of future responsibility, but I reminded him that she isn't American, isn't Jewish, is five years older than he, doesn't speak English, and had never gone to college.

"All these things will be problems for you someday."

"That's fine," he said. "I'm marrying her anyway."

Being family—to me—means you fall in line behind your loved ones' decisions once they're made, even if you don't understand them. When Sam joined a fraternity at Washington University, my parents and I were shocked. We considered ourselves constitutionally antifraternity. My father had quit his; I not only didn't consider joining, but kept a frat paddle emblazoned with GDI—God Damn Independent—propped in my window. We all felt contempt for fraternities, with their ritualized revelry and compulsory bonhomie. And now my brother was joining one. "Being in a fraternity . . .

must be okay," I told my parents, slowly, working it out for myself, trying to adjust, "because Sam's doing it."

Marrying Yuri must be okay, too, because Sam was doing it. Once I realized that he was determined, I took them downtown—Yuri's reaction, seeing the Chicago skyline from the Kennedy Expressway for the first time was to clap her hands together and say "Sugoi!" which means "Amazing!" We went to the basement of the Cook County Building to get their marriage license, to Tiffany's on Michigan Avenue to buy their wedding bands, to Shaw's Crab House to celebrate the betrothal. "Order anything you like," I grandly announced, snapping open my napkin, and Yuri, innocently taking me at my word, ordered the steak and lobster combination while I struggled to arrange my face into a generous smile.

They planned on getting married at City Hall (people getting hitched by the government in Chicago invariably say they are tying the knot at City Hall, even though the adjacent County Building is where the ceremony actually takes place). But I knew that, come the fall, Edie and I were to be wed at a lavish ceremony at a fancy downtown hotel—the Intercontinental on Michigan Avenue. I didn't want Sam to resent me for the rest of our lives because he got married in a two-minute ceremony among strangers at the clerk's office in the basement of the Cook County Building while I got married in black tie with a hundred and fifty family and friends across the street from the Wrigley Building, in a landmark hotel that has bas relief carvings of Babylonian lions, the ceremony followed by a reception featuring a twelve-piece swing band and fresh fruit salad tucked inside hollowed-out pineapples.

"Sam," I said. "Get married at my apartment. I'll throw you a party." He agreed.

A wedding needs to be officiated. A rabbi was out—the bride wasn't Jewish. And though some rabbis will overlook that detail, the more germane point was: I didn't know any rabbis. But I did know Art Petacque. Among my occasional duties at the *Sun-Times* was writing Petacque's column—he was the paper's crime reporter. A droopy-faced, sixtyish man with bushy eyebrows, he was famous for bestowing mobsters with their colorful nicknames: Johnny "No Nose" DiFronzo and such. Petacque was the uncle I never had; he taught me to smoke cigars—the alternative was to breathe his stale cigar breath while I wrote his column. Art was old school, which meant that he didn't write his own stuff—none of those guys did.

Art couldn't even type. He reported stories—reported them well, impersonating a police detective or a deputy coroner if necessary—and someone else would type them up as he pulled scraps of paper and scribbled-over matchbooks from his pockets and dictated a rambling narrative that his rewrite man, sometimes me, would transcribe and mold into some kind of coherent shape. I can still hear his hoarse, booming, voice: "She was a *hoor*! Lived in a hoorhouse! A joint called the Four Deuces! Thirty-one years of age!"

Getting by in Chicago isn't just a matter of who you know, but who the people you know know. The connections of your connections. So even though I did not know any judges, personally, I knew Art Petacque personally and, most significantly, knew that Petacque knew people.

"Art," I said. "I need a judge to marry my brother."

"I'll get you a judge!" he thundered. "I'll get you the most famous judge in Chicago! I'll get you Abraham Lincoln Marovitz!"

Marovitz was indeed the most famous judge in Chicago, though I had never heard of him. The man was a living scrapbook of twentieth-century Chicago. He was born in 1905 and graduated from the Chicago-Kent College of Law at age nineteen, back when you could become a lawyer without first going to college—he had to wait until he was twenty-one to get his law license, however—and became an assistant Cook County state's attorney in 1927. In the 1930s, he went into private practice, representing gangland figures. He defended Gus Winkler, suspected for a time to be the machine gunner at the St. Valentine's Day Massacre. He took Sally Rand, then at the height of her fame as a fan-dancing stripper, the star of the Century of Progress fair, to the opening of the Palmer House's Empire Room in 1933. He swore in Richard J. Daley each of the six times he was elected mayor, and was appointed to the federal bench by John F. Kennedy. The year before my brother's wedding he swore Richard M. Daley into his first term of office.

"I haven't married anybody outside my chambers in ten years," Marovitz complained to me in his reedy, elderly voice, over the phone the next day. "But Artie says I have to do this. There's something you have to do first, though. You bring the happy couple to my chambers so I can meet them—I don't marry anybody I haven't met."

I saw trouble coming a mile away. "Look Sam," I told my brother. "Teach her to say, 'Yes your honor, I understand.' Five words. Can you do that?"

No problem, he assured me.

So now the three of us, dressed nicely for the occasion, arrive at Marovitz's office in the Dirksen Federal Building. His souvenirs spill out into the hallway, including an enigmatic painting of a black Abraham Lincoln done by a convicted murderer Marovitz spared from Death Row. No other judge would dare clutter the hall around his office door with personal memorabilia, but Marovitz is no other judge.

Inside, his secretary shows us to chairs in his enormous chambers. The decor defies description: part law office, part steakhouse foyer. There are photos of Lyndon Johnson, Carl Sandburg, older and younger Daleys (the latter signed "To my uncle Abe"). A picture of boxer Jack Dempsey inscribed "My old pal." Marovitz and Truman, Marovitz and Pope Paul VI. Thank-you drawings from children, a letter from David Ben-Gurion. "When are you coming to Israel again?" the nation's founder asks. Bronze molds of Lincoln's hands, of Lincoln's death mask. Rows of books. More medals, crystal obelisks, golden gavels, plaques, paperweights, and assorted doodads than you can imagine.

After a few minutes, Marovitz emerges from an inner room, an eighty-five-pound, eighty-five-year-old man, bald with white hair combed straight back on the sides, his face covered with spots and blotches, but with warm eyes. He is wrapped in a purple brocade smoking jacket with black satin lapels. He talks to my brother; he tries to talk to Yuri. Finally Marovitz turns to me. "I can't *marry* this girl," he says, emphatically, with a wave of his hand. "*She* doesn't know what's going on. *She* could be a *slave*."

I open my mouth to answer, but Sam jumps in. "Don't worry your honor," he says. "We'll have a translator there."

Walking out, I ask my brother: "A translator, Sam? Where are you going to get a translator? It'll cost you hundreds of dollars."

"Oh, the old guy doesn't know what day it is," Sam says, dismissively.

An image forms in my mind: everyone I know is gathered in my living room. The judge walks in, looks around, doesn't see a translator, and walks out—he's a federal judge, he can do whatever he wants.

* * *

Everyone I know is gathered in my living room on Logan Boulevard. I had to borrow my in-laws' folding chairs. Edie's parents bring a big tray of bagels and lox—making this an honorary Jewish wedding, in my eyes, despite the lack of rabbi or a Jewish bride. The room is filled with Edie's relatives—her brother and sister, their spouses and children, her friends, plus mine, college buddies, and pals from the paper—the rare wedding where the guests are friends of neither the bride nor the groom.

Judge Marovitz walks in with Art Petacque, who is carrying a box of cigars as a present. The judge looks around, doesn't see a translator, and is unruffled. ("Look your honor," I had said, phoning him a few days before the ceremony, trying to put a bright spin on things. "We're having a *lit-tle* trouble with the translator. But the bride's going to be wearing a white dress. They're going to be exchanging rings. Even in Japan that means something.")

Marovitz speaks for nearly twenty minutes, an eternity for a marriage ceremony. He talks about his parents, whom he adored—he wears cufflinks with their photos, his mother on one sleeve, his father on the other. His standard joke is about his mother, a Lithuanian immigrant, attending a settlement house talk about Abraham Lincoln. She saw the beard and heard that Lincoln was shot in the temple, so naturally assumed that the greatest American president was Jewish, later giving Marovitz his unusual middle name. Not quite true, but everybody always laughs. He tells bromides about marriage—he has performed more than six hundred ceremonies, he says, and all but two or three were successes, and he doesn't expect this one to bring down his average. He recites nineteenth-century doggerel about kindness, repeats puns dating back to 1920s comic Joe E. Brown—Marovitz was executor of Brown's estate. I grin fixedly. Sam, having begun to nod his head in agreement at the start, now has to keep nodding. Yuri looks lovely, in an ivory dress with puffy satin sleeves and lace gloves.

The vows finally exchanged, the guests launch themselves at the lox platter. Judge Marovitz departs, accidentally leaving behind his black judicial robes. When everyone has gone, I suggest to Edie that, since she is about the same size as the judge, this is her chance to commit an act of carnality while wearing federal judge's robes. We can get them dry-cleaned later. Being a fellow Chicago-Kent College of Law graduate, however, and a responsible officer of the court who takes her duties seriously, she declines.

* * *

In 1990, Toyota completes the transition of the design of its Celica from a boxy car with cat's-eye taillights into something rounder, sportier. The first time I see the new model I whistle in admiration, hurry across the street, run my hand over its pleasingly curved rear end. It seems very Porsche-like, with headlights that flip up dramatically. I buy one, a rich red with a hint of orange, and go pick Sam up at the Kyowa Bank on Michigan Avenue to show my brother the first new car I have ever owned and then take him to a celebratory dinner.

"Whaddaya think, huh?" I say, beaming, gesturing around as he climbs into the car.

"I got fired," he says. "Just now."

With his Japanese wife and his ever-improving command of the language, Sam was no longer the charming foreigner who knew a few words of the mother tongue, but something his bosses viewed as unsettling. Not a valued employee with key language and business skills, but a kind of imposter, a man wearing a disguise, seizing their culture, parroting their speech, stealing their women. An uppity white guy. The Kyowa Bank didn't like that.

Sam doesn't stay unemployed long. He marches over to the Midland Hotel, an upscale establishment on Adams Street in the Loop, and gets a job as the night clerk. The hotel is around the corner from all the banks and brokers on LaSalle Street. He's in the right neighborhood, just not at the right job.

Our parents come to visit, staying of course at the Midland—being the night clerk, he gets them a deal on the room.

"What did the folks think about your working there?" I ask him, carefully, after they leave.

"I think they were disappointed," he says. "But they didn't offer to pay the rent."

That's Sam—pithy, practical. His first nickname as a toddler was "Plain Sam"—his line. My sister and I, attentive older siblings, would coo "Wonderful Sam" and "Cute Sam" and he'd object, indignantly insisting: "No—pwain Sam!"

Not so plain, really. He could toss off a casual observation that would help guide me for the rest of my life, vibrating truth across the years like a tuning fork. After Los Angeles, when I was back at home, trying to crank out a novel, agonizing over the chasm of failure that was opening up under my life, we were parsing the situation. "You think getting a novel published will make you magically happy?" Sam said. "You could have it published and in your hands and you'd still feel the same way you do today. You have to make up your mind to be happy." That's exactly what he said, when he was seventeen years old. I never forgot it, because he was right. Circumstances only go so far to make a person content—happy is something you decide to be, whatever life is serving up at the moment.

That philosophy notwithstanding, Sam isn't happy working nights at the Midland Hotel. So he uses contacts made there to snag a better job, running a Japanese-oriented limousine service out of the Claridge Hotel on Dearborn, something he does well, managing the crew of eccentric, sometimes criminally so, drivers and the expanding fleet of cars. He adds services, buys a 20-person bus, and finds work for the bus. A huge Japanese shopping mall—Yaohan—opens up in Arlington Heights, a suburb with enough Japanese residents to print its own Japanese-language phone book. Sam approaches a Japanese old-age home in the city, Heiwa Terrace on Lawrence Avenue—would its residents pay twenty dollars a head for a weekly run to the new suburban mall? Yes they would. Then he approaches the mall. Would it pay him ten dollars a head to regularly bring a busload of well-off Japanese seniors to shop there for two hours? Yes it would. That strikes me as a kind of genius—a Chicago genius, not just for cashing in on both ends of a deal, but for speeding something to a place where it is worth more, the crops in the field to the city, the manufactured goods back out to the farmers. From Montgomery Ward realizing that if he prints a catalogue he can sell directly to the countryside to a street kid icing down ten-cent bottles of water and carting them to the park on a hot day to sell for a dollar apiece, the germ of the thought is the same: let's get this to where we can make some money off it.

The years dribble by. Sam builds the business, a constant process of education. He buys new limousines, which must be registered. Sam goes to the Elston Avenue office of the Illinois Secretary of State to register a new limo. The paperwork requires the signature of the seller. The clerk behind the counter draws his attention to the blank line.

"The seller is in St. Louis," says my brother. "How am I supposed to get his signature? I need to put this car into service."

"No he's not," replies the clerk, a woman in her fifties with a gruff, five-pack-a-day voice. "He's downstairs—I saw him there."

"What?" says my brother, baffled. "He is?" Sam walks downstairs, holding his official form, into the first-floor lobby, looking for the guy who sold him the limousine in St. Louis. This is nuts. He huffs back upstairs to the clerk.

"He isn't there," Sam says. "I looked, but he isn't . . ."

"Look again, honey," she growls, getting annoyed. "You're not listening to me. I'm telling you he's there. I'm telling you I saw him there. Go look harder."

Sam leaves the office again, a little stunned, and is heading down the stairs to look around for a second time when realization dawns. Ohhhh. He takes out a pen, and a moment later he hands the completed form to the clerk.

"Found him," my brother says.

* * *

Why did Edie and I get married at the Intercontinental? Why not get married in our living room, the way that Sam and Yuri did? It isn't just that we had the money—though we did. Edie had left the corporation counsel's office and was a litigator at Jenner & Block, a big downtown law firm. So much for my smirking at the Chicago-Kent College of Law. That was part of the reason we were finally taking the plunge. We had dated for seven years—I loved her, but was afraid of settling down, afraid of setting my life in stone as it was, forever. Afraid of making the wrong decision. Afraid of being with someone. Afraid of being alone. Afraid, generally, the leitmotif of anxiety that runs through my life.

But I was thirty, had a smart, beautiful woman who loved me, a woman whose new job paid nearly twice what mine did, a woman who would soon be snapped up by some smirking jerk Jenner lawyer if I didn't act immediately. Everyone I knew thought I was crazy for not having married her years earlier—Edie felt this with particularly deep conviction—and eventually, after needless and agonizing deliberation, I decided that everybody I knew was right.

A deluxe wedding went down easier. It fed my hunger for grandiosity, my need to feel significant, and to me, significance meant both fanciness and being in the city. A swell hotel in the suburbs wouldn't have counted, and we never considered one. This might sound very strange, but when I think about getting married, it is not standing under the wedding canopy that comes to mind, nor the vows, nor the first dance with my beloved, but hurrying through the hotel's industrial kitchen to get to the spot where I was supposed to enter the room at my cue. It's quick-stepping up Michigan Avenue beforehand to Field's at Water Tower Place to buy a set of cufflinks and shirt studs, which I had neglected to obtain. The main event is never as interesting to me as the artifice behind it.

One moment especially stands out, a few hours before the ceremony. It takes a woman a lot longer to get ready to be wed than it does a man, and I decided to go somewhere to kill time while Edie fixed up her hair. The Intercontinental has a nearly Olympic-sized swimming pool, the biggest hotel pool downtown, all Spanish tile and terra-cotta. Johnny Weissmuller, the future "Tarzan," trained for the 1932 Olympics in it. To pass the time before the wedding, I swam laps. There was something very calming, doing that, and also in recalling that, shortly before getting married, I was quietly cutting through the water, the only one in the pool, on the fourteenth floor of a fancy hotel on Michigan Avenue.

Sam was my best man, and met me there. We shaved together at the hotel health club, getting ready for the wedding. "Yuri's pregnant," he told my reflection in the steamy mirror. "I just found out."

"Do me a favor," I said. "Don't tell the parents until tomorrow."

* * *

Sam and Yuri's daughter, Rina, is born that April. He phones from Rush University Medical Center with the happy news.

"That's great," I say. "Congratulations. I'll come by tomorrow to see her."

There is a silence. "Aren't you coming now?" he asks. I look at my watch— 3 p.m. I need to be at work at five. Just enough time to get there, glance at the tot and leave.

"I have to be at work at five."

"Neil," he says. "There's no one here."

Hurrying through the hospital to their room, clutching a Steiff toy cat, I come across a clear plastic bassinet, just sitting there, unattended in the hall, containing what is obviously my new niece. Rina has a shiny mass of black hair, sticking straight up—just like Sam's did when he was born. He and Yuri are living now in their first condo, on Summerdale Avenue. When he told me he was buying the place, my immediate thought was: *That's the street John Wayne Gacy lived on.* The mass murderer who killed thirty-three boys and buried most of them in a crawl space. On Summerdale Avenue— ten miles west in Des Plaines, true, but the street is still the same. A lot of baggage for an address. I didn't share that thought, however—it seemed a killjoy older-brother comment. Besides, it's a long street, and a hazy historical connection to a serial-killer clown isn't a reason not to live someplace.

Edie and I, newly married, buy our own place. Not on Logan—the wide boulevard strikes us as too suburban, ironically. There is nowhere to walk. And we feel the encroachment of Humboldt Park, which has gangs. On New Year's Eve, we stay away from the back porch, worried about gunfire from the south.

So we relocate east, to Pine Grove Avenue—a four-bedroom duplex, with a section cut out of the living room ceiling to create a wall of bay windows eighteen feet tall. I like to lie on the couch in the living room, tuck my foot between the cushions, and let my eye scan up that wall—first to the lower set of eight windows, then to the upper eight. Luxury.

The corner of Pine Grove Avenue and Oakdale Street is within the boundaries of Chicago, but East Lake View, as the neighborhood is called, is not one of the areas people have in mind when rhapsodizing life in the city. Not because it isn't nice—it is, nicer than most. But lacking either Gold Coast opulence or humble Bungalow Belt charm, East Lake View skirts the extremes, the clichés. It's a jumble. Our building is 1930s brick, functional, vaguely Shakespearian, with elegant stone insets—and across the street is a grim, charmless 1960s beige brick-faced concrete four-plus-one apartment building. That's how the neighborhood is—a few mansions, a few awful 1970s mansard-roof townhouses, an elegant old eight-story brick courtyard apartment building crowned with scalloped stonework with a flat and featureless strip mall jammed flush against its base. The businesses on Broadway are a hodgepodge of frame stores, pizzerias, shoe repair shops, a chili stand, a music store, a bike shop, a deli, an adult book store.

Two blocks south and two blocks east is Lincoln Park, with a gold statue of Alexander Hamilton, facing toward the city, and one of Goethe, "the Master Mind of the German people," erected by Chicago's German community in 1914, six weeks before World War I broke out. They had to put the statue into storage when the United States entered the war, to prevent the defenders of liberty from seeking vengeance upon it.

(The statue, by the way, doesn't physically represent Goethe in the slightest, but is the perfectly formed, well-muscled heroic ideal of an eighteen-foot-tall Roman, and once you contrast the two—Goethe himself was short, balding, toothless—you begin to see where the Germans went astray.)

Across the street from Chicago's tribute to the author of *Faust* is the Elks National Veterans Memorial in all its neglected glory. Not that they don't keep the place up; they do. It's immaculate. But few people visit. While the monument at Diversey and Lakeview would be the center of many smaller cities—it's bigger than the Jefferson Memorial—it is a safe bet that, whoever you are, however long you have lived in Chicago, even if you live a few blocks away, you have never actually stepped inside the rotunda dome. I'd wager that most Chicagoans don't even know it's there. Which is a shame, because it is incredible: enormous, wrapped in pillars and ringed with friezes, filled with intriguing tributes to soldiers, bronze statues, plaques, twenty-six different types of marble. The ceiling inside is painted, à la Sistine Chapel, and there's something cool about having neoclassical murals with dogfighting biplanes in them. The structure is a tribute to Elks who lost their lives in World War I but, given its utter desolation—on average, three people an hour visit, though some days, no one comes at all—whenever you go there, you'll probably be by yourself. It's an unintentional tribute to the waste and ruin of war, because nothing underscores the tragedy of sacrifice more than an ignored memorial.

A block west of Pine Grove is Broadway, with its taco joints, liquor stores, generic chains, and quirky shops—one storefront, Soupbox, cleverly changes character with the seasons, a caterpillar offering steaming crocks of homemade soup in the winter, then in the summer transforming into Icebox, a butterfly hawking fruity sorbet. Soupbox opened in 1995, and I almost didn't mention it, because in my eyes it's new and so maybe ephemeral. Then I realized: Soupbox has already been on Broadway several years longer than there was Prohibition, and nobody hesitates to remark on *that*, especially in Chicago.

Beyond Broadway, Boystown runs west toward Halsted Street and north toward Belmont, stretching beyond to Addison. I remember wondering, before we bought our place on Pine Grove, whether living so close to one of the nation's gay epicenters would be a problem for me—I believe I asked myself that question when I looked out the window of an apartment that I was touring and saw a line of graffito, "Steve, please blow me," or words to that effect, boldly printed in large white block letters on a black tar rooftop across the street. The honest answer was no, that it might occasionally push me out of my comfort zone, but it wouldn't bother me in any significant way, and nothing in seven years of living there made me regret that decision. I'd sometimes stop into one of the local gay bars for a beer, and their attitude seemed to be, if I didn't mind drinking it there, they didn't mind serving it to me. The atmosphere of open gayness was something new, to me, something different, an adjustment, but I wasn't afraid that my children would catch it. Though there were transvestite hookers who came out along

Broadway after midnight, and I do admit, returning home late, I'd track them out of the corner of my eye and wonder where precisely it was that I had decided to start my family. Since then, straight people increasingly began to live in Boystown, just as gay people feel more comfortable settling throughout the city, a sign that the persecution that once forced them to cluster together for support and protection is growing weaker.

In addition to the streetwalkers, the neighborhood had its satisfying city characters—a homeless lunatic we referred to as "the Wicker Man" because he had a large straw coolie hat and dressed in layer after layer of filthy burlap bags. The gadfly writer and thinker Jon-Henri Damski lived around the corner, in a single room at the Belair Hotel on Diversey, and he would come shuffling up to me in his green army parka, Cubs cap, and broken eyeglasses to compliment—or complain about—something I had written. He was an exuberant man, and must have complimented more than he complained, because I liked him. He seemed like gay Chicago's Socrates.

The alley that runs by our building has a name, announced on a standard green city street sign: WOOGMS Alley, which stands for the Wellington-Oakdale Old Glory Marching Society. The street one block north of Oakdale is Wellington. It boasts some impressive Edwardian stone mansions, and in 1963 the occupant of one of them, Albert Weisman, was given a large American flag, and impulsively donned a Napoleonic hat and led a few neighborhood kids in an impromptu parade. They repeated it the next year and a tradition was born, on Memorial Day and Labor Day, bookending the summer. By the time we moved in, his son Tony had taken over, and the parade had become a big, semi-organized affair, covered by TV news and featuring a high school marching band and the Jesse White Tumblers (White, longtime Illinois secretary of state, organized the acrobatic squad in 1959; the former gymnast doesn't tumble himself anymore, though even in his later seventies he would sometimes still get in on the act, standing on his head to provide a barrier for his tumblers to leap over). The parade slogan is, "Everybody marches, nobody watches," and while the parade has grown, whoever feels like joining in is still invited to march. We'd hear a drum calling the neighbors to assemble—how nineteenth-century is *that?*—and hurry downstairs to gather before the impressive Weisman home, listen to a speech of welcome from Tony, and be led in the Pledge of Allegiance. There was a definite whiff of the squire greeting his yeomen on their saint's day about the whole thing.

Your life in the city is built on happy events, such as marching down the middle of Sheridan Road, smiling at all the babies in strollers while a brass band plays. But even stressful moments carry the seeds of pride, in the surmounting of them. One morning, the buzzer rings and I open our front door and look down the stairs to see a nicely dressed but frantic young man. He lives across the street, he breathlessly explains, has locked his wallet in his car, and needs money to take a cab downtown to get to his office, where the spare key is kept. I can be as dense as the next guy, but for some reason—maybe the improbability of keeping your spare car key at your office—I experience a moment of clarity. "You live across the street?" I say. He nods gravely. "What's your address?" Our eyes meet. Of course it's a scam—he doesn't know the address. He guesses, and misses by a half dozen blocks. He turns, muttering, and leaves.

Another morning, I look through the living room window and see that a city crew has begun to tear up the sidewalk in front of our building. I hurry downstairs. What are you doing? Replacing the sidewalk, a worker tells me. I gesture to the walk they are ripping up: perfectly good, almost pristine. Well, I got the order right here, he says, pulling out paperwork for one block over.

When people insist that you must live in the city to be a Chicagoan, to the extent that I agree with them, I'm thinking of the wallet scam and the torn-up sidewalk (which they quickly replaced, by the way, denying me the pleasure of complaining to my alderman about something so patently wrong). At such moments you feel your Chicagoness most acutely, a reminder that, almost by definition, being a Chicagoan demands a certain level of savvy. You can be born here, live here, and work here, and spend every minute in Chicago, but if you're still a sap, you never really belong.

* * *

The debate over who is a Chicagoan, I believe, really is a philosophical argument over whose version of the city—and everyone has a different one—is the real version, the genuine, authentic, and legitimate version. Everyone's argument can be boiled down to the same essential point. They're all saying, each in his or her own particular way: it's mine. *My* city is the true Chicago, the solid and lasting and real Chicago, while you exist perched in a borrowed lean-to of fraud, delusion, and illegitimacy. I have yet to come across anyone who ever offered a view of city life where people such as the speaker are the unwelcome interlopers, the marginal strangers, and someone else is the true heir to the spirit of Chicago. Never.

Some groups get better press. Between the *Studs Lonigan* trilogy and nearly half a century of Daley rule, not to mention scores of lesser novels and lesser politicians, it is easy and, to some, automatic and correct, to assume that the true Chicago is indeed "a lower middle-class, Irish American, Catholic environment," to use James T. Farrell's phrase, and nobody outside of those strictures can even pretend to belong.

Many people believe that. But it's not a rule, not a law, not written in the municipal code. It's an outlook, a perception, one tied not permanently to the essential core of Chicago life, but to the city of a certain time and a certain place. The Irish do have history and weight of numbers—they were the first immigrant group to come to Chicago en masse, digging the canal that helped create the city, and they grabbed the levers of power, elbowing aside the traditional Anglo-Saxon Protestant mandarins, and kept control long after the German community outstripped them in population. But that doesn't mean it won't change, and that the average Chicagoan won't someday be seen as a kid named Manny Lopez or Song Lin.

With that in mind, the situation becomes clear. The bedrock, unarguable reality is that everyone only has a piece. No one experiences Chicago in its entirety. Because you can't; it's impossible, there's too much of it. Pull back to see the whole city—a gray silhouette glimpsed from the Metra train as you cross the switching yard at Western Avenue, or a printed circuit of gorgeous little buildings seen in crisp perfection through the airplane window taking off from O'Hare, or a distant, elaborate jeweled egg jutting out into Lake Michigan as you motor north from Hyde Park on Lake Shore Drive, so beautiful you're tempted to pull over and just *look*—and you miss the all-important human-level details. Swoop in to savor the details, however, draw your fingertips over the spiky leaves and curling ribbons of the Louis Sullivan ironwork, and you run out of time long before you run out of city. Spend your life on one block and you may feel you belong, there, but you miss everyplace else. Wander the city, however, and you are never truly familiar, never really at home anywhere. Which is why Chicago is a mystery that can never be solved—you come upon it, a detective arriving on the scene, flip to a fresh page in your notebook, lick your pencil tip, and begin your investigation, make your choices. Where should I live? Who should I talk to? What should I do? What should I notice? What's worth paying attention to? What are the important parts, the relevant facts? Dig as hard and as fast as you like—your tale still ends long before you solve the puzzle, long before you reach a final conclusion, although, if you're lucky, you've lived a good story and been to interesting places and done exciting things, even as Chicago eludes you.

7

In the sleeping room

ARRIVE AT THE DIVISION Street Russian Baths on a weekday morning in the 1990s and a shabby, copper-skinned man everyone calls the Chief will greet you with deference in the small parking lot out back. He hangs around there most days, keeping an eye on the Cadillacs and Lincolns of the big shots, guiding them in and out of tight parking spaces. You give the Chief a couple of dollars, if you have a heart, but only when you return—this isn't a shakedown; he isn't one of the wiry black kids haunting the streets around the Chicago Stadium, whose air of juvenile menace suggests that a little something up front might be a good investment in the paint job of your car. No, the Chief is harmless, old, played-out—a bum, to use the term of a harsher, more direct age, or if you prefer euphemism, a member of the homeless community, though he certainly has a home, somewhere, even if you probably would not care to visit it. The Chief does not ask for pity; this isn't charity. The Chief is on the job, working, and your payment is a consideration for services rendered.

Go up the front steps and pull open the heavy glass door. Slide fourteen dollars through a barred window and into the hands of a clerk, often Jimmy Colucci, the owner's son, a heavy man in a white short-sleeved button-down shirt, his black hair slicked back, who sits impassively among the ancient trappings of manhood: plastic packages of square white Hav-a-Hanks, yellow bottles of Vitalis hair tonic, a cardboard display offering a row of black Ajax Unbreakable Pocket Combs. He takes your money and gives you a big chunk of Ivory soap, a soft, folded, well-worn goldenrod-colored sheet, two small, rough towels, and a steel key on an elastic lanyard. Return the key later and you get a dollar back.

If Jimmy's dad, Joe—a tiny, aged man—is there, glimpsed through an open door in the little office, doing the books, pop your head in and say hello, and he'll growl something in return. Compliment him on how well he looks. Go ahead.

"I'm a cripple!" he snarls, gesturing to his aluminum walker.

Having respected the formalities, take your soap, your towels, your sheet, and your key and go down a long hallway—a narrow hallway, not properly constructed, not to code, decorated with cheap frames containing yellowed *Herald-American* front pages commemorating Pearl Harbor and the end of World War II, a poster for 1940s middleweight champion Tony Zale, who ran a Catholic Youth Organization training ring on Wabash Avenue after he retired, plus advertisements for Kaiser-Frazer automobiles—Joe was a Kaiser-Frazer parts distributor and used car dealer for forty-two years, the owner of Parkside Motors before he bought the baths.

In the back are gray metal lockers, and as you approach, a nameless aroma hits you—a dry, vaguely pleasant fragrance, like a baked gym sock.

Take off your clothes, stash them in a locker, wrap yourself in the sheet, then pad downstairs, the key around your wrist. You enter a low-ceilinged basement room, the walls a mismatched hodgepodge of streaked, garish linoleum tiles and glazed yellow brick. There are two tables and two men—squat, hirsute, burly Mexicans in gym shorts and shower clogs—giving massages to the great pink hillsides of older gentlemen, face down. A half-hour massage is twelve dollars, plus tip. Averting your eyes, you step around the tables, unwrap, set aside the towels and the sheet—there are no hooks, nowhere to hang anything up, so place your towels carefully on the tile lip of the placid cold pool, by the door to the sauna—turn on showers that don't spray but pour, then step under the gushing spigot. The showers are not secluded by any kind of wall or partition, but out in the open in one corner of the room. Nobody else cares about that, and soon you don't either.

Wrap yourself in your sheet, if you like. Leave one towel by the cold pool, saving it for later. Bunch the other one up, delivering a quick blot to your face so you can see, taking it with you as a pillow. Then pull the heavy glass door open and scoot dripping into the sauna itself, the superheated heart of the Russian Baths.

* * *

I might never have gone to the Division Street Russian Baths if Edie and I hadn't had a big wedding. But with guests coming in from out of town, and a day between my bachelor party on Friday night and the wedding Sunday evening, I thought my groomsmen—Jim, Robert, Kier, Sam—might like to sweat out their excesses on Saturday morning.

The Russian Baths were one of those Chicago places you hear about, one of those fabled spots in the city, like the Checkerboard Lounge or the Granada Theatre that you know are historic and know are still there, and sincerely intend to visit, someday, but never quite get to. Then suddenly they're gone and you missed them and you wish you had found the time to go, if only to be able to say that you were once there.

Despite having never been inside, going to the Russian Baths struck me as a very Chicago thing to do, an experience that might please the out-of-towners. That's what made me want to go. But I had to verify the baths first. To be thorough. Because you never know. I didn't want to unwittingly drag my brother and my best friends to a gay bathhouse the day before my wedding. That seemed like a bad idea.

Checking out the baths to see if they qualify for a post–bachelor party visit is a reminder that part of being a Chicagoan is an exercise performed for the benefit of others. Years go by when I—and probably most Chicagoans—don't step inside the Art Institute, or take a boat cruise, or attend a baseball game, unless it is to impress a guest from out of town. I'd go so far as saying we need the outsiders, to motivate us, to spur us, to remind us how wonderful this place is, to prompt us to try new things and to appreciate glories we've grown overly familiar with. To notice aspects ourselves, to spark our pride, renew our love for the city because we get to see it reflected in someone else's eyes. I never realized that driving downtown with a reasonable expectation of being able to park on the street is an enviable marvel until I saw the amazement on the faces of friends from New York City. They couldn't believe it.

Going to the Russian Baths seemed a lost ritual, a vanished custom, an exotic species of flower that grows on this one spot and nowhere else. The baths are not a practical matter. Not anymore. Once upon a time they were—a hundred years ago many dwellings didn't have private baths, or had baths that were shared and foul. When the Russian Baths opened in 1906 there were fifty bathhouses in Chicago, some independent businesses, others run by the Chicago Park District, even a few built at public schools whose students could not reasonably be expected to have the chance to wash at home.

Not that lack of private bathrooms was unique to Chicago. When Louis Armstrong took the train up from New Orleans in August 1922 to play with King Oliver's band, he went straight from Illinois Central Station to Lincoln Gardens at 31st and Cottage Grove, blew his horn, went home with Oliver for a red beans and rice dinner, then took a taxi to the boardinghouse where Oliver had rented him a room at 3412 South Wabash. On the way, Oliver told him it was a room with a private bath. "What's a private bath?" Armstrong asked. In New Orleans, Armstrong reminded his mentor, you bathed in a washtub in the backyard.

Chicago public bathhouses survived a surprisingly long time beyond the general advent of indoor plumbing—past World War II, through the 1950s. In 1965, the Chicago Park District still ran eight bathhouses, and recorded more than sixty-five thousand visits. The baths were always open, twenty-four hours a day, because people worked three shifts. Men labored in steel mills and slaughterhouses and coal yards—not the type of filth and grime you wanted to wash off in your own home if you could avoid it. That same year, there was a fire at the Loop Turkish Baths that sent patrons scurrying into Randolph Street wrapped in towels. When the Turkish Baths closed to repair the fire damage, the manager discovered that the front door had no lock. The bathhouse had been open, continuously, for fifty years.

The last Park District bathhouse closed in 1974, the year Joe Colucci bought the Russian Baths, calling it a hobby for his retirement. His last private competitor, the opulent Luxor at Milwaukee and Damen, whose opening ribbon was cut by Mayor William "Big Bill" Thompson in 1923, closed in 1984. (Mike Royko, comparing the two institutions, said that while the Luxor was "once considered the finest steam bath joint in town" and was preferred by Nelson Algren, the Russian Baths still "had more class.")

Reconnoitering the Russian Baths didn't seem a mission to be done alone, so I recruited Sam. We showered and entered the sauna, which is not the warm cedar room found in health clubs, but a searing tiled chamber where men sit on two tiers of wooden benches, dark with age and water. Around the room, three taps, full open, blast water into overflowing black rubber buckets. At the far end of the room is not the usual scattering of hot stones in a square metal box, but an enormous oven, filling the wall. Inside, eight tons of superheated granite rocks, each the size of a loaf of bread, which could be spied through a clanking metal door. You charge up the oven by opening the door, nudging the latch up with a worn scrap of 2×4, then dipping a plastic bleach bottle cut into a scoop into a large bucket of warm water—cold water would crack the stones, supposedly—and flinging the water into the glowing mouth of the oven, where it explodes into hissing steam. It takes a bit of finesse, a sideways toss—if you throw the water straight in it will vaporize and blow straight back out, a scalding gust. That I can vouch for. The older guys tell you how to do it—in times past, only the oldest man in the room was allowed the honor of tending the oven; now anyone can, but you have to do it right or you'll hurt yourself.

Sit on the lower level, at first, to acclimate yourself to the temperature. When you are ready, you literally rise through the ranks, climbing to the higher tier, where the tough old birds sit, hands on knees, defiant of the heat—which rises, remember—while you cringe and cower and protect your head by draping it with a wet towel.

The men inside—and there may be three, or six, or none—come in all sizes: tall, short, old, young, hairy, smooth, lean and muscular or spindly-legged with beach ball bellies, black or white or brown, lobster-faced or chalk-skinned. Though strangers, they talk to each other, strike up conversations—about construction projects, about whiskey versus beer, about which is a better workout, punching the heavy bag or riding the exercise cycle. How does Daley the son stack up against Daley the father? How bad is official corruption? ("In the zillions," someone speculates.)

Some wash each other with oak leaf brooms, or rough natural sponges the size of basketballs, and for a tip—as with the Chief, you pay later—a massage guy will step away from his table, if he's not occupied, and scrub you down with oak branches while you lie there, an incredible ritual to find still being performed at the cusp of the twenty-first century. Our social structure has veered in such a way—we are all so isolated, so atomized, so removed from each other's bodies and from our own—that nowhere except here will a stranger wash you with a big soapy sponge. It seems almost illicit. (Nothing about the Russian Baths ever struck me as even remotely erotic, though sometimes I'd see an unfamiliar face looking around with a certain hopeful air, an open, inquisitive expression that made me suspect he had come here expecting a different kind of bathhouse. And one editor at the paper, an old Vietnam correspondent, claimed that, in decades past, a Division Street hooker or two would occasionally be snuck into the back rooms—he dramatized this claim with an excited, Yiddish-accented cry of "da cahksuckers are here!"—though he is the lone person in my experience to suggest this, and while I have my doubts, I don't want to be naïve either.)

The oak branch scrub-down seems an ancient practice, something men did in Carthage, and in the years I went to the baths, the oddly comforting thought often occurred to me that if a Roman senator walked down those stairs and into this room, he would know exactly what was going on here and exactly what he should do.

If you've asked for a massage, one of the Mexican masseurs will step into the steam room and wordlessly gesture you out when it is your time, then lead you to one of the tables. You climb atop the table, settle yourself, close your eyes. He pours baby oil on your back, kneads and chops and squeezes your flesh. A bone-cracking rubdown, pressing hard with his forearm, with the heel of his hand, a massage that is supposed to hurt and does, so much that at times you worry you're being permanently damaged, that your spine is being snapped, your neck broken; at moments you are at the point of crying out for him to stop. But you don't, you endure, the moment passes, and relaxation descends upon you like a peaceful summer evening. Time slows, you fade out of consciousness. Then he's done, signifying it with a dismissive tap, and you stand, blinking in the light, and climb the stairs to the sleeping room, a bit groggy, like a small child going up to bed.

The sleeping room of the Division Street Russian Baths is long and thin, with a high ceiling and half a dozen old metal beds, single beds with head- and footboards of rounded iron tubes, cool and smooth, slightly pocked with age, each bed tightly made with a charcoal-colored rough woolen blanket, topped with a fat fresh white pillow. Nobody pulls the blanket back and gets under the sheets, but rather men rest on top of the covers, and several human forms, curled and inert, like casts of bodies from the streets of Pompeii, are already sleeping when you slip into the dim room after your massage. You pick an empty bed and gently lower yourself onto it, the springs creaking. You lie there, gazing placidly up at the ceiling fans quietly whirring in the twilight—a faint glow from the open transom, along with soft sounds, breathing and the occasional rasp of a snore, plus various clanks and splashes and bits of conversation filtering from outside. Above you, flickering against the pressed-tin ceiling, long ago painted white, shadows from the spinning fans, fluttery gray shapes that fade to black as you drift off.

I always thought of that room as a portal to another era, as a teacup salvaged out of time, spared from otherwise relentless change. As if one room on Ellis Island had somehow magically survived a century, and immigrant bricklayers from Sardinia were still there, sleeping, undisturbed as the years rolled on, exhausted from their long journey, waiting for the results of their tuberculosis tests.

* * *

Saul Bellow was a patron of the Division Street Russian Baths. He took John Cheever there once, and set a scene in *Humboldt's Gift* at what was already, in the mid-1970s, a lingering anachronism. "As I kid I went to the Russian Bath with my own father," it begins. (Bellow uses the singular, "Bath," but I always used "Baths." It was "Division Street Russian Baths," plural, on membership cards, and "Baths" is carved in stone across the front of the building.) "This old establishment has been there forever, hotter than the tropics and rotting sweetly. Down in the cellar men moaned on the steam-softened planks while they were massaged abrasively with oak-leaf besoms lathered in pickle buckets."

Bellow's hero, Charlie Citrine, reneges on a $450 poker debt to crazed mobster Rinaldo Cantabile, who ruins Citrine's Mercedes in order to impress upon him the importance of paying one's debts. Thus educated, Citrine agrees to pay. The transaction is to take place at the baths, which Citrine finds "more or less unchanged" from when he was a child: "The old guys at the Bath do seem to be unconsciously engaged in a collective attempt to buck history."

The place is not so much about cleanliness as about cheating time:

Things are very elementary here. You feel that these people are almost conscious of obsolescence, of a line of evolution abandoned by nature and culture. So down in the super-heated subcellars all these Slavonic cavemen and wood demons with hanging laps of fat and legs of stone and lichen boil themselves and splash water on their heads by the bucket.... There may be no village in the Carpathians where such practices still prevail.

"Splash water on their heads by the bucket." Not to quibble with a Nobel laureate, but that doesn't do the process justice. It isn't the sleeping room, or the conversation, or the history of the baths, or its famous customers, that are the main appeal to me. It isn't the boxing club decor, or the little speckled linoleum lunch counter upstairs, where, after the heat, the massage, and the sleep, my brother and I sometimes enjoy a shot of whiskey and a plate of herring. Nor even the square plastic dispenser filled with ice, so after the sauna you can drain glass after glass of ice water; not even the joy of drinking very cold water when you're parched, baked dry, and really thirsty. It isn't just getting clean—you can do that at home, though not the deep, glowing, subcutaneous clean you feel walking out into the brisk air of Division Street after a morning at the baths.

No, the moment that make the Russian Baths worth fourteen dollars—not that I am ever asked to pay after Joe Colucci finds out I am a newspaper reporter—happens inside the sauna. You sit there, sweating, talking to the other men.

The minutes pass. Someone charges the oven, and you immediately feel the heat as it rolls, an invisible wave, off hissing granite rocks, rising to the ceiling and spreading throughout the room. You can almost taste the heat in your teeth, a physical presence. You sit, taking short breaths, lest the air sear your lungs. You get hot. Hotter and hotter. Very hot. Unbearably hot. The tops of your ears are burning. You look around at the other men, Chicago men, stoic as Buddhas, placid as fire hydrants. What to do? You could flee, and accept the deathless shame of weaklings and cowards everywhere. Or you could embrace the solution to this awful heat as represented by three open spigots gushing water into three black rubber fire buckets, the water cascading over the sides and splattering, steaming to the floor. You could stand up, grab one of the black buckets in both hands, heavy with its load, move to the center of the room, raise the bucket, pausing for one deeply felt second, lingering at the brink, holding the bucket at chest level, your fists wrapped around the bucket's lip, the muscles in your arms and chest tensing, girding your courage, then leap across the chasm, tip the bucket upside down over your head, tilting your face back, roaring as you douse yourself with ice-cold water.

Relief. Sweet God it felt fantastic. You can't imagine how invigorating. You snapped back to life and all its possibilities. Drenching yourself in cold water is only daunting the first time or two. After that, you look forward to it, yearn for it, for the slow buildup of murderous heat, the freezing slap back to life. I never took my groomsmen to the Russian Baths; they were not Chicagoans, and they all balked at the idea of getting naked in front of each other. Most guys I knew—and I invited almost every man I ever held in any regard—flatly refused. They didn't see the point.

I did. If Sam was busy, I'd go by myself. Sometimes just to get clean after work. At the end of an eleven-hour day spent watching Dr. Robert J. Stein conduct autopsies at the Cook County Medical Examiner's Office—including the decomposed corpse of a drifter that had lain on the floor of a transient hotel room for two weeks in the August heat, until it began to drip into the room below—I rushed straight from Harrison Street to the baths and reveled in the chance to scrub the smell of dead bodies off myself, forgetting that, after finding rejuvenation in the sauna, I would have to go upstairs and put my clothes back on and they would reek of death—death as found in the morgue, which smells of meat and bleach and refrigeration. I put the clothes on, cringing, then raced home to strip them off again, and couldn't go into the meat section of a supermarket for a month.

Sometimes the need was social, even mental. I wanted to escape. I wanted to go somewhere familiar, to see people I knew. To see the Chief, to chat with Joe Colucci or his son Jimmy. To have the pleasure of being welcomed, of being recognized somewhere. Sam could usually find the time to go with me—limousine guys, like newspaper reporters, have flexible schedules, and we could steal the three hours it took to do the baths properly. He and I met there so often that, eventually, the times I went alone, one of the masseurs might say, "No brother today?" I liked that immensely, because it made me feel as if I belonged.

Once, and only once, when I was a teenager, my Grandma Sarah—Sarah Bramson, a tiny, bird-like, poker-playing member of the Jewish Singing Society—sent me on an errand down the block to pick up something at a bakery on Cedar Road in Cleveland. The baker knew my grandparents, of course, smiled and said something pleasant at meeting Sarah and Irwin's grandson, and I remember standing there, in front of the glass case of sweets, thinking, even then, as a teenager accepting my white box wrapped in white string, that this is nice, that this must be what people who live in one place around their family enjoy all the time. This must be what home feels like. Because while I grew up and spent my entire youth in the same house in Berea, we didn't really know anyone there, not well, and had no close friends and no family nearby—the East Side of Cleveland, where my grandparents lived, was an hour away—and it all seemed a temporary bivouac, as if we might break camp and depart at any moment.

Maybe because of this tentative attachment to my actual home, I can't help but yearn for substitute homes, for the routine welcome certain places offer. I tend to go to the same handful of restaurants—Harry Caray's, Petterino's, Gene & Georgetti—not just for the food, but for a welcoming maitre d', a friendly waiter, a smiling owner, a place to eat where somebody knows me. Yes, part of that is vanity—the local demicelebrity craving recognition like a drug. But part is the kind of overwhelming loneliness that a city both causes and balms.

Every year Joe gave me a new cardboard membership card, which I treasured beyond its value for use getting in free on the rare days when he or Jimmy weren't at the front window to wave me in, carrying the last one in my wallet for years, long after the baths closed. I might be a Jew born in Ohio, whose grandparents were dead and whose family and friends, with the signal exception of my brother, were fallen away or scattered around the country. I might be a night-shift reporter at the less popular newspaper in town. But I was also a card-carrying member of the Division Street Russian Baths, and the Russian Baths were Chicago.

* * *

Toward the end of the decade, the baths began to seem empty, moribund.

"No people because it's Monday morning?" I asked, hopefully, of one of the masseurs when I found myself the only customer at 8 a.m. one day in 1998.

"No people every day," he glumly replied.

Joe Colucci died in 2000; his son Jimmy died three years later—I wrote both their obituaries. Joe's was a bit of trouble—it turned out that his business activities extended beyond Kaiser-Frazer car parts and traditional Russian schvitzes. But we'll get to that.

The Russian Baths closed in 2006, stayed closed for about a year, then reopened for a while. The third generation, Jimmy's son Joey, tried to run it. Joey brought in a Moroccan partner, redecorated the haphazard 1930s boxing club interior into a sponge-painted terra-cotta and rose faux Mediterranean 1970s effect, like Jake LaMotta in a tutu. They brought in a hair stylist and a manicurist, offered mud wraps—the Russian Baths looked like a Bulgarian beauty salon by the time they were done with it. I can't say I was grief-stricken when the place finally closed for good. The building remained, and every time I went down that stretch of Division Street, I would hold my breath as I approached its block, relaxing only when the rectangular gray façade with its five arching windows came into view. It was still there. There was still hope.

* * *

The city shifts. The parts we dislike sometimes disappear, and few mourn them. Not many wish there were still a sprawling stretch of railroad yard right next to the Art Institute instead of Millennium Park. Hoboes, perhaps.

You want the city to grow, to change—new places, new buildings, new people—to give it energy, to make it live. When a few Chicagoans were getting upset over Marshall Field's State Street store changing its name to Macy's after Federated bought the chain, I had to point out that Louis Sullivan's Carson Pirie Scott Building—as classic a Chicago landmark as there is —wasn't originally built for Carson's. For the first five years it belonged to a retailer called Schlesinger & Mayer. That's who built it. People forget that today's unacceptable upstart is tomorrow's cherished icon.

A city is like a language—constantly in flux, with new words being born, old ones falling out of use. Whether you approve of the change or not isn't the issue. Every dictionary is outdated the day it goes on sale.

Without change, a city is a museum, perhaps beautiful, like Venice, perhaps something you could love. But a relic, under glass. Change is the definition of life, and change is what gives a city its drama and vitality.

And yet. . . .

You want some of the familiar to remain. Constancy is an important part of what makes any city what it is. The modern sections of truly old cities— the office high-rises in London, the apartment blocks around Paris—might be technically within the city, and might even have their own charms, but they never seem to add to whatever ineffable special something makes a city a place to yearn for and live in and love. In Rome, nothing they will ever build is going to supplant St. Peter's or the Colosseum. But Chicago is a far newer city, and nothing here is so old and so ingrained that it forever dwarfs everything yet to come. As beloved as Wrigley Field is, its owners are constantly talking about tearing it down. The Water Tower, the small crenulated limestone castle in the center of Michigan Avenue, a survivor of the 1871 fire (as well as several efforts to get it out of the middle of the street) may be revered, now, but it isn't quite beloved. Maybe the truth of Oscar Wilde's famous dismissal of the Water Tower as "a castellated monstrosity with pepper boxes stuck all over it" eventually sank in. (Wilde is a member of an elite group I call the "People You Don't Think of as Ever Being in Chicago But Were Club," which includes Winston Churchill, Albert Einstein, Golda Meier, who lived here, and Lt. Col. George Armstrong Custer. I'm tempted to include Abraham Lincoln, who wandered the streets for years—he was nominated here in 1860. We know Lincoln was in Chicago, yet somehow his image didn't stick; maybe because of its association with Springfield.)

Despite its past, like Lincoln the Water Tower isn't the city symbol that comes to mind when we think of Chicago—it isn't even in the top three, not anymore. Posters advertising Chicago in the 1960s showed the hip new Marina City corncobs. Now Marina City seems fusty, dated. A new city is entitled to new icons.

Each of us gets to choose our special places. The quirky metal sky bridge, fourteen floors up, connecting the two towers of the Wrigley Building—which, like the City Hall/County Building block, is actually two different buildings constructed at different times, though this easier to see with the Wrigley Building since, if viewed from a certain angle, it is clearly a pair of separate glazed white terra-cotta structures. The Wrigley Building has two addresses: 400 and 410 North Michigan, 400 being the building with the four-sided clock tower, completed in 1921—in its cornerstone, a time capsule contains boxes of Spearmint, Doublemint, and Juicy Fruit gum manufactured in 1920. The second, northern structure, 410 North Michigan, was added in 1924.

The Wrigley clock and I shared a moment together once. Everybody at the newspaper was required to work New Year's Eve 1999, because of the quaint concern that society would come to a grinding halt due to unforeseen computer glitches brought on by the change to the year 2000. The staff gathered in the newsroom, ready for action, but as midnight approached, it became clear, from what wasn't happening at the places where midnight had already come and gone, that nothing unforeseen would take place within the world's vital computer systems. No electrical grids were collapsing, no darkened cities were erupting into riot. At 11:45 p.m., I stood up and said to myself, "I am not ushering in the new millennium sitting in the *Sun-Times* newsroom." I fled the cluttered, fluorescent-lit fourth floor, left my colleagues, walked downstairs, out to the middle of the Wabash Avenue bridge, leaned on the rail, alone in the pleasant December cool, and watched the minute hand of the Wrigley clock inch toward midnight, when fireworks exploded over the lakefront.

The biggest New Year's midnight of my life was spent with the Wrigley clock for company. Yet as beautiful as the clock may be, it is the little enclosed bridge, with its romantic decorative flourishes, that makes me inexplicably happy every time I see it. Installed between the two buildings in 1933, the bridge is like a refugee from some alternate universe art nouveau Venice that never came to be. There is a popular misconception about the sky bridge—in fact, I'd wager almost nobody knows why it's really there, or even what it's made of.

First, it's not aluminum, as it appears, but Allegheny nickel. Nor was it built because William Wrigley got tired of taking an elevator downstairs to go to offices in the other building. That is just a story. The Wrigley Company had no offices in the north tower at the time the bridge was built, and besides, William Wrigley wasn't a wander-from-office-to-office-making-small-talk kind of guy. The Wrigley Building was the first significant commercial building built north of the Chicago River on Michigan Avenue, which at the time was still Pine Street, a shambling road of factories and dilapidated structures leading up to the old Water Tower. That's why Wrigley built such a fancy building—glazed terra-cotta in six shades of white—to stand out, to draw prosperous people across the river, and why he put a restaurant and a bank in it, to make such a remote spot appealing to commercial tenants. The bank did have offices in both buildings, however, and because the buildings had two different addresses, the bank risked running afoul of the Illinois law forbidding branch banking. Thus the sky bridge, to make the two buildings one for legal purposes. Or at least that is what Philip K. Wrigley, William Wrigley's son, said, late in life. In 1933, the public reason given for the bridge construction was that the Wrigley Company wanted to expand into the new tower. Maybe both reasons are true.

It seems a shame to linger on one building when there are so many others, so much architectural beauty in Chicago. The glass-ceilinged lobby of the Rookery at LaSalle and Adams, redesigned by Frank Lloyd Wright and restored to its pristine 1905 gilded splendor. The ziggurat on the old Britannica Building, topped with its cobalt blue beacon. The soaring waiting room at Union Station—and yes, that scene from *The Untouchables*, the baby carriage bouncing down the stairs, adds to the appeal. It's like stepping away from your daily commute to visit a Hollywood set, enshrined in permanence, the dips in the center of the stone steps mute evidence of the millions of feet that trod them, the closest Chicago comes to the footworn alleys of an ancient city like Jerusalem or Rome. The view south down to the Board of Trade, a deco fantasy topped by that thirty-foot stainless steel statue of a faceless Ceres, was cool even before the Joker flipped an eighteen-wheeler while battling Batman in the middle of LaSalle Street in *The Dark Knight*. Now it's extra cool.

Chicagoans take an outsized pride in movies being set here because there was a drought of about ten years, after *Medium Cool* in 1969 focused on the riots around the Democratic Convention, and an offended Mayor Daley completely choked off film production. It didn't start up again until after he died and Jane Byrne put the city government at the disposal of John Belushi and Dan Aykroyd for their valentine to Chicago, *The Blues Brothers*. (Cook County government was even more cooperative, a generosity not unrelated to the fact that Murphy Dunne, the keyboardist for the Blues Brothers Band, is the son of then Cook County Board President George Dunne.)

That decade hiatus left the general sense that movies aren't made in Chicago, an impression that lingered long after film producers began routinely shooting here again. We're used to movies that take place in New York and Los Angeles, and there's still a certain "Hey, look, it's us!" frisson of pleasure and sense of significance that comes from watching one set in Chicago. Not to mention the insider satisfaction of being able to pick out the inconsistencies and physical impossibilities that every film serves up. A smug feeling: you know this place, but others don't. (I think that's why I enjoy giving directions, why I will swoop in on a couple consulting a map and offer my services. Mainly because I'm a nice guy and want to help, but also because I have the knowledge they lack. There is a joy in telling people something they don't know. A French family once haltingly asked me where the John Hancock Building might be. I smiled, savoring the moment, extended my arm, pointing my finger, slowly raising it to indicate the building looming directly in front of us: "Voila!" I said.)

History and Hollywood have a way of mingling, of competing. Sometimes, driving visitors up Lake Shore Drive I'll point out the old Conrad Hilton in the distance and say, "The 1968 riots took place right there." And sometimes I'll say, "This is where the ending of *The Fugitive* took place."

The past puts a gel in front of your eyes making the beautiful even prettier. You come up out of the tunnel at Wrigley Field and see the grass, and the ivy on the wall, and the el beyond, and you have to be dead not to tingle with delight, to not look at the field and think, first, "It's so *small*," and then, "Babe Ruth stood right *there*, and pointed at the center-field scoreboard for his called shot." (Supposedly—though no less an authority than John Paul Stevens, the former US Supreme Court justice, claimed that Ruth really did point to where his homer would go, and that's good enough for me, since he was there, as a child, at the historic third game of the World Series in 1932.)

City Hall has that same jeweled box feel—the lobby, with its quirky barrel-vaulted ceiling, is almost completely unchanged over a full century— the brochures at the bronze information kiosk have been updated, but that's about it. Too solidly built, all marble and bronze, to ever wear down, so integrated a design that nobody dared remodel it, leaving the space exactly as it was in 1912. You can be trucking through, maybe just to nip out of the cold—the building has a pair of block-long central corridors cutting straight through, one north and south, the other east and west. It only takes a little imagination, a narrowing of the eyes, and you can see a city resident, a lady in 1913, wearing a wide Edwardian hat with a pheasant on it, hurrying ahead of you, dragging along a small boy in a sailor suit with one gloved hand while the other crumples the letter that left her fuming and prompted her to take a streetcar downtown to complain to the civic authorities about some outrage.

Not that something has to be old to inspire love. But it does help. Old things are beloved because they've survived, because they're beautiful and expensive and well made and we'd never build them today, and they inspire you to marvel at the span of time, and realize that we dwell in the glorious shells of our ancestors' ambitions.

Or, in the case of the old Sun-Times Building on Wabash, the not-so-glorious shells. You have to wonder what they were thinking. Constructing the Sun-Times next door to the Wrigley Building was like placing an overturned galvanized metal tub next to a spun-sugar Victorian wedding cake. Actually, we don't have to wonder. It isn't as if the thinking of the past is unavailable. The Sun-Times Building was built in 1957, "the latest in design and excelling efficiency," with aluminum trim, a heliport on the roof, and train tracks that went right up to the basement, to whisk the big rolls of newsprint straight to the mighty Goss presses. At the time they were thinking we'd all live in Tomorrowland, with robot maids and backpack rockets. They were zipping into the bright shiny modern world of their imaginings. When you understand that attitude, the wonder shifts from puzzling how they were oafish enough to build a trapezoidal metal monstrosity next to such rococo porcelain beauty, to appreciating that they didn't also tear down the Wrigley Building while they were at it, to accommodate the monorail they hoped to run someday between the Sun-Times Building and the hoped-for lakefront space port.

In a 1965 guidebook on famous Chicago buildings, architecture critic J. Carson Webster praises the Sun-Times Building for its modern look, contemporary plaza, and interesting exterior walls. The Wrigley Building, on the other hand, he finds suffering from "rather commonplace ornament derived from Renaissance designs" that has "achieved fame through traits other than architectural merit." He speculates that perhaps people notice the Wrigley Building merely because it's so well illuminated at night.

Just because automatically embracing whatever is new while backhanding anything old is philistinism doesn't mean that the new can't sometimes be an improvement. The shiny pale metallic-blue Trump Tower, impossibly thin, like a skyscraper on Mars, is gorgeous in spite of who built it. I'm proud that I can be walking up Wabash Avenue, catch sight of Trump Tower surging into the sky, and think, "Wow," without a single regret that it replaced the Sun-Times Building. I worked there for seventeen years; it was enough. We mustn't be slaves to nostalgia, even when it is our own cherished past.

When I first caught sight of the NBC Tower under construction, in all its deco majesty, complete with stylized flying buttresses, peeking from behind the gothic horror show of the Tribune Tower, I wanted to drop to my knees in awe. Who cares that it's a rip-off of Rockefeller Center? It's splendid. The Harold Washington Library sits in majesty, a ten-story cube of rose granite and brick with immense green winged metal froufrou decorating the roof's summit and cornices. The newspaper printed the various contenders in the architecture contest to choose the library's design, and wonder of wonders, the design that I liked best was the design finally selected. I felt a little-boy thrill—"My design won!"—though the city hesitated, debating whether to actually add the huge metal flourishes called for in the plans. They were expensive, and officials balked, until Mayor Richard M. Daley demanded they be included, a sentiment that mitigates the general scorn I feel for him.

And the Bean—Anish Kapoor's hundred-ton stainless steel sculpture in Millennium Park. For decades, you couldn't shoot a movie set in Chicago and not have the camera pause in front of the Picasso on Daley Plaza. No more. Now a movie can explore the beauty of the city and completely ignore Picasso's rusty baboon, preferring to marvel at the infinity of the

Bean's curving mirrored surface. Everyone was immediately intrigued by it—partially due to the allure of their own reflection, no doubt. The Bean offers visitors the gift of themselves. You have to always resist the tendency to think of Chicago as an aggregation of streets and structures and events, and the Bean is a perfect physical reminder that the city is also the people in it. Maybe it'll be even more enjoyable a hundred years from now, when visitors will be able to reflect upon all the faces that have been mirrored in it. (Or maybe it is even more marvelous now, to consider all the faces that *will* gaze upon it in the years to come.) There was no adjustment period needed; the Bean was pretty damn fun fresh out of the box, one of the few pieces of major public art that sparked no controversy, no criticism, no outcry, no debate. It was love at first sight.

That sometimes happens. The slender beauty of the Park Hyatt, a sand-colored skyscraper just west of the Water Tower. I stood in the street, looked at it for the first time after it was completed, and regretted my entire professional life, wished I had spent my career as a corporate lawyer parsing the dry language of mortgages, just so I could have my coffee and read my morning paper on one of those balconies for a decade or two. Frank Gehry's billowing metal band shell in Millennium Park—proof that a structure can be radically different, completely out of character to its setting, yet still somehow fit in. The second North Avenue Beach House, an adorable whimsy built to look like an ocean liner docked on the lakefront, with its red stacks and blue portholes, far superior to the run-down 1938 original it replaced.

Chicago has so much splendid architecture, it offers a vast wonderworld that one can easily march off into, if not careful, never to return. No one would suggest that architecture is overlooked in Chicago, but there are glories of the city that are generally ignored. For instance, Chicagoans are strangely detached from the river that had such a key role in forming their city. If they list the things they love about Chicago, the lakefront is always right up there, along with ball fields, buildings, parks, festivals, parades, concerts. They might even mention smells, such as the delicious cocoa aroma wafting from Blommer Chocolate on a summer night or the caramel air lingering at the entrance of a Garrett's Popcorn shop.

But the river? Maybe because they usually only see it downtown, where the two branches, north and south, meet at Wolf Point and the river widens, a barrier to cross, a wind-scoured span to hurry over, maybe glancing down at ducks or scullers from the Loyola team, only really noticing it when there are sailboats or one of those enormous empty barges heading to pick up crushed limestone, or sand, or dry cement at the enormous quarries and concrete plants down river. They are so big, those barges, it seems they couldn't make the turn, and when I see one I can't help leaning on the rail for a minute, both to monitor its progress and to wonder where the other passersby could possibly be going so important that they can't find the time to even glance at such a monstrous vessel.

The Chicago River gives us all those bridges—thirty-seven operable drawbridges, more than any other city in the world. And it seems perverse to love the bridges—and who doesn't feel a thrill watching a bridge go up, the bedrock certainties of the street suddenly rearing into the sky?—and yet not also love the river. The Chicago River provides a false coastline—you can see a panoramic sweep of buildings along Wacker Drive that would otherwise be obscured by other buildings, but are left open by the water. The new *Sun-Times* offices, just west of the Merchandise Mart, in the old Apparel Center, are on the river, and every day when I arrive at work, I make a ritual of stopping, putting my hand flat on the top of a stainless steel bollard, sweeping my gaze, from the clock atop the Boeing Building to the Willis Tower, the emerald parabola of 333 W. Wacker to the needle spires atop 225 W. Wacker, all the way to the gilded pinnacle of the aptly dark Carbide and Carbon Building, the wavy Aqua Building, the upward-pointing index finger of Mather Tower, a slice of Marina Towers, and a corner of the huge bulk of the Merchandise Mart, hard to the left, with its nine big American flags flapping boldly along the river. El trains move steadily above car traffic on the rust-red double-decker bridges—going north and south above Wells Street, and east and west on the Lake Street Bridge—as across the river Metra trains snake in and out from Union and Ogilvie stations. If the moment I'm pausing before going into the building I happen to see the el go by, looking like little toy trains on a vast diorama, emerging magically from behind buildings, for some reason that strikes me as good luck. Maybe it comes from seeing too many TV shows and movies, which of course must have the train going by in the shot, to add visual interest, to make the scene complete. Plus everything else: the cabs in line in front of the building, the tourists heading out from the hotel with their maps, the tattooed, pierced art students catching a cigarette, the car traffic starting and stopping on Wacker Drive. I take it all in, and softly repeat a line of Jesse Jackson's, the exclamation he made as a teenager arriving in the city for the first time: "God, I am in Chicago." I say it aloud, every day, as a mantra, a spell, a morning incantation to ward off ever taking the city for granted. The world never becomes dull, I remind myself, it is we who dull ourselves, sometimes, while scratching away at our routines, digging for wonders. Everyone becomes blunted, and everyone must constantly sharpen themselves to keep their edge.

The river is not nearly so imposing a spectacle anywhere else in Chicago. Up north, the river is hidden by buildings and trees, and becomes a brown glimmer barely glimpsed from bridges. To see it, you almost have to be on it. Once I canoed ten miles down the Chicago River—an outdoorsy New York magazine was publishing a special canoe issue and realized the whole thing was turning out a bit too pious, so hired me to go down the river in an aluminum canoe, as a bit of levity to cut the birch bark reverence. I dragooned my friend Larry, made big roast beef sandwiches, grabbed some cigars and a bottle of Chilean Riesling ("I need," I told the liquor store clerk, "a good canoeing wine").

Paddling the river was hard work and fun and I recommend it to anyone. I was surprised to discover that, canoeing down the center of the Chicago River two miles from downtown, at times you could just as well be on a river in rural Michigan. A canopy of trees lines the banks, the noise of traffic fades, the buildings hide, and you feel like you are deep in the woods, while gently paddling through Chicago, the only sound the lapping brownish-green water. Hitting the main channel was less bucolic—Larry and I put our backs into it frantically as a big Wendella tour boat loomed up behind us—but it was worth it to pull the canoe ashore on the dock at North Pier and toss it atop his Land Rover, which his wife had indulgently driven downtown to collect us. Larry worried, at first, about the canoe scratching his paint job, and I had to remind him that you can't spend years puttering around in your four-wheel-drive sports utility vehicle, with brush grills over the headlights and, no doubt, special Rhino Charge Evasion Tires, only to balk the one time it's actually being used for its intended purpose. Doesn't happen often. Not many canoes are grounded in downtown Chicago nowadays, though maybe there should be—it's a unique way to see the city, and a nod back to Marquette and Jolliet, who arrived in the same fashion on this very river more than three hundred years ago. What would they have thought, could they have seen what that swampy sandbar would become? They'd be terrified, no doubt.

* * *

This is what makes Chicago the place it is: you can't be familiar with it. If you fancy you are, you're not. Not all of it. You can't fully fathom even a portion of the city, because the parts you know keep changing. The building that used to be there—gone. A vacant lot on its way to becoming something else. What are they building now? And what was there before? The mind gropes, constantly adjusting to the continuous change. A new block goes up, a plaza is created, a new row of trees planted. You take a different route, on a whim, turn down a different street and see something you've never seen before. You can be in a part of the city you know very well, when suddenly you spy something *new*.

An old iron water main burst at LaSalle and Lake, the rush of water quickly undermining the street and opening up an enormous sinkhole. A woman in a hurry, thinking she could drive through a puddle, went around the barricades and submerged her compact car to the roof into the crater. Nearby city workers rescued her. I was standing there a few hours later, notepad in hand, looking at the top of the car, and found myself talking to someone in a hard hat—an assistant commissioner from the Water Department—about all the tubes and pipes and infrastructure affected by the break. I started doing stories on *those*, on the city that is hidden, literally just below our feet, if we are willing to notice. Water mains, sewer pipes, telephone cables, service conduits, heavily shielded electrical lines, fiber optics, thermal cooling tubes. And those are just the operative veins and arteries of the city—there are all kinds of defunct technologies down there too: pneumatic-tube message systems and wood-encased Western Union telegraph wires. To this day, crews from the Department of Water Management still occasionally dig up a water pipe made in the 1800s from a hollowed-out hemlock log. Many iron water mains are so old and decayed—relics from 1900—that only the earth around the pipes holds them together. Dig too close to some mains and pressure from the water within will burst them.

I toured the Jardine Water Purification Plant next to Navy Pier, nearly fifty years old and still the largest water treatment plant in the world, pumping out a billion gallons of water a day into Chicago. I visited each of the four water cribs perched on the horizon in Lake Michigan—intakes for the city's water system. For over a century men lived on the little castle-like round brick structures, caring for them. In winter, to keep the intakes clear of ice, the tender would lower a quarter stick of dynamite on a rod and blast them open.

The underground networks are forgotten and unimportant until the moment they're not—such as in 1992 when workmen driving a pile into the river pierced the old subterranean railway tunnel system, once used to deliver coal, flooding many building basements in the Loop and forcing an evacuation of the central business district in the middle of the day, causing more than a $1 billion in damage. When I turned on the TV in my apartment on Logan Boulevard at lunchtime and saw workers fleeing their offices, my first thought was that it had to be some kind of nuclear device—why else would they evacuate the Loop? Downtown that afternoon, hurrying from the paper toward City Hall, I saw one of those surreal sights that a crisis can create—six mounted Chicago police officers, first one, then two, then a line of three, riding their horses in triangular formation up an otherwise deserted Wabash Avenue. Then I got to City Hall and found all the emergency vehicles parked in the street—light towers and cranes, ambulances, fire department pumpers, and a command center. I remember looking at all that equipment and thinking, "God bless America." There are many nations where they'd be gathering men with buckets.

Unless it's flooding or burning, you usually have to remember to look for infrastructure, to seek it out. The several windowless faux buildings that Commonwealth Edison built discreetly downtown—electrical stations disguised as offices—might escape notice until you realize their front doors aren't real and don't open. Chicago fire hydrants are patented—no other city can use them, and you can instantly tell whether you are in Chicago or the suburbs just by looking at a fire plug and seeing if it has three outlets, as hydrants in the suburbs do, or only two outlets, which means you're in Chicago.

Even streetlights: illuminating alleys was a big deal in the 1950s, repre-senting the banishment of crime and urban decay, and the mayor might show up to flip the switch. Streetlights do more than just provide illu-mination. They set a tone even during the day. The clustered globe lights along Wacker Drive and Michigan Avenue are supposed to evoke belle epoque Paris, beginning with their lovely names, "Boulevard Electroliers." The mute sentinels of electrical boxes and stoplights. My idea of a good story would be to go to the foundry in East Jordan, Michigan, where the Chicago sewer covers are made, watch them poured, glowing red from the furnace, and end with a city crew muscling one into place. Manhole covers are round so they can't fall into the holes they cover, the way a square cover could if turned.

So when a tall, lean, elderly flack for the Metropolitan Water Reclamation District of Greater Chicago named Ed McElroy asked if I wanted to tour the Deep Tunnel, he didn't have to ask twice. The Deep Tunnel is basically a storm sewer, though one 109 miles long, up to 25 feet in diameter, 300 feet under the street and costing $10 billion. Without it, basements in Cook County would flood more frequently than they already do. The idea behind the Deep Tunnel is the exactly same idea that caused Chicago to elevate its streets in 1858, famously raising the six-story Tremont House hotel while the guests were still in it, using five thousand jackscrews in the basement (operated by George Pullman, who would go on to railway car fortune and fame): to keep a city built on a swamp drained. "A world-class sewer system" is not high on the list of points of pride among Chicagoans, but we wouldn't be here without it.

To go down the Deep Tunnel, we donned white hard hats, earplugs, and yellow slickers, descended into the earth in a square metal cage lowered on a cable by a crane, arriving in an underground cavern where we boarded a small electric train and went two miles to examine the work, staring at the groundwater glistening on the walls of the tunnel until we reached an enormous drilling apparatus cutting through the dolomite limestone bedrock, the huge, triangular-toothed drill-face a circle twenty-seven feet in diameter, spinning like some science fiction monster robot, howling and cacophonous, the crushed rock borne over its back on a roaring conveyor belt. The lights glowed eerily in the dusty air; it was like watching the pyramids being built, except underground, a realm that few people will ever visit. I liked it so much I went back a second time. McElroy bragged to me that once storm water was properly drained away, the river would be a lot cleaner—why, soon they would even be bringing a bass fishing tournament to Chicago.

Whatever spot you decide is significant becomes significant, at least to you. It can be a huge public works project. It can be the smallest thing. When Edie lived on Melrose, there was a small hole in the sidewalk across from Nettelhorst Elementary School. A shallow depression—water collected in it—in the outline of a crude heart, like a child's drawing, maybe eight inches wide, the size and shape of two open hands held together at the thumbs, palms out. Every time we'd walk down that sidewalk, we'd stop at that spot and kiss over the heart. Or at least one of us would stop, abruptly, silently in our tracks, setting the trap, noting with glee as the other walked on—gotcha! dontcha love me?—waiting for her, or sometimes him, to realize that a cherished custom was being neglected and hurry back for a teasing complaint and a kiss.

* * *

My Chicago is not yours, it is not anybody else's, and if you're wondering whether I realize that I'm lucky, I do. It may sound simplistic to say that Chicago is the places you go and the things that occur there, the people you meet and spend time with, but it's true, and it's why every person occupies the same city yet comes away with a completely different experience. Chicago is not the same place to someone having his egg on the balcony at the Park Hyatt as it is to someone sleeping in an alley three blocks to the west. Nelson Algren lived in one Chicago, Hugh Hefner another. I'm not saying that my Chicago is the best Chicago or the true Chicago or any Chicago other than the one I found here. If your Chicago is a better, truer, more real and alive Chicago, at least in your own estimation, well then, that's just great, buddy. Don't get a swelled head about it.

While residents tend to stick close to their routines—an endless loop between home and work and back with occasional detours—one big advantage of being a newspaper reporter is that your routine demands that you have no routine; it calls on you to range across the city and see what's there.

Not that swinging by a place is the same as living there. Not close. I've been inside every Chicago Housing Authority project in Chicago— the high-rise Robert Taylor Homes and Cabrini-Green apartments, the low-rise Altgeld Gardens and Lathrop Homes, plus senior CHA projects nobody has ever heard of. Most of the high-rises are gone now—to my vast surprise. I would have bet anything that they'd be around for the rest of my life; I think most Chicagoans would have, and it was a shock when they were pulled down, one after another.

The projects were not frightening places, to me, so much as they were gritty and depressing and infinitely sad places—people with nothing trapped in airless rooms watching old televisions. Elderly residents who no longer noticed their kitchen was crawling with cockroaches, or noticed but no longer had the strength to care. "Their lives are wasted—both by themselves and by society," M. W. Newman wrote of the residents of the Robert Taylor Homes in 1965, before the place got really bad. "They're second-class citizens living in a second-class world, and they know it, and hate it."

One evening, on the night shift, I was writing about gangs using vacant CHA apartments as bases—they would break through the cinder block walls between units, so they could operate out of one apartment, and if the cops came bursting in one front door, they could escape through another, into a different hallway.

As I was heading out on the story, an editor asked me if I wanted to wear a bulletproof vest. The paper has bulletproof vests, just in case society crumbles and we have to cover it. I stood there and imagined showing up at the Robert Taylor Homes in my bulky blue bulletproof vest, maybe with a helmet and clear Plexiglas face shield too, getting as close as I dared to an exhausted black lady wearing a small hat with a flower sticking out of it and a dark cloth coat, dragging herself home from the bus stop after a long day, lugging two heavy shopping bags of groceries. "Madam," I'd shout through a bullhorn, assuming a protective crouch, my voice crackling and fuzzy, "tell . . . me . . . about . . . your . . . life."

I looked at the editor. "Thanks Larry," I said. "But I'd rather die. If people can live there their whole lives, I can visit for an hour."

That wasn't bravery. I didn't feel at risk; with my white skin and sports coat, everybody assumed I was a cop. I thought I carried my own little bubble of protection with me wherever I went—it would be a hassle to kill the white guy—which I didn't realize was obliviousness until after I went to the projects with an African American photographer, normally the calmest, most confident guy I know. I could see the fear in his eyes, and he couldn't get us out of there quick enough, and that was a low-rise. I might naïvely feel safe, but he knew we were at risk, if only from the stray shot, fired at somebody else three blocks away.

You walked up the urine-scented high-rise project stairs—the elevators were always broken—and knocked on doors and never knew what you would find. A boisterous group of adults having a party in the middle of a weekday afternoon, pulling on forty-ounce plastic bottles of malt liquor. A subdued mother watching TV on the living room floor with her three solemn little girls—say four, six, and nine—and they all came to the door to talk to a visitor about how they couldn't go outside, because of the gangs.

They didn't mind talking, and they were in no rush because they had all the time in the world. I kept looking down at the intricate beadwork and braiding woven into the girls' hair, and it dawned upon me as we talked that if you were a loving mom, and you couldn't send your children out to play, and couldn't go outside yourself, you might endlessly and laboriously do their hair, as a sign of love and pride and to pass the empty hours. It was beautiful, but there was an aspect of horror to it, too.

But my Chicago, sliding by a housing project, visiting for an hour, leaving and never going back, gaining another story to put in the paper and a notch to put on my pride belt along with being inside the scoreboard at Wrigley Field and climbing halfway up one of the TV masts atop the John Hancock—yup, been there, done that, and did I tell you that I've seen Muddy Waters play the blues?—is completely different than the perspective of those who lived there. Some hated it and couldn't get out quickly enough and never returned; others clung to it and wouldn't leave. When the buildings were torn down, some residents fought to stay. It was their home.

For people who never went there, however, the projects *were* terrifying. Just the thought of them was scary, and so they'd joke, as people do about things that frighten them. After I waved off the bulletproof vest, as I was leaving the newsroom, notebook in hand, the night editor called me back. "Hey," he said, standing up, grinning, holding out an open black felt-tip pen. "Lift up your shirt—I want to write 'Hello Dr. Stein' on your chest."

Dr. Stein, remember, was the medical examiner at the Cook County morgue.

8

"How long is it supposed to *last*?"

THE MORNING MY SON Ross was born, a yellow school bus stopped at a red light with its back end hanging over railroad tracks in Fox River Grove and a train hit it. When the phone rang, we thought it was the doctor returning our call. It was the city desk, telling me to get over there *now*. I was walking Edie back and forth in our bedroom, wristwatch in hand, timing her contractions. "My wife's having a baby," I told them. So they sent someone else to the Northwest suburb; many people, it turned out.

Meanwhile, we walked up Broadway, Edie stopping to brace herself against a parking meter whenever a contraction hit. But instead of getting stronger and closer together, the contractions grew weaker and further apart until they stopped altogether. By midmorning, Edie was at the apartment of an artist neighbor, cooing over her birth announcement designs, and I started to worry that the paper would think I had shirked the assignment— the baby wasn't due for two weeks. Another reporter had dodged a story and gotten into trouble. Still, I dithered like Hamlet until Edie said, "Honey, I'm not having this baby right now. Go to work."

I walked a block east to Sheridan Road and caught a cab to the paper, babbling to the driver about the baby on the way. At the office, reporters at the Fox River Grove crash scene fed me information to weave into the story. Seven students on the bus died.

We put the newspaper to bed at 1 p.m., the late afternoon edition that the *Sun-Times* still hawked to commuters on their way home from work.

On my lunch break, I strolled up Michigan Avenue and stopped in the F.A.O. Schwarz toy store to contemplate a Steiff toy dog. My beeper went off: a call from Edie. I walked back to the paper—an unbelievably leisurely thing to do, given the circumstances—and phoned home. "How far apart are the contractions?" I asked. "I don't know!" Edie wailed. I quickly gathered my things, gazed hard at the office commotion, then left and didn't come back to work for a year.

* * *

Directly due to Ross's birth, I went from being a reporter chasing news at any editor's whim to a regular columnist, with my picture in the paper and everything, free to choose my own topics and write about them in my own way, and no career advancement was ever achieved in a more accidental fashion. It happened like this: in 1995, after years of trying, Edie became pregnant. Being in the Chicago Newspaper Guild meant we were subject to union work rules, and at some point in the free-to-be-you-and-me 1970s, someone stuck a clause in our contract stating that not only could mothers take up to a year unpaid maternity leave after the birth or adoption of a child, but fathers could too. Of course management would agree to that—the provision cost them nothing, and how many guys would actually take a year off? Nobody would, and indeed, nobody ever did before I snapped at the offer (nor, now that I think if it, has anyone done so since). Most men can barely manage two weeks at home with a new baby before they go shrieking back to kiss the hem of their jobs. Besides, they can't afford it.

But I decided to take the full year off. Because I'm the Best Father in the World. . . .

Just kidding. No lofty impulse was involved in the decision. Paternal diligence had nothing to do with it; I had never had a child before, so had no idea what raising a child meant. Not because I was a good husband either. It wasn't that I was eager to help my wife change diapers. What was going on in my mind was this: we had some money from the book I was writing. Edie had just left Jenner & Block after six bank-account-fattening years there. The paternity leave would be a chance to step away from the paper, to finish the book, maybe work on other things and have a steady job waiting when I was done, if I still wanted it. The new-child aspect was incidental, an opportunity, another crack in the wall between me and where I wanted to be. I had never ceased waiting for that big bear hug of success; working at the paper was still the Day Job, in my mind. I didn't even subscribe. "They're supposed to give money to *me*," I'd rationalize. "I'm not supposed to give money to *them*."

That was the crux of my thinking. I wasn't taking a year off for the baby's benefit, nor for my wife's, but for my own. I was thirty-five.

Just before the baby was born, our incoming editor-in-chief, Nigel Wade, a big, beefy slab of a New Zealand press lord—shock of pale yellow hair, untamed eyebrows, complexion the color of the center of medium rare filet mignon, wearing pink-striped shirts with white starched collars and French cuffs—blew into town from our mother paper, the *London Daily Telegraph*, to spend a few weeks kicking the tires of the *Sun-Times*. Most employees hide beneath their desks under such circumstances, laying low to avoid the potential new boss; fear, I suppose, or a reluctance to be seen as apple polishers. But for me, with my shark-like hunger to promote myself, that just wasn't a concern. I latched onto a group going out with Nigel for drinks the night before he left, bringing along my latest book, a series of meditations on failure. "Something for you to read on the plane back to London," I said, pressing the volume into his hands.

* * *

Rushing home the day of the Fox River Grove tragedy, I found Edie on the bed, in pain. Grabbing her overnight bag, I coaxed her to her feet and toward the door. As we passed the white wicker basinet, set up and ready in our bedroom, she clutched at it.

"What if I'm a bad mom?" she cried. "*What if I don't love the baby!?*"

"I'm sure you'll be an excellent mother," I said soothingly, prying her hands off the basinet and leading her out of the room. "Either way, let's go find out."

There are many good hospitals in Chicago, and I wanted my son to be born at one of them. Then he could always say "I was born in Chicago"—something his father could never claim. It was important to me. But my wife's obstetrician was at Evanston Hospital, which had, Edie assured me, an excellent women's center. I tried arguing, but with the birth process as fraught as it is, I couldn't see insisting. I knew that if I did, and through some miracle prevailed—always a long shot when dealing with Edie—and if anything went wrong, God forbid, it would be All My Fault. I couldn't risk that, not for something as insubstantial as birthplace bragging rights. So with my wife's contractions coming faster and faster, we raced—not to the adequate-for-an-uncomplicated-delivery St. Joseph Hospital, three blocks from our condo, nor downtown to the world-renowned Northwestern Memorial Hospital, three miles away, but twenty miles to Evanston, with my wife writhing in her seat, bracing herself against the dashboard, yelling "I'm going to have the baby in the car!" while I laid on the horn and weaved in and out of traffic.

Practical tip: if you want to be noticed by the staff of a hospital emergency room, crawl in on your hands and knees. It attracts their attention magnificently.

Ross Edward Steinberg was born at 5:45 p.m., one hour and forty-five minutes after we arrived at the hospital. He was not born within the borders of Chicago, but was born with ten fingers and ten toes, which is all that's important. He can fudge the rest. ("I was born in Evanston"—that isn't something you hear people say, is it? "I am an American, Chicago born"—now *that* sounds a lot better, doesn't it? The opening words of *The Adventures of Augie March* pack such an emotional punch that people read them and forget they're part of the fiction—that author Saul Bellow wasn't born in Chicago, he wasn't even born an American: he was a Canadian, Montreal born. But try opening a novel like that.)

I cuddled Ross, sang the opening stanzas of the "Air Force Song" ("Off we go, into the wild blue yonder, climbing high, into the sun . . .") that my father used to sing to himself, and had a complex, vindictive thought about Nazis that can be boiled down to: "Fuck you, Nazis, we're still here, popping out Jews while you're rotting on the ash heap of history."

Edie still smiles recalling how the Speed Demon drove home from the hospital the next day, gingerly, as if the trunk were filled with dynamite, scowling with concentration, sweating, hunched over the steering wheel, hands in the ten-and-two position, checking his mirrors and his wife and newborn in the back seat, thirty-five miles an hour down Lake Shore Drive in the right lane.

Back on Pine Grove Avenue, Edie and I settled into the exhausting grind of new parenthood. Being the father of a newborn is like being tortured by the Red Chinese: deprived of sleep for weeks at a time, forced out of bed in the middle of the night, trudging back and forth repeating meaningless slogans while some small foreign person screams at you in a language you don't understand.

If nothing else worked, I would put Ross in the car and drive him to sleep in big dead-of-night loops around the empty North Side neighborhoods, swinging past the deserted hulk of Wrigley Field, its famous sign dark, the radio playing softly, the driver himself half asleep, the baby fussing, unseen in his car seat in back, then sometimes fussing and sometimes quiet, until, finally, a steady quiet, filling the air like music, and I would gratefully point the car toward home.

* * *

Two months and one week after Ross was born, Nigel Wade called, on his second day as editor-in-chief of the *Sun-Times*. "Steinberg!" his voice exploded from the telephone, in that distinctive British bellow of his. "This *paternity leave*"—childless, he infused the words with sarcasm if not disgust—"how long is it supposed to *last*?"

"Gee Nigel," I said, "another ten months—why?"

"Ohhh, that's a pity," he said. "I rather hoped you write a *column* for us."

"Or I could start Sunday," I replied in one breath. Which I did, writing the column freelance from home while still on leave, working in my small office downstairs, convinced then and now that if Edie and I had not had a child and had I not taken a year off, had I stayed at the paper as the night-shift reporter slumped in a corner, wearing fingerless gloves, covering fires, and haunting the criminal courts at 26th and California, that Nigel would never have offered me a column. I would have been just another ambitious malcontent, another stymied writer working below his ability, another drop in the algae-covered retaining pond of talent stagnating at every newspaper in the world. But departing just before he showed up gave me a twist of mystery, and the book showed that there was some skill there, too, enough that Nigel wanted to reel me back and claim me as his catch, his invention.

Something all those focused, relentless, gerbil-on-a-wheel, don't-lose-a-step career climbers ought to keep in mind: sometimes you win by walking away.

* * *

Well, "win" might be overstating the case. One column a week in the *Chicago Sun-Times* does not make you J. J. Hunsecker, the all-powerful newspaperman holding out his cigarette to be matched by a fawning pub-licist in the "Sweet Smell of Success." Nor does two a week. Nor three. Nor four. The drawback to my story is that you end up with me—an obscure newspaper columnist writing at a time when the rising waters of technology are drowning newspapers, flooding the commentary business, inundating it with foaming swirls of frothy opinion, perspective, and raw verbiage, a watery planet where most drown while a few thrash and splash and struggle to stay afloat and the prospect of going under seems only a matter of time. My life may not be *Citizen Kane*—no dandling politicians on puppet strings, no nudging world events like chess pieces, no white sand beach of cash to gratefully recline upon, safe and dry. But if I don't view my life as significant, who will?

The week I returned to the newspaper after my paternity leave, my third book came out, the several fist-muffled coughs of notice dwindling within days into the echoless silence and permanent oblivion that most books receive. No shame in that. The paper allowed me Fridays to write my column, but the rest of my week belonged to the city desk. I was still a reporter, mostly. My first day back on the job after a year at home with the baby is clear in memory only because the desk sent me to cover a press conference that Sen. Paul Simon was holding at the Bismarck Hotel. At the hotel, Simon's gathering wasn't to be found—not in the lobby, not in the ballroom. I combed the place, wandering with increasing urgency through empty hotel corridors. Maybe it would be impromptu? Maybe in an upstairs meeting room? I conferred with a hotel manager, waited until when the press conference was supposed to start, then phoned the desk and told them there must be a mistake—I was here at the Blackstone, but there was no press conference.

"The Blackstone?" the desk said. "It's at the Bismarck." I immediately realized what had happened; both places occupied the same niche in my brain, as two similar run-down, dark, and mediocre old-line downtown hotels whose names begin with *B*. Almost twenty years after arriving in Chicago, I was still getting lost. I hurried over to the proper hotel, but the press conference was already over. I did not, I feel obligated to point out to novice reporters, react by constructing an imaginary press conference to try to pass off and hope nobody noticed. You take your lumps. Own the sin and move on.

9

Annals of the paper tube trade

THINK OF POTATO CHIPS. What could you say about them? What's the *interesting* part about potato chips? That they're salty? That they're made from potatoes? Not exactly a revelation.

The most interesting thing about potato chips is how they're produced. Which might come as a surprise, because it's a simple process. You take the potatoes, you peel them, you cut them up, fry the slices in oil, sprinkle salt on the chips, and put them in a bag. What's there to say?

That's the beauty of going places, of watching processes, at least for me. It's surprising, and an education.

"You take the potatoes." From where? Where do you take the potatoes from? You need lots of potatoes, tons and tons and tons. They arrive on semitrailer trucks, sturdy "chipping" potatoes, grown for their thin skin and low moisture, driven straight from North Dakota, the trucks constantly pulling up at the Jays Foods factory at 99th Street and Cottage Grove Avenue.

Simple question: How do you get the potatoes off the trucks? Stretch your mind, let your imagination wander. You're a smart person—you must be, you're reading this book. What do you come up with?

Never in my life had I wondered how potatoes would get off a truck and into a potato chip factory—watching manufacturing is an endless series of stumbling across answers to questions you never thought to ask—but had you asked me, beforehand, how it was done, I would have squinched my eyes shut, taken a deep breath, and guessed, refining my hunches into an ascending order of probability: (1) men with shovels, (2) burlap bags of potatoes tossed onto conveyer belts, or (3) huge wooden bins of potatoes moved by forklift trucks.

I assume your guesses would be along similar lines.

Wrong, wrong, and wrong. That's why it's so hard to write fiction—you can't make this stuff up. Imagination is almost inevitably impoverished by what is found in the living world.

The semitrailers are detached from the truck cabs, then backed onto enormous hydraulic lifts that tilt them forty-five degrees, causing the potatoes to tumble out the back like Raisinets spilled from a box of movie candy.

But that isn't the amazing part.

The newly arrived potatoes are immediately sorted, through a jiggling process, divided into big potatoes and small potatoes. Then the big potatoes go one way, and the small potatoes go another. They never come back together again. The potatoes are handled completely separately, with certain production lines making chips out of big potatoes, while other production lines make chips out of small potatoes.

"Why?" I asked. That was one of those questions that stayed with me, like asking Dr. Chasnoff if I could see the cocaine babies.

Any idea? I've run this question by a hundred people over the past decade. Maybe two hundred. Nobody ever has the faintest clue. Big potatoes one way, small potatoes the other. Never come back together. Separate production lines. Whatever for?

Ready? Wait for it. . . .

The big potatoes, I was told, become big potato chips that go into the big bags, while the small potatoes become small potato chips that go into the small bags. Because if you put big potato chips into a small, lunch-sized bag, you'd have about five chips in each bag, and even though they weigh an ounce, the consumer would still feel ripped off. *"Hey man, that's not enough chips!"* With smaller chips, you can fit more chips into a lunch-sized bag.

I love that, loved learning details like that, loved knowing that the reason there is no possessive in the name—not Jay's, but Jays—is that there is no Jay. The company, which began in 1927, was originally called Mrs. Japp's Potato Chips, after Leonard Japp Sr.'s wife, right up until Pearl Harbor—two days after Pearl Harbor in fact—when Japp made the nimble executive decision to change his company's name to avoid association with the wartime slur, scrapping his own and adopting the more neutral Jays.

The challenge to writing a story about making potato chips is that you are confronted with a complex process, from the arrival of the potatoes, and their unexpected method of getting dumped, to the makes-perfect-sense-once-it's-explained sorting, to the range of flavors and sizes made. How to present it? What to say first? I wandered and watched and asked and jotted, taking in the slicers, the fryers, the conveyor belts, the radial filling machines, the chutes, hoppers, and gently vibrating slides, the chips being not so much moved through the plant as gradually massaged forward, jostled in the direction they're supposed to go, the outer layer of a mass of chips a yard deep gently shearing away like the face of a melting glacier.

Gradually, it dawned on me what the factory was all about. Making the chips is indeed the easy part. The true challenge, the complex and difficult part of the process, is moving the chips through the factory. The real story is about how to move tons and tons of potato chips without breaking them, because Jays sells chips, not crumbs.

"A potato chip is a delicate thing," my story began. "Fragile. A pound of pressure will crush it. So when you're moving 250 tons of chips through your plant, as they do every day at Jays Foods, you need to have a system."

When I look back over more than a quarter century of writing for the *Sun-Times*, from that first story on thrift-shop bakeries to today, what stands out is, left to my own devices, how much attention I gave to factories, plants, and processes of all kinds. I watched hogs slaughtered, rabbits skinned, and hens plucked, saw cap guns molded, lampshades sewn, cell phones and lava lamps assembled, steel poured, goat cheese mixed, and globes glued—at Replogle Globes in Broadview, where the spheres couldn't simply roll along a conveyer belt or an assembly line, which would damage them, and so were suspended on hooks and moved around the plant on an overhead chain system, a giant clockwork cosmos of green and blue and black and sepia worlds floating in all directions at varying levels and speeds.

I watched pinball machines being built—Chicago was once the world's pinball manufacturing capital. I followed a rabbi as he certified that Canfield's soda pop factory was kosher, saw elevators inspected, watched water mains being laid, and walked through the heart of the Tevatron high-energy particle collider at the Fermi National Accelerator Lab when it was shut down to be cleaned.

The production of food is particularly fascinating to me. Jelly beans are tumbled in drums that look like cement mixers, gradually aggregating like pearls. Gummy bears are made in molds of cornstarch that are washed away after the candy has cooled, so there is no trouble getting sticky, tiny bears out of their molds. Hard candies were the most amazing of all. At the Brach's plant on Kinzie, at the time the largest candy factory in the world, I watched how they form the designs at the center of sucking peppermints—the flags, the Christmas trees, the hearts. They do so by creating a giant mint, two feet across, forming the design by hand, with fingers and forearms covered in powdered sugar, then muscling the giant hundred-pound mint onto an extruder, which turns and evenly compresses it into a long rope of candy that is sliced into individual quarter-sized mints, each with the miniaturized design in the center. It's the same process used to create Venetian glass beads.

They say you should never see sausages being made; I have seen sausages being made—big Polish sausages, along with bratwurst and frankfurters at the Vienna Beef plant, and was still able to have a couple of hot dogs that day for lunch. To be honest, they tasted even better, because I knew the effort that went into making them, and that became a ritual for me, to get back on the horse, to have a turkey sandwich after visiting the turkey farm, a pork chop at the Mexican diner across the street from Park Packing, one of the last pig slaughterhouses in the city that was, remember "hog butcher for the world." (Not always easy—after a photographer and I visited an indoor chicken farm on West Chicago Avenue when the heat wave of 1995 turned its name, Williams Live Chickens, into an empty boast, he swore he would never eat chicken again. I somehow managed.)

Nor was I on an academic quest to document Chicago's fading manufacturing base. It was just fun to go to these places. They were glad to see me and I was glad to go. They were filled with fascinating details—the purple ink the USDA inspector uses when pressing his Illinois-shaped rubber stamp onto pig carcasses at Park Packing is made of blueberry juice. The Schulze & Burch Biscuit Company at 35th and Racine claims to have invented the saltine cracker.

There were no other reporters—usually nobody, or very few, thought to write about whatever I was examining. There was never any rush. There were often free samples. It was happiness. If I had to rank experiences I've had as a reporter in terms of personal enjoyment between, say: (a) discussing politics one-on-one with Barack Obama, (b) sitting in the Bulls locker room, talking with Michael Jordan before a basketball game, (c) being a guest on the *Oprah Winfrey Show*, and (d) eating a fresh Maurice Lenell pinwheel cookie plucked off the production line at the company's Norridge factory, there would be no question in my mind: (d) the warm cookie. It also led to the better story.

Why? Because the first three subjects—Obama, Jordan, and Winfrey—have all been reported on for years by an army of journalists far better than myself. What are the odds that I could manage to come up with a fresh morsel during my brief time with them? Close to zero. Their carcasses have been picked clean. But where are you going to find somebody who's been to the Maurice Lenell Cooky Co. plant at Harlem and Montrose—it's "Cooky" with a *y*, for murky historical reasons related to the spelling skills of Swedish immigrants—and watched them churn out the pinwheels and almond crescents and jelly stars they used to bake there by the millions every day? Good luck, and you can't go there yourself, not anymore. The place is long gone.

My colleagues who spend their careers ferreting out corruption, combing through tax records, hurling questions at politicians at press conferences, tend to regard my focus on manufacturing with puzzlement if not contempt. They don't come out and say it, but I have a sense. It sometimes seems a struggle for them to say good morning without adding: you *like* doing what you do? You think it's good journalism? You find it *interesting?*

Yes I do. The fact that many people will stick their hands—heck, their arms up to the elbow—in the public trough, given half a chance, does not surprise me. Why should it? Corruption sure happens often enough. Graft is neither new nor unique; plus, like all crime, it is draped with a depressing sameness. How can anyone pretend to be surprised by it?

I'll tell you what's surprising. What's surprising is to be touring Allen Edmonds, the largest men's shoe factory in the United States, two hours north of Chicago, and when you ask a woman answering phones in the customer service department what is the most unusual request she ever received, she answers that one customer sent in a few pairs of his father's old dress shoes to be refurbished and included his father's ashes, requesting that the company mix the ashes in with the hot cork used to recast the soles of worn shoes. That was unexpected.

Unexpected, though not the really surprising part. The really surprising part is that Allen Edmonds honored the request and mixed the remains of the dead man into his shoes so his son could tread on them, could have a bit of his father's soul in his soles. They are a full-service shoe company.

Thus in my career I pretty much let politics slide, the white noise in the background. I have many regrets in life, but that choice is not one of them. There were still plenty of reporters at Rod Blagojevich's trials without me. Now that I think about it, it's incredible that I survived being a daily columnist at all, since the kabuki of journalism demands that villains be found, that reporters sniff out misdeeds like pigs rooting for truffles, that waste and error be dug up and waved over one's head. Look, got another one! And here! And there! Again and again and again.

I never attended a mayoral press conference. Not once. The mayor never says anything at those; the best the press can do is provoke maladroit phrases and snigger at them. That gets old. Those who do ritually attend every press conference and city council meeting, of course, portray them as epic events of vast and resonating significance, but then, given the time they spend there, they kinda have to.

When I said that I took off the year after Ross was born, there is an asterisk to that: the week in August of the 1996 Democratic National Convention. The paper asked that I come back to lend a hand, because so much news was going on and the city desk was short-staffed. Of course I said yes.

Now most columnists, particularly those who are new and trying to prove themselves—I had been writing the column for less than a year, remember—would have pushed to get inside the United Center, would have stamped their feet, grabbed somebody's credentials and forced their way in, just to write from the convention floor and to be able to say they were there and to report on whatever momentary, meaningless political fuss was going on inside at that hour. And the week I was back, I did consider doing that. It crossed my mind. But that seemed not good journalism, but showboating. We had plenty of reporters inside already, experienced political hands, so for me to try to elbow one aside would be ego. Besides, my editors might say no, and then I'd have my marginality confirmed. So I took assignments as they came, listened to Al Gore deliver a speech to the Israeli lobby at the Park West, observed a surprisingly well-organized protest by an anarchist group—yes, anarchists can organize themselves—and never got inside the convention hall.

The important stuff was happening outside anyway. The 1996 convention is significant to Chicago because it helped revitalize the Near West Side and bring the city back into the national eye. Reporters groping for an easy metaphor needed only contrast Chicago in 1996 to the city in 1968 for the always satisfying, now-we-come-full-circle story. The mayor was still a guy named Daley, but look how much else has changed. Riots then but flowers now. And the city did look good, with Washington Street and Madison Street rolling through the West Side dolled up with black wrought iron fences and planter boxes in the middle of Fulton Market. Those I saw—they were very pretty. But frankly, I was happy when the week ended and I went back to pushing Ross's stroller around East Lake View. If you ask me what a year taking care of a new baby is like, that is my central memory. Sitting on a bench in Lincoln Park on a lovely spring day, reading the newspaper, with one foot on the stroller, gently rolling it back and forth, glancing over the top of the paper to see if the baby is still asleep. Yup, still asleep.

* * *

What is it with manufacturing? Why that? Maybe because, as a writer, I don't produce anything tangible myself—words on paper—so I admire somebody who can do a solid piece of metal casting. Maybe it has to do with appreciation of a different kind of power—I find myself admiring hydraulic presses, rotary cutting blades, overhead cranes, arc welders, the massive might of boilers and machines. The blinding eye of blast furnaces. Once I met a blacksmith, Erwin Gruen, who had a shop in the basement of his art gallery in River North. I could have written a column about him, but his tools—his anvils, hammers, tongs, rasps—were so beautiful, I sold the idea to *Chicago* magazine, just so they'd run photographs of his workshop, something I knew the paper would never consider. (Well, that, and to give his personal story full play. Gruen was a rarity not only because he was a blacksmith in downtown Chicago, but because he had been a Jew living openly in Berlin throughout all of World War II. It turns out that even murderous Nazi fanaticism had its practical limits. They never came for the skilled Messerschmitt engine mechanics.)

The place doesn't have to be an old-fashioned blacksmith shop—it was fascinating to go through Ford's enormous, ultramodern Chicago Assembly Plant on Torrence Avenue, a kick to watch the Kawasaki robots rush in to weld a growing automobile chassis, turning and probing like hungry birds, casting off sprays of sparks. The place was huge, spotless, and almost devoid of people—the robots had replaced humans, which was how Ford could compete with China. I was proud to realize that Ford has not one, but two huge, complicated tasks it must achieve—the first, obviously, is assembling thousands of different components into one nearly flawless automobile. The second, equally challenging, task is getting the right pieces from all over the world to the right places they need to be, at the exact moment they need to be there, because unless every bolt and cover and plate is precisely in the proper place when a worker—human or robotic—reaches for it, the whole line comes to a halt. What amazed me was that the Ford system is so finely calibrated that the parts that will be assembled into cars in the afternoon are sometimes still on the trucks on their way to the factory that morning. Ford figured out—well, the Japanese figured out and Ford learned the lesson from them—that instead of paying for parts and then paying to warehouse the parts for weeks and months until needed, it's better to pay for parts and immediately put them together into a car and sell the car as quickly as possible. Every hour a part sits in a warehouse, waiting to be used, adds a sliver of a penny to the overall price of an automobile.

But cars were an exception. Generally, the more obscure a process, the happier I was to explore it. I went to the factory that makes pads that cover fine wooden dining room tables, in part because I truly felt like an adult the day I was in my dining room on Pine Grove Avenue, placing my order with an elderly table pad salesman who had come with his big square salesman's case containing samples of the various levels of pads—the Budget, the Select, the Elite, the Athena—which he explained to us with a flourish, progressing from the merest gossamer covering to a thick sheet of armor plate that you could set a hot rivet on without damaging the table underneath. Having impulsively purchased an enormous bird's-eye maple dining room table on our honeymoon from a furniture maker in Maine, with children on the way we needed a table pad, the first of many small, expensive surprises that family life would bring.

That was the trick to these stories—to find the emotional element. The story wasn't about table pads; it wasn't about protecting fancy tables; it was about a step into the middle-age cautiousness—we must shield this table top from sticky lollipops!—that the pads represent, plus the earnest way the people at Superior Table Pads went about their business.

My feeling is, no matter how dull a process seems, there is always a secret something hidden within that is fascinating, if only it could be found, and my job is to plunge into the unpromising places that few bother to go—an explorer in the Land of the Dull—and ferret out that buried secret something, discover the treasure and drag it into the light for everyone to appreciate. The only factory that ever called me and pitched itself was an establishment called Cougle Commission Company. The owner had noticed

I was writing about factories and wondered whether I would write about his. Well, what do you do? I asked.

"We cut up chicken," he said.

Do you raise it? I asked. No. Do you cook it? No. "We just cut it up."

I know a challenge when I see one. And I wanted to reward his moxie. He asked. Most people never ask. Many don't even return my phone calls when I call to ask. After I toured the Vienna Beef factory, I went back for Vienna's two-day hot dog venders' course, the grandly named Hot Dog University. It was fascinating, surprisingly so, the challenge of cup sizes, the dilemma of whether to let your customers dress their own dogs or do it for them (it saves time if you let customers do it, but they can get greedy with the expensive tomato chunks, literally eating up your profits). In the Vienna Beef cafeteria, I ran into a young man who was about to open a hot dog stand on Franklin Street. Oh, I said, I used to write about a hot dog place across the street from where you're opening, Harry's Hot Dogs, but he closed. Here's my card—let me know when you open and I'll ballyhoo you in the newspaper and maybe you can become my new colorful hot dog guy.

Nothing. Never heard from him. I was stiffed by a hot dog stand. Now I can't even bring myself to eat there, and I've wanted a hot dog, at times, and had to resist. This is bad, I know—to harbor resentment against a hot dog stand. Sad, but a glimpse at the mindset that made me want to reward Cougle. So I toured the place. At first I feared I had finally met my match. What was there to say? Lots of refrigerated rooms, lots of chicken, obviously, in huge plastic bags (the company exists in a niche—if you are the Peninsula Hotel, and you need 1,500 five-ounce chicken breasts for a testimonial chicken dinner, you can't order those through the local grocery store—the order's too big. Tyson and the other giant chicken processors don't do that kind of thing—the order's too small. Cougle is a chicken middleman).

I knew I was getting closer when they ushered me into the room with sixteen women busily cutting up chicken. At first I focused on the knives— how often do you sharpen them? Every thirty minutes, and once a week Chicago Knife comes by, brings us new knives, and takes our old knives away for expert sharpening—rather like a towel service.

That's close. I made a mental note: call Chicago Knife. But that didn't help me with Cougle. I studied the women cutting their five-ounce chicken breasts, sometimes nipping off a tiny piece the size of a fingertip, and eventually realized something was missing. No scales. How, I wondered, can you cut a five-ounce chicken breast without a scale to weigh it?

Beny Quinonez gave me a weary, hey-idiot look.

"I've worked here for thirteen years," she said, holding a chicken breast in her hand and lightly jostling it up and down. "We don't have to weigh them. I can tell. I can hold this chicken breast in my hand and say within a half an ounce what it weighs."

The people at these factories always amaze me. Not just because of the skills they have and what they know. But because they're happy—or if not happy, at least content, or seemingly content—which might be deceptive, given that I'm usually coming by with some boss. Content enough to show up, to do their work for years, and not go crazy. Here I have a job where I can basically do whatever I want, go wherever I please, more or less, wander places that interest me, stay as long as I like, look around and then leave and never come back, or come back, as I choose. Write about them, don't write about them, it's up to me. Complete freedom. And you don't have to ask me twice to complain. And then there are people such as Christ Kostakis, who debones whitefish for a living. I met him because I had an idea—wouldn't it be neat to begin a story with a fish being netted at, oh, Lake Superior, to see it pulled flapping and sparkling out of the cold waters, and follow it to a gold-rimmed plate at the Ritz-Carlton Dining Room? Sounds fun. I was visiting the Chicago Fish House, a wholesaler at 1250 W. Division Street, trying to set up the story.

Kostakis's job as a whitefish deboner was to stand in a forty-degree room for eight hours a day. The room couldn't be warmer or the fish would spoil. A hundred pounds of whitefish an hour were brought in big plastic bins and set on the table he was standing at. He couldn't sit; he had to stand up because the room was so cold. No machine could do the work, because it would mangle the delicate fillet and leave it ragged. Kostakis would lift a piece of fish out of the bin, run his naked left hand gently over the white flesh, caressing it, probing for the thirty-two tiny pin bones, some as thin as a blade of grass, which he removed with a needle-nose pliers held in his right hand. His left hand had to be kept bare.

"You don't see the bones—you feel them," he explained. After he had removed the bones, which he dropped to the floor at his feet, he carefully set the fillet into an empty bin and reached for another fillet. One hundred pounds an hour. Eight hours a day. He had worked there a dozen years when I met him.

He seemed happy. Most people seem happy. Or at least claim to be. Wherever I pop my head in, I find people who have, in one way or another, made a life for themselves, usually by coming to Chicago from somewhere else. Wherever they had come from—Greece, Mexico, Poland, Korea, India—they all say the same thing: life was so much harder at home than it is here. The pay is so much better here. They're so lucky to be here, they say, doing this dirty job that their children, invariably going away to college, will never have to do. I try to learn from their example.

* * *

If you look north out the window of a Metra train shortly after it heads west from downtown, you will see a large sign: "CHICAGO MAILING TUBE CO.," spelled out in sleek, foot-tall letters, a sans serif, machine-age font, affixed to a low red building.

I see it almost every day, taking the train to and from the suburbs.

After seven years of watching that sign slide by as the train slowed to pull into the Western Avenue Station—or gained speed, pulling out—I began to idly wonder about the cardboard tube industry. Now *there's* a business you just don't see splashed in the newspaper every day. What could it be like?

Soon afterward I was climbing the stairs to the spartan second-floor offices of Chicago Mailing Tube, where Ken Barmore, ninety, was waiting to tell me about buying the company in 1949.

"There wasn't much to buy," he recalled. "One machine and six or seven people; nobody knew anything about the company."

Chicago Mailing Tube was founded by three partners in 1902. Back then it sold a lot of snuffboxes—squat cylindrical containers similar to chewing tobacco tins. The containers were delivered to stores around town by horse and wagon, and the company still proudly holds several city licenses for delivery horses.

No horses anymore. But it does have forty or so human employees, and a number of spectacularly complex machines, producing cardboard tubes in a splendid, Dr. Seussian frenzy: ribbons of brown paper flying off enormous spinning spools, puffs of steam, rivers of glue pumped from three-thousand-gallon vats, quivering, hissing pneumatic lines and roaring spindles, a grinder turning scrap tubes back into paper pulp, emitting a deafening pounding noise that made me think of frozen turkeys raining down upon a sheet metal roof.

The production process is called "spiral winding"—three-inch strips of brown paper are coated with glue, wrapped tightly around a metal core, or "mandrel," then squeezed by thick rubber belts. "The pressure is terrific," said Barmore, pointing to belts compressing the tubes. "You get a finger under there, it's going to be flat."

There was no large/small potato conundrum, no precision-fingered chicken ladies to give fascination to the cardboard tube company—I counted on the sheer out-of-left-fieldness of the topic, a certain Behold the Humble Paper Tube quality: we think of tubes beneath paper towels and toilet tissue, but they also hide in plain sight—as Parmesan cheese containers, charity cans, crescent dough packages, and masking tape roll cores. Tiny tubes hold bundles of wires in cars, and huge tubes form concrete pillars in building construction. "We used to make cores for machine-gun bullets for the Joliet arsenal," Barmore said.

There actually is a potato chip/mailing tube connection—local potato chip manufacturers lingered while other food companies folded or were gobbled up by international chains because chips are so expensive to ship—puffed-out bags take up a lot of space while containing not much of value. You don't want to be shipping potato chips from China if you can avoid it. Ditto for mailing tubes. "It's kind of like we're shipping air," said Keith Shimon, Barmore's grandson. "The ten-inch tubes really fill up a truck."

The owners of Chicago Mailing Tube radiated pride over the quality of their product. "This is a competitor's tube," said Barmore, standing among a forest of tubes in the "sample room," appraising a cylinder as tall as him, explaining how the lengths sometimes need to be precise within a fraction of an inch, say if they're used in manufacturing. He carefully eyed the end of the tube he held. "It's got a bad cut on it. It isn't square. A lot of companies, they couldn't use that."

How does a man get into the cardboard tube trade?

"I wanted to get into the farm machinery business, but I couldn't make any kind of a deal," Barmore remembered. "I'm a farm boy, from Monroe, Wisconsin. A dairy farm. I know cows."

Why not stay down on the farm?

"I hated it," he said. "I hated milking cows."

This was during the Great Depression—Barmore was Monroe High School Class of '34—when collapsing milk prices had farmers dumping milk at the side of the road because it wasn't worth selling. "Things were very bad," he said. "Believe me, it was hell." He got a job candling eggs for twelve dollars a week, then a job repairing farm machinery, then one driving a bus in Rockford, then was put in charge of ordering coal for Central Illinois Electric and Gas. "How many pounds of coal to make a pound of steam, how many pounds of steam to make a kilowatt," he said. "I was figuring that out." He worked too many other jobs to list them all.

That one-thing-leads-to-the-next path of life takes people on stunning, almost ludicrously serpentine journeys. We are dice in fate's cup. Not just people, but companies too. I was touring Strombecker Toys—they made low-priced playthings you'd find in dime stores: paddle balls, jacks, building blocks, cap guns, jump ropes, plastic army men—seven hundred different kinds of inexpensive toys. They were the largest producer of bubbles in the world—or, rather, of those little jars of solution with wands inside. The bubbles, you make yourself. I was there because I had happy memories of their TootsieToy cars, which my mother would buy me for a dime, fished out of a big bin in the hardware store in Berea. The owner gave me a tour of the clangorous factory, and then we sat in his office—its shelves lined with vintage TootsieToy cars that I eyed, hungrily—and I asked him the usual question: how did the company start?

Dan Shure, the Strombecker CEO, said his company was begun as the *National Laundry Journal* by brothers Sam and Charles Dowst in 1876.

The *what*? How does a trade publication for the owners of laundries become a manufacturer of toys?

Like this:

Samuel Dowst visited the 1893 Columbian Exposition, just as so many Chicagoans did, where he saw the famed Mergenthaler Linotype machine. Up to that point, pages of type would be set up by hand, by typesetters reaching for metal letters from bins, setting them in a row to form words, and locking the forms in place to be printed. The Linotype machine did away with this system by shooting hot lead into molds, creating one-use lines of type. After printing, the metal alloy was melted back down and used again. Of course the owner of a magazine would be interested in this.

Besides the magazine, the Dowsts sold to subscribers various small items that a laundry might need, such as buttons, collar stays, and cufflinks. Watching the Linotype machine work, injecting lead into letter-shaped molds, Dowst had an insight: the Linotype machine could be used to make more than type—it could also make buttons, collar stays, and cufflinks. He persuaded his brother to buy one.

At the time, the laundry business was fiercely competitive. In the years before home washers and dryers, washing clothes was such an arduous process that any halfway solvent household either employed a washerwoman—like Bigger Thomas's mother in *Native Son*—or sent its dirty clothes out to a laundry to be washed. One way laundries attracted customers was by appealing to their children by offering them prizes, the same way fast-food chains attract kids today by giving them toys with their meals.

Soon the Dowsts used their Linotype machines not only to make buttons, but to make laundry promotional items its subscribers could give to their customers' children—a little flat iron, for instance, for the Flat Iron Laundry.

At the same time, Shure's great-grandfather, Nathan Shure, had come to Chicago from Lithuania in the 1880s and started his own trinket company, Cosmo Manufacturing, which in 1912 began supplying little toys to a Chicago company that had decided to include small metal tokens as prizes to boost sales of boxes of its candied popcorn and peanut confection, Cracker Jack.

By the dawn of the century, the laundry magazine business had completely fallen away, and the Dowsts were making dollhouse furniture, lucky charms that girls wore on bracelets and baked inside cakes, and small die-cast metal cars. Shure's great-grandfather bought the Dowsts' company in 1926, and ten years later it began supplying Parker Brothers with tokens for its new game, Monopoly, including the original flat iron it had begun making for a laundry thirty years earlier. (Originally, Monopoly players were charged with hunting up game tokens themselves, and would use buttons, coins, or Cracker Jack prizes, which kids collected. Parker Brothers quickly decided to save them the trouble and simply include tokens in the boxes so the game would be ready to play.)

Other toys followed. As unexpected and delightful as its corporate history was, what really shocked me at Strombecker Toys was how they made cap guns; the same process that the Linotype machine used, hot metal poured into a mold. After it cooled, a worker removed the unfinished gun—all the parts treed together in a single piece—by pulling it out of the mold with a pliers, one splayed gun at a time, so the various pieces could be cut apart and assembled. He then greased the mold with a big wet brush for the next toy gun. The barrel that tumbled the pieces after they were separated, to grind off the sharp edges, was made of wood—a grimy, black, wood-staved, iron-banded barrel that looked like it came to Chicago on a clipper ship. The eight pieces were assembled by hand in thirty seconds.

It seemed an astoundingly low-tech way to produce a $2.99 cap gun—a Pony Boy Western-Style six-shooter—a process that shouldn't have lasted as long as it did and seemed to me couldn't last much longer. It turns out I was right; it didn't.

* * *

Strombecker Toys is gone. Jays Potato Chips is gone. Replogle Globes, gone. Sara Lee closed its bakery here. Maurice Lenell too. The Chicago Fish House is now a car dealership. Radio Flyer makes its red wagons in China. Wrigley's, which began making gum in Chicago in 1911, sent its gum production overseas in 2005. Brach's closed its West Side plant—a thousand jobs sent down to Mexico. I went through Cooper Lamp, a large plant just east of the Kennedy Expressway, to write a story for *Granta*. The magazine didn't use any pictures, which seemed a shame; the rotary cutting blades looked beautiful, like exotic starfish arrayed upon a wooden board. So I asked *Chicago* magazine to do a photo spread, and the magazine just had time to photograph Cooper before the company went out of business.

I thought I was just uncovering interesting stuff, but I was also chronicling a vanishing part of Chicago—of America, really. In the first decade of the twenty-first century, the United States lost a third of its manufacturing jobs, and industry had already been declining for decades before 2000.

Almost every economic trend went against producing things in the United States. Take Strombecker Toys. The stores that carried their products—Woolworth's, Ben Franklin's, little mom-and-pop places—went out of business. The big outlets that didn't go out of business, like Toys "R" Us, stopped carrying toy guns in the mid-1990s and pushed big-ticket brand names far more than inexpensive paddleball games and die-cast cars. Everything could be made far cheaper overseas anyway. Strombecker merged with Processed Plastic Co. of Montgomery, Illinois, in 2004, and in early 2005 it closed its main plant in Chicago, moving its cap gun and bubble solution production to China.

Sugar tariffs designed to prop up the American sugar industry made it economically sensible for candy companies to flee to Mexico, where sugar costs a quarter of what it does here—and of course labor is far cheaper. The Union Stockyards closed in 1971 because it is less expensive to transport steaks than to transport cows. United States Steel closed its enormous South Works in 1992 because Japanese steel plants did a better job of making steel than we did.

Transportation put Chicago where it is and stoked its growth, then manufacturing came in and built a great city, and anyone who loves Chicago has to pause to soberly consider what will become of the place if all the factories completely disappear. My guess is they won't—that extrapolating Chicago into a city entirely without manufacturing makes the same mistake that Daniel Burnham made looking to the future and seeing a city with thirteen million people, a case of being blinded instead of illuminated by the past. Trends shift. Incomes will rise in China, eventually; politics will change. There are already signs of renewal. Some companies that shipped production overseas are allowing it to trickle back. And some companies, such as Chicago Mailing Tube, never left.

It's a testament to the resilience of the city, to its scope and adaptability, that Chicago survived its significant losses by pushing into new areas, into engineering, technology, cell phones, the Internet. "The Merchandise Mart was built here because Sears was here, Marshall Field's was here, Montgomery Wards was here," said Chris Kennedy, then president of the Mart's holding company, sitting in his fourth-floor office, which was festooned with memorabilia from his father, Robert F. Kennedy. "Now Fields and Wards are gone and Sears is just holding on." So the Mart, the largest commercial building in the world, transformed from a massive showroom allowing department stores to connect with their suppliers to a place where rich people go to outfit their high-end kitchens and bathrooms, as well as a site for trade shows—for wedding suppliers, antiques, or outdoor furniture—and business offices. It still makes money. Which is the key thing in Chicago, like everywhere else.

* * *

Not everyone can handle the transformation. Along with much of its manufacturing, Chicago has also lost a chunk of population. Another 200,000 people left in the first decade of the twenty-first century—it wasn't just me—bringing the 2010 population to 2.7 million, down nearly a million people from 1950. Chicago shrank, but it did not decline, at least not the way Detroit and Cleveland and other midwestern cities did. It used its crossroads location to remain a hub of business. You can still go to the enormous trade shows at McCormick Place—the housewares show, the specialty foods show, the restaurant show, the auto show—and see product reps from China who must come to Chicago to sell what they make. The influx of conventioneers wheeling their sample cases, the gigantic displays, the squads of salesmen, the mounds of product, are breathtaking to behold. I'm always grateful to have the chance to visit a show, and at the end of a footsore day, even more grateful that I don't make my living this way, selling colorful plastic mixing bowls or pouring my hopes and dreams and time and money into trying to start up another gourmet cookie company. The centrality of the city during the canal and railroads days has been maintained, miraculously, into an age when one big airport is the same as another. At least so far. Maybe computers and the Internet will someday moot the idea of being in a city at all—the online world will be our Daley Plaza. But not yet.

Why not? I hate to squint into the distance and make claims about what people need or don't need to do. Predictions of the future inevitably reveal the anxieties of whatever historical moment they are made in, rather than serve as augury, and accurate assessments of what is to come are more due to chance than to wisdom. People guess about what's going to happen and, later, we look back and view anyone who happened to be correct as some kind of oracle. Maybe the need to gather in cities is as intrinsic to human beings as the need to wear top hats, and someday we will become an atomized whir of individuals connected online but not geographically, working in our scattered cabins and apartments and yurts.

Or maybe not. Maybe people will always have a strong desire to gather in a place with other people, a place where things are happening, satisfying some yearning that goes back ten thousand years to when we slept in big piles in caves for warmth, and a basic element of human life that's not going to be undone because of a few new electronic gadgets. While the immediacy and reach of the Internet upended a spectrum of industries, I can't help but notice that it didn't dent colleges—not yet anyway—and you would think the ability to immediately access the world's information for free might do that. But the social and career dynamics that universities offer young people dwarfs their educative function, at least so far. Maybe because students learn from each other, from the sharing of ideas.

Or maybe my freshman buddies and I were right. Maybe college really is about the beer.

Social necessity sure hasn't stuck to newspapers. I suppose at some point I should say a few solemn words over the industry. Newspapers framed our perception of the city—you lived in a different Chicago if you read the *Tribune* than if you read the *Sun-Times*, or if you read the old *Daily News*, or, God forbid, the Hearst *Herald-American* (those who decry tabloid television as a symptom of our crass modern age haven't flipped through the jarring, axe-murder and love-nest world of the Hearst papers). What surprises me now is realizing how many years we spent thinking the problem was one of content—that if only we changed our approach, our layout, our graphics, our story size, then the readers would come back. I suppose that's natural—we're in the content business. To a hammer, the saying goes, every problem looks like a nail.

In the end—not that this *is* the end, though it sure feels like that sometimes—it wasn't the content, wasn't the stories, wasn't a matter of quality. Every newspaper, good, bad, and indifferent, ended up cooking in the same pot. It was a technological shift—that sounds so obvious, but its implications were too stark to accept. Once, in order to get the weather forecast, the sports scores, the movie listings, the latest doings, you had to buy a newspaper. And now you don't—all of that is online for free. And the advertisers, who once had to be in that newspaper to reach the public, can find them online. You can do almost everything a newspaper did online: sell your garden tools, check the stock market, and glean enough of a rough approximation of what is going on in the world to get through your day.

The stuff journalists thought was important—the exposés, the columns, the in-depth reports on famine in sub-Saharan Africa—turned out to be something people could live without, or with much less of. I compare it to gas stations. It was nice to have Jack come out of the Clark station in Berea and pump our gas and clean the windows of my mother's car and say something pleasant and give a stick of gum to us kids in the back seat. But the bedrock truth was that, to save a nickel on a gallon of gas, we would do away with Jack. We could get our gum from other places.

Jack was superfluous, as daily newspapers might end up being, almost certainly in print, perhaps online too, though I hold out hope that we are evolving into some new form—like the Merchandise Mart—into something with a future, into energetic websites that, rather than disgorge amateur opinion and aggregate other sites, have employees who actually go out into the living world and see for themselves what's there, who have been around for a while and bring a certain knowledge, depth, perspective, and accountability, in theory. Some consider that elitism, but collecting and analyzing news still seems to be an important societal function, though of course I'm biased. Maybe armies of regular folk will do that for free on a consistent basis—news will be something that your neighbor tells you he saw, the story come full circle. But I have my doubts—reporting is hard enough to do when you're paid.

Whatever comes, individuals will have to adapt, if they can, to maintain a constant nimbleness to get by, as we do in our own jobs, transforming to the task at hand. I certainly do. Some columns are light and frothy—a tea party for dogs—and some stark and tragic: a disabled girl testifying at the trial of her attacker. Different subjects, different audiences, require different tones. The ability to shift to suit circumstances is a mark of professionalism. You write differently for the sharp, satiric monthly *Spy* than for the sweet and simpering *Brides*. "Give the lady what she wants," was the slogan at Marshall Field's, but I keep it in mind when dealing with editors.

You make instantaneous changes and long-term ones—I went from being a reporter to a columnist, a bachelor to a husband, a newlywed to a father, from living in the city to living in the suburbs, from being a guy who drinks to one who doesn't. As far as going from somebody who writes for a living to somebody who does something else, well, as Seneca says, leave tomorrow's woes be—maybe they'll come, maybe they won't—and don't make a down payment on future sorrow by feeling bad about it now.

* * *

I could see Sam making the same kind of shifts, in his job running the limousine company. He'd be browbeating an erring driver on one line, then get a phone call from his Japanese masters on another, and his whole demeanor would change. He'd snap forward, a little, at the waist, dipping his head slightly. "Hai!" he'd exclaim, every inch the deferential Japanese underling. There was a lot of that. When I tried to explain what Sam's job was like, this is the story I would tell: He was racing to meet a top Japanese executive at the airport—too important a client to delegate to one of his drivers. He had to do it himself. Traffic was terrible and though he had allowed plenty of time, it was a footrace to get to the right airport gate, where he joined the line of waiting Japanese subordinates moments before the executive arrived. The underling bowing next to him turned and regarded him coldly. "You were almost late!" he hissed, bent over at the waist.

"You were almost late." Even the boss of a limousine company is not the boss of his customers. It's a lifelong commitment to being a lackey. Sam isn't that sort. Like me, he can chafe at taking orders. Unlike me, who tends to float and wait for what fate would deal, Sam had the courage to toss in his cards when he became dissatisfied and call for another hand.

* * *

At some point, the *Sun-Times* stopped being the day job and started being my life. Sam wasn't going to let himself be a limo guy, but I could accept spending my career as a newspaper columnist. That was a good thing, in itself, and nothing else had to happen. Success had come up from behind and given me that big hug, finally, but so gradually and so tenderly that I didn't realize it, not for a long time. Maybe, as with the Sears Tower, it was the threat of loss that made it beloved. I always thought the Sears—whoops, Willis—Tower was brutish and ugly, until after 9/11, when realizing that we might have lost it made it cherished, almost beautiful. Only as a world without newspapers began to take shape in the murky landscape ahead did I understand how much I loved writing for one.

Why? Maybe it was just the shifting routine, the chance to dig into things that fascinated me and present them to others. What is a newspaper? It's a gang of people who know a lot about their individual fields—politics, science, business, the arts, sports—who fan out over the city, every day, to identify the most important stuff going on right now and write about it in the most interesting, factual way possible. Being part of that wasn't a fate to be accepted—it was a gift to be cherished and clung to. It took a few decades, but I finally figured that out. Being a journalist might not mean belonging to a growth profession—I never got rich—and perks such as job security and a decent retirement were tossed over the side as the paper struggled to stay afloat. But it did offer learning and humor and challenge, quirky colleagues, and a sense of life richly lived, a tang of the romantic that being a content provider for a web server company will never impart, as least not to me. I was crossing the Orleans Street Bridge, talking to a pal who had grown downhearted about our trade. I reminded him of the great opening sentence of Isak Dinesen's *Out of Africa*: "I had a farm in Africa, at the foot of the Ngong Hills."

"Don't you see?" I said, excitedly. "Someday, your grandchildren are going to ask you what your life was all about, and you're going to begin, 'I was a newspaperman in Chicago . . .'"

10

"A byutafl day in the palka"

WHEN ROSS WAS NEARLY three years old, the Chicago Transit Authority commissioned artist Steve Musgrave to create a poster promoting the Crosstown Classic. Though the two teams routinely played exhibitions, the White Sox and Cubs had not faced each other in a regulation game since the 1906 World Series. But baseball changed its rules to include interleague play in 1997, so now the rivals would battle it out for city-wide bragging rights in games that counted.

The poster struck a balance between the two teams, with the word "Cubs" against a blue ribbon, "Sox" against a black one, a fat, brown mitt in the center holding a ball emblazoned with the dates—June 5, 6, 7, 1998—and the slogan "Take the CTA Red Line to Wrigley Field and Comiskey Park" running twice around the border. The poster, done in hues of infield green and base-path brown, gave off a distinct whiff of a 1930s travel advertisement, a vintage A. M. Cassandre feel. The CTA sent the *Sun-Times* transportation writer a copy of the poster, which was to be handed out on the Addison and 35th Street el platforms to fans arriving for the games, to thank them for taking the train. He stuck the poster up with thumbtacks over his desk.

When I saw that poster, I had two thoughts: first, that it was beautiful and I wanted one for myself. And a second, more gradual realization: that if I took Ross to one of the Crosstown Classic games, then not only would I have this cool poster to frame and admire for the rest of my life, but it would be a poster of the first baseball game my older son and I ever attended together.

That seemed like a plan.

So I phoned the CTA and asked them to send over another poster. And I told Ross, a few months shy of three, that we would be going to a real baseball game together. This pleased Ross very much—he had never played baseball on a team, but had played catch with his dad in the park and knew what a baseball was. His brother Kent was not yet a year old and deemed not quite ready for the crowds and commotion of Wrigley Field.

The day of the game, I put on my old Cubs cap, grabbed an even older Cleveland Indians cap, and stuck it on Ross' head. Though I had lived and died for the Indians, for a brief time as a boy, as an adult my interest in sports waned—I would go to a baseball game to cover it for the newspaper, or to play host to visitors, or to accept someone else's invitation to a social outing. But it was not a personal passion; I would never consider going to a baseball game by myself, for my own enjoyment.

This was different. My father had never taken me to an Indians game, not once. That task was delegated to my grandfather, who took me to a game when I was six. The next game I attended was when I was thirteen, old enough to be dropped off at Cleveland Municipal Stadium to meet a buddy from summer camp. My father came to get me when the game was over. This hands-off approach to America's pastime, not to mention to fatherhood, was not a legacy that I was interested in passing along to the next generation.

Ross was very excited, singing snatches of "Take Me Out to the Ball-game" in the mirror and occasionally bursting out with spontaneous cries of "Strike one!" and "Strike two!" We bid farewell to his mother and brother, and I took him by the hand and we headed to Wrigley Field.

We brought along my Little League mitt, a mid-1960s, squarish Sears model, devoid of any ballplayer's endorsement. A Charlie Brown mitt. We would need this, I carefully explained to Ross, to snag the foul balls that came our way, and since he was a lefty, just like me, he could use it too.

I hadn't gotten tickets—I figured we'd buy them at the park, though the Cubs-Sox series was completely sold out. But from covering playoff games for the paper, I knew a secret: that no matter how hot a game, no matter how news stories breathlessly relay the impossible prices of those precious few tickets trading hands, two minutes before the national anthem there are always tickets selling for face value or less outside the ballpark, if you're willing to take the risk that you won't find the people selling them. Sometimes the box office has last-minute seats that become available, though this time I checked and there was nothing—not for the very first Crosstown Classic. We hung around and ran into a busload of fans with a couple extra to sell. Tour buses are a good source of tickets, because they're easy to spot pulling up, and somebody usually misses the bus. I bought a pair on the first-base side, terrace boxes, section 228. A little far back, but not terrible. Nor was it two minutes before the game—I had given us a lot of extra time to find a scalper and get inside before the crush of the crowds. We went through the turnstile more than an hour before the ceremonial first pitch.

When we came up through the tunnel, I had Ross in my arms, and studied his sweet face closely, the way I had looked at him when I eased the first spoonful of ice cream he ever tasted into his mouth. There was no big smile for the inside of Wrigley Field, as there had been for vanilla ice cream. In fact, he was immediately confused, even upset, as I carried him up toward our seats. Something was wrong. "What is it?" I asked, and he indignantly sputtered that the players were all down there, on the field, while we were up here, walking up stairs, away from the action. In the wrong direction! He had his "baseball mitten," he protested. He had his hat. He was ready. He wanted to play.

His confusion was understandable. I immediately realized that while I had told him we were going to a baseball game, I had neglected to explain that we were going to the game as spectators, not participants, and how would he know otherwise? It isn't like I watched much baseball at home.

Sometimes a child's qualms can be soothed away, and sometimes trying to be calming only intensifies them. As I struggled to make him understand that we were here to watch, not play, as I tried to bribe him with the hot dogs and sodas that awaited us, the promise of a souvenir, I could see him grow more and more unhappy. My magical dad and lad moment—our first baseball game—was slipping away.

Desperation inspired my next decision. It was an hour before the game. The stands were just beginning to fill, the field given over to players stretching, tossing balls to one another. The Wrigley security staff had not yet assumed its game-time diligence. An idea bloomed . . .

"Okay, I'll tell you what," I told Ross. "I think they have enough players. But let's go ask them if you can play. If they say yes, then fine, you can play. But if they say no, we'll come back and just watch the game today and no complaining, okay?"

He agreed—fair is fair—and I took him down to the rail separating the stands from the field. If I have learned one thing from being a professional journalist, it is that you can get away with a lot if you pretend to know what you're doing. Confidence is the key to many locks. In one smooth motion, without any hesitation or looking around, I went through the gate in the railing and down onto the field.

I had never been on the field at Wrigley before—I take that back; I had been on the field once before, but only in a dream. Literally, it was one of those dreams so vivid that it stays with you for the rest of your life—I remember sitting in the dugout, seeing the field at eye-level, then looking down at my legs, at the blue pinstriped uniform, thinking, "Hey, I'm on the Cubs. I'm wearing a uniform. I'm a player. I've got to make sure my dad sees this." And then I woke up.

Now I was actually on the field, in the waking world, with my three-year-old son in my arms. We walked up to the first player we saw—some languid, rail-thin Sox rookie. He looked about twenty. I didn't notice his name.

"Can this little boy play with you guys today?" I asked.

"Not in that cap he can't," he replied, flatly, without smiling. I looked at Ross. He was wearing my Cleveland Indians cap. Of course. The Sox. The Indians. Rivals, or at least competitors—the Sox at the time would have to do a lot better to rival the Indians, who spanked their bottoms as a matter of routine. The Indians were a team that had gone to the World Series the previous October, the second time in three years. Still, it was the right answer for my purposes.

"Oh, I'm sorry," I cooed sympathetically to Ross, turning away and heading back toward the stands. "He says you can't play today. But that's okay—we'll watch the game, and see how it's done. Maybe we can play next time."

He was fine after that—sat through the entire game, no squirming, no complaining. We had tried; that was all we could do. I couldn't recall a single play of the game if you put a gun to my head—sports has a way of rolling off me like rain off a newly waxed car hood. It's the parts off the field that remain sharp. The miniature blue Cubs bat I bought for Ross as a souvenir. The line at the concession counter, where we stood behind a Hispanic man with a neatly trimmed beard, holding an even younger boy, practically a baby. Our eyes met.

"I'm saving everything," he gushed. "The ticket stubs. Even the food wrappers." I smiled, understanding completely. The little Cubs bat is still in the toy box in Ross's bedroom. The poster is framed on the wall. I've never gotten tired of looking at it.

* * *

Children change everything. Your relationship with your wife, with your parents, your view of yourself, of your city. You fear the city more on their account—I would have never left Chicago, except at the prospect of my sons' sharp minds being blunted by tilling the stony field of Nettelhorst Elementary School.

But you also love the city more because of them, because children are like guests who never leave, and you find yourself revisiting the things you enjoy most about Chicago, in order to share those parts with the next generation, in the hope that they will love them too, so they will become the kind of people you like most: people similar to yourself.

Or, in the case of the Cubs game, you show them things that they *might* love about the city, to expose them to the standard rituals. I couldn't make Ross or his brother Kent into Cubs fans—that would involve an ongoing fraud on my part, and what would be the point? But if they didn't become fans—and they didn't—it wasn't going to be because their father never took them to a game. We cheered at baseball games, football games, basketball games, hockey games. Hockey—I love them that much.

We went to all the tourist sites, up to the top of the Willis Tower, down to the Coal Mine in the Museum of Science and Industry, which, to celebrate a century since the first heavier-than-air, powered flight tried to fly a replica of the *Wright Flier* off its North Lawn. The thing never left the ground, but it felt significant to stand in the crowd and watch them try. After forty-five minutes, though, we slipped into the museum, and, coming out an hour later, we were surprised to find that a festival of kites had sprung up while we were inside. The sky was filled with kites of all colors and descriptions, swooping and diving and fluttering against the blueness.

As Indian Guides, we slept in the science museum one night, between the giant walk-in heart and the suspended Spitfire fighter plane, an experience that sounds more fun than it actually is. The floor is very hard.

The Adler Planetarium, the Shedd Aquarium, circuses, both Ringling and Medinah, zoos, both Lincoln Park and Brookfield, the Children's Museum at Navy Pier, puppet shows, playgrounds, parks, fountains, kiddy concerts—for one birthday, the week before Halloween, Ross took a few pals to Symphony Center to hear the Civic Orchestra of Chicago play scary music for silent movies. There is a parallel city of children that exists almost independently of the city of adults, and you get to know the fun kid restaurants: Ed Debevic's, Margie's Candies, the Rainforest Cafe, pizza parlors.

Ross started talking at eleven months and never stopped, and the things he would say astounded me. We were at a third-birthday party for a classmate in his preschool at that mecca of toddlerhood, Chuck E. Cheese's—there was one not far from our place, in a suburbanish mall west on Fullerton. The big moment—the arrival of Chuck E. himself or, rather, some poor minimum-wage teen in a big gray cartoon mouse costume—was at hand. The recorded fanfare blared, the canned howdy-kids voice crackled over the speakers, the children cheered, and Ross leaned in to me. "Dad," he said, sotto voce, as if imparting a secret. "Do you think it's appropriate to have a mouse at a restaurant?" He was three.

Children can change your relationships with your coworkers, your friends, your sources, your readers. Or at least they did for me. I wrote about the boys from the very beginning, because I found them interesting, even though my kids were the one thing my boss ordered me *not* to write about, almost immediately, the first year Ross was born. "Steinberg!" Nigel Wade said, "Every time you write about your *son*, I get the impression you did not know what else to write about." Luckily, I had a comeback: "Every single column I've ever written for the paper, without exception, I picked the topic because I didn't know what else to write about," I told Nigel. "There's never a Plan B." I simply ignored his edict—another key journalistic trait, knowing when to ignore the boss—and readers who tell me they like the column inevitably mention the boys in their next breath.

Because I had my own office at the *Sun-Times*, it was a simple thing to bring Ross or Kent downtown with me, and I often did when they were small. At any given day during winter, spring, or summer break, Ross would be sprawled on the floor reading a book, or Kent, playing with soldiers. I tried not to bring them both at the same time—too much of a handful, and I did have work to do. So they took turns, first one and then the other.

We usually stopped by Harry's Hot Dogs, at Randolph and Franklin. Harry Heftman was in his nineties and would always sit at our booth and talk to the boys, as I tried to make them grasp that before them was a man who'd been three years old when the *Titanic* sank, who remembered the end of World War I and coming to Chicago from Hungary in 1922. The boys, of course, were more excited to eat foot-long hot dogs and french fries for breakfast, a practice that my wife vigorously objected to. "Okay, okay," I told Edie, defending our customary spree. "They didn't have foot-longs and french fries for breakfast—they had sausages, toast, and hash browns. Is that better?"

Harry's Hot Dogs also had a television, which was often turned to the *Oprah Winfrey Show* when we were there, and Ross took a liking to it—I think he was thrilled by the edgy subject matter. So we'd sit and watch for a while after breakfast, and for the first time, I began to have the slightest appreciation for the show myself, a reminder to parents that while we are teaching our children they are also teaching us.

One day in July, when Kent was newly five, he and I went to work together, and Edie decided to take Ross downtown and rendezvous with us in the afternoon. Kent played quietly with his Night Attack G.I. Joe during the editorial board meeting. After lunch we repaired to the Lake Shore Athletic Club to swim. "This is the life," he said, closing his eyes and tipping his head back while lounging in the whirlpool. "No Rossie. No mommy to boss us around."

When we met Edie and Ross later at the Art Institute, Ross had a pen clipped to the collar of his mustard-colored t-shirt. When I asked him why, he showed me a piece of paper folded up in his pocket. "For taking notes," he said.

Wonder where he got *that* from. . . .

We wandered the galleries. At the time, the museum displayed a bronze of a powerful backside set on a plinth in the middle of the central staircase. I drew attention to it, as I always did. "Now if you get separated, remember, we'll meet up at the Big Butt," I said, and the boys smiled, delighted at this bit of daddish naughtiness. Practical tip: if you are trying to get small boys interested in fine art, ask them, as they proceed through any museum, to point out all the bare backsides they notice and yell "Butt!" They won't want to leave, and you can worry about telling them who painted and sculpted all this stuff in future years.

The Art Institute is one of the world's great art museums, and it contains the famous treasures that museumgoers crave—Grant Wood's *American Gothic*, Edward Hopper's *Nighthawks*. But those are only familiar to people old enough to know a little something about art. I was interested in what, besides posteriors, would catch the boys' attention, at five and six—the armor, obviously. But Ross also planted himself in front of Seurat's enormous pointillist masterpiece *A Sunday on La Grande Jatte—1884*.

He looked at the painting for a long time.

"I like this one," he said.

Not everything met with his approval. Van Gogh's bedroom in Arles. "Why is that in a museum?" Ross demanded. "An eight-year-old could do that," he said, then, correcting himself, "a *newborn* could do that."

That night, after tucking Ross in and singing him his songs, I noticed a piece of folded paper on his dresser and picked it up and took it with me when I left the room. It was the notepaper he had taken to the museum. "Srot," he wrote. "A byutafl day in the palka." Not bad for a boy whose formal education consisted of a year of kindergarten trying to convey, "Seurat, a beautiful day in the park."

* * *

I try not to regret leaving the city, try not to conjure up a shadow me who never left, whose wife went back to work at another big law firm. I try not to torture myself with the deluxe Chicago life that these Imaginary Steinbergs would now be enjoying. Though occasionally I do, picturing the swell Armitage Avenue graystone we'd live in, the fancy overseas vacations we'd take, the problems in life that would have never come my way, moving a Sham Chicago Me through this fantasy city life like a little girl walking her daddy doll through an elaborate Victorian dollhouse.

Parents banded together and greatly improved the Nettelhorst Elementary School—I could have been part of that, though whether we would have fixed it fast enough to benefit my own boys is an open question. Still, some people stayed and fought a battle that I had shrieked and run away from at the first whiff of gunpowder. Now by third grade, 85 percent of the students in the Nettelhorst School meet or exceed state reading standards, almost a complete inversion of what it was in the mid-1990s. Kudos to them.

You can't go back and change the past. The necessary time-travel technology just isn't here yet. And regret is a chimera. We always imagine that had we done something different, our life would have worked out better. We never imagine alternate routes being worse. We never say, "Oh, if only I had married this person or gone to that school, then my life would *really* be in the toilet." Though that could have happened just as easily.

So whenever I'm in full regret mode, pining for the life we would have had in the city, I always draw the little puppet opera of regret to a close by observing to myself that I have no idea what would have happened. One of the boys could have accidentally stepped in front of the 151 bus. Then I'd spend my life desperately regretting that we had not moved to the safety of the suburbs. All the benefits of the city would then sour, would be poisoned, becoming the siren call to ruin, the sweet-smelling bait that had lured us into disaster. People who move out of the city are thought to be abandoning it, but there is an argument that they are poised to enjoy it more, because they can swoop in and experience the best while missing out on the harder parts. Maybe that's why full-time residents resent us so—we're like wedding guests who skip the ceremony but show up for the reception.

* * *

Having children also changes your relation to the people you know in the city. Once I turned in a column that mentioned that Ross had come downtown with me three days in a row, prompting a rare visit to my office by the managing editor. He had hundreds of employees, he said. *They* don't have offices. If I write in the paper that I let Ross come to work with me, they'll complain. I didn't want to spike the column, so I revised the ending to include my boss's ban on bringing my children to work, and my sigh of relief. I liked having the boys come down, but it was also a distraction, an interruption to my routine. Easier to keep them at home, and now it was officially forbidden, the matter was out of my hands. Give the lady what she wants.

When Chris Kennedy, the president of the Merchandise Mart, read that, he was outraged. He phoned me: the heck with my bosses—a man should be able to bring his children to work with him as much as he likes. Next time the boys wanted to come down, he said, you turn them over to *me*.

A different man would have thanked him and let that offer fade. But

I am not that man. So next time Ross had a vacation day and wanted to come downtown, I informed Chris. He asked us to present ourselves at his offices, and we were met by the man in charge of renting out space in the Merchandise Mart, who did the whole dog-and-pony show about how they remodel offices, complete with panels showing sample carpet swatches and squares of tile. Then they gave Ross a Merchandise Mart t-shirt and a Merchandise Mart hard hat with his name on the back and put him to work on a scaffold, setting screws with a power drill (on a scrap 2 × 4, to keep him occupied, not as part of the project—I don't want anybody in the Mart worrying that their false ceiling wasn't properly installed by qualified union labor and might come down on their heads).

After Ross's day working at the Mart, my ability to judge Chris Kennedy and his projects and pronouncements, well, it was compromised. Or at least I worried it was compromised. He might argue that I was extra hard on him in the column, trying to avoid charges of favoritism. It's hard to tell. When Kennedy decided to quit the Mart, he told me first and let the *Sun-Times* scoop everybody else, so there are good aspects along with the bad.

The value of knowing people, the grease that connections can provide, is central to the Chicago experience—we learn it without being taught. I didn't have to lecture the boys on the importance of contacts; it's instinctual, inborn. The family was in Washington, DC, on vacation, and for an afternoon I slipped away to do some research at the Library of Congress while Edie and the boys saw the sights. When they came to meet up with me, at the end of the day, I wanted to show Ross the Main Reading Room—it was so beautiful, a gilded dome, a marvel of arches and stained glass, a Victorian glory of murals and friezes and statuary, and Ross is such a lover of books, I knew he would be delighted to see it. So I took him up to the guard—you have to be a registered researcher to enter the Library of Congress, which I was. Ross wasn't, but I figured: the kid's seven years old.

"Can I slip this boy in for a moment to look at the Reading Room?" I asked, nodding hopefully, displaying my Library of Congress ID card. I'm sorry, the guard said, only researchers are allowed in the reading room. "But I *am* a researcher!" insisted Ross, thumping his chest and stepping up to this rent-a-cop. "I'm researching James Monroe. And I always take good care of my books and papers." The guard, of course, didn't budge, and as we turned away, Ross said to me, in a whisper, "Dad, do you think it would help if we told him I'm friends with Mrs. Creighton?"

Mrs. Creighton was the librarian at Greenbriar Elementary School in Northbrook.

That attitude—I know people, I'm in with all the librarians, cut me some slack—is a very Chicago attitude, and reassured me that while my sons had not been born within the borders of the city, and might be growing up in the leafy suburban paradise of Northbrook, but they were becoming Chicagoans nevertheless.

* * *

There is a downside to all this. The connections you make also bind you, limiting your mobility. I'm certainly not constantly slagging Harry Caray's Restaurant. Part of that is due to the fact that the food is good, the decor a splendid museum-quality collection of baseball memorabilia, the staff as gracious to me as you'd expect them to be to a customer who has eaten there fifty times, at least. Maybe a hundred. Maybe two hundred.

But there is also the matter of Grant DePorter, the managing partner of Harry Caray's. He's very hands-on, in that he's always there, prowling around. He likes to keep regular customers happy, picking up the occasional check, pressing envelopes containing his endless supply of primo tickets to the Cubs and Blackhawks.

I like to think that, despite the perks, if they started poisoning people at Harry Caray's, I'd lead the charge to condemn the place. But you never know. I'm terminally biased when it comes to them, and for a simple reason.

One day, Grant DePorter said, "Neil, would you like to throw out the first pitch at a Cubs game?"

"God no," I answered, instinctively, then reconsidered. "But I know somebody who would . . ."

Kent was seven then, playing on a Northbrook Park District team. The thing about throwing out a first pitch is that everybody's watching. Whether you get it to the catcher or fling it into the dugout is immediately cheered, or booed, and that kind of thing can haunt you for the rest of your life. The strain of thinking about doing it would counterbalance, for me, whatever joy there might be in the doing. So I passed the buck to my son, worrying that I was setting the kid up, prodding him to do something his old man was too scared to try. But he seemed eager.

Throwing out the first pitch would be meaningless if the kid botched it.

A great part of success is preparation, so I measured off sixty feet, six inches on our driveway, and we went out and practiced, me in the catcher's crouch, mitt out, him making the throws. We practiced a lot—again and again, Kent flinging, me standing up with a groan and strolling to the curb to retrieve the ball thrown out of my grasp, too far to the left or to the right.

The day of the big game, Ross came downtown with me that morning, then we headed to the ballpark, while Edie and Kent left the car at the Skokie Swift station and took the el down. As game time approached, Ross and I sat in the stands, wondering: Where are they? "Maybe you'll have to throw the pitch out," I said to Ross, who made a face. That wasn't going to happen. I might end up throwing out that first pitch after all.

Finally, about twenty minutes before game time, Edie and Kent bustled over, breathless, Kent wearing a little Cubs uniform that Edie had bought for the occasion, with white baseball pants and long blue kneesocks. They had been trapped on the el after the train they were riding sat inexplicably at a station for half an hour. Edie was just at the point of deciding to pull the emergency door release and go to the street and search for a cab, when the train started moving again. There was no time to marvel over their adventure.

Kent and I hurried down toward the field, moving past Andy Frain ushers, who would make eye contact and initially hold their ground until I announced, "This is the boy who is throwing out the first pitch," and they would dip their heads and defer, stepping aside to let us pass. Kent and I approached an official, who told us to sit in some seats by the dugout and wait.

We sat together in the bright sun. Kent for some reason handed me his hat, and I fingered the brim nervously, jabbering away—last-minute advice, cautions, exclamations of excitement. The full Polonius. Kent was silent, very focused, narrowing his eyes, examining the field as if measuring it. I kept on talking until he finally said, "Dad, be quiet." I wasn't offended—I shut up. Shutting up is an art form, one that requires practice. A skill not everyone can master. Holding the hat, I felt like Willy Loman holding the pennants before Biff's big championship at Ebbets Field in *Death of a Salesman*. It was unsettling how important this all had become for me. I felt like I was experiencing the greatest moment in my life, and was simultaneously thrilled and horrified by the realization. Part of me was saying, "THIS IS IT!!!" and part of me was saying, "*this* is it?"

Finally, we were beckoned to the field. I handed Kent his hat. When I had gone down onto the field with Ross, six years earlier, it had felt covert. Now it felt like the most public thing in the world, with all forty-two thousand fans looking at us. An official called Kent over—I thought of hovering, but didn't. This was his moment. I stayed back, against the wall. Kent received some instruction on what to do. The man introduced Kent to the catcher, then stood for a moment, his hand on Kent's shoulder. There was more waiting. Kent tossed the ball he had into the air and caught it, tossed it and caught it, again and again.

Suddenly it was time, and Kent was trotting to the mound with a hero's easy gait. He did not pause. He did not look back at me. He did not compose himself or show any sign of hesitation. He did not linger. He reached the mound, set his foot on the rubber, eyeballed the catcher, found his target, went into a windup I didn't know he had and fired a strike. Not a looping arc toward the catcher, but a frozen-rope strike. At least in my memory. The crowd erupted. I cheered, as best I could while taking videos with one hand and still pictures with the other. As we walked back to our seats, a guy in the stands shouted, "Sign him up!"

To this day, if you go into Harry Caray's Restaurant on Kinzie Street, among the wall-cluttering array of baseball memorabilia, bronze plaques, uniforms in cases, and famous balls in special stands, there is a photo of Kent throwing out that pitch at Wrigley Field. It's in the far room, next to the big picture of Joe DiMaggio and Marilyn Monroe.

I can't help but think of some little kid, eating dinner with his family, maybe his first meal in Chicago, seeing, among all these legendary players, the incongruous photo of a seven-year-old boy, scowling with concentration, in his windup on the mound in what is obviously Wrigley Field on a bright summer day. He'd have to wonder about that boy—who is he? How did he get to pitch for the Cubs? What is his picture doing here in this gallery of heroes?

That lucky boy is my son, Kent Zalman Steinberg, and he got his chance because there are many ways to build clout in the city and yes, you can eat your way toward it.

11

"You gave the money *away?*"

IF YOU EVER FIND YOURSELF aboard a bass fishing boat, hang onto your hat. Seriously, grab the brim or it's gone. The big twin 250-horsepower engines on a twenty-one-foot Triton blast you across a body of water—such as Lake Michigan—at seventy miles an hour, with only a tea-tray's worth of bottom actually touching the surface as you catapult through a cheek-flapping gale, then pull up at a sweet spot, identified earlier from the air, and abruptly come to a dead stop so you can cast your line in silence, dropping your hook atop the head of a waiting bigmouth, if all goes according to plan. The sport is an unexpected combination of drag-racing and chess.

A few weeks before we moved to Northbrook, the Bass Anglers Sportsman Society brought its $100,000 BASS Bassmaster Classic, which had always been held in the Deep South, to Chicago, in an attempt to expand the base of bass fishing fandom.

This was the sort of offbeat story that editors liked to dump in my lap—something wacky requiring a certain touch—and I was sent to participate in the Bassmaster Pro-Am tournament, which was, basically, a mini-fishing competition before the main event designed to get the city's press out onto the lake and fishing. By then I was writing three columns a week, a task the *Sun-Times* gave me two days a week to accomplish. The other three days I was still a general-assignment reporter. That's how the paper always is, a lean and frugal operation that demands a lot from its employees. The *Sun-Times* won't give you a new pencil unless you hand in the stub of the old one.

I was paired with Gary Klein, forty-two, who had spent his entire professional life bass fishing and had earned $500,000 the year before, doing so. Nothing is more humbling than to meet a fellow your own age who is lapping you many times on the money track by being a good fisherman. Reminds you of your place in life.

The idea was that the expert would instruct and educate the reporter in the fine details of the sport, guidance I needed, having never fished in my life. But this was also a competition, albeit a small one, and pro that he is, Klein wasn't about to waste time teaching some doughy newspaperman how to cast a line. We spent a sun-dappled afternoon, with me clinging to the bill of my baseball cap, which I liked, while he rocketed the boat around the lake's shallows, staying near the shoreline, pulling up short to stop and flick the rod, then blasting off again in search of more bass.

When we returned we found out that we had won—well, Gary Klein won; I hadn't caught a fish or even properly cast a line. But I was in the same boat with the guy who caught the most fish, and that was enough for me to be presented with a check for $1,000 at the concluding ceremony.

The *Sun-Times* did not have a thick ethics policy at the time, the way the *Tribune* did. If we had one at all, I'd never seen it. "Don't get caught," perhaps. But I knew that accepting $1,000 from a subject I was writing about, not only at that moment, but in the future—the actual tournament was being held later in the summer, and the idea was that I'd be covering that, too—would be bad.

I hadn't been nimble-minded enough to simply refuse the check; somebody hands you $1,000, you tend to say "Thank you" first and think later. At least I do. But now that I had the money, what to do with it? Simply giving it back to the Bassmasters seemed both a waste and a failure of imagination. They had plenty of money already.

Luckily, one of my previous incarnations—in the paper's endless quest to figure out what to do with me—had been as the charities, foundations, and private social services reporter. Trying to perform that function, I discovered it could be very difficult to burrow through a philanthropic organization and actually meet individuals being helped. These groups are very good at hosting parties; getting invited to lavish dinners was never a problem. But if you wanted to talk to a real person aided through the good work of an agency, or watch the group doing what it supposedly does on a daily basis, when it isn't hosting gala evenings, that was often difficult to arrange.

The story I always tell is of someone phoning from the Lighthouse for the Blind. They were having their annual Glitter Ball and Women's Auxiliary Silent Auction, or some such thing. Did I want to go? Of course not, I said. But what does the Lighthouse for the Blind do? Oh, the woman said, we teach children to read Braille. *That* I wanted to write about. Who knew people still learned Braille? I would have thought that computers would have eliminated Braille long ago. "Find me a child learning Braille!" I demanded. That proved impossible, at least for this particular flack, whose task no doubt was to promote the Glitter Ball. It irked me so much that I would occasionally phone this poor woman, demanding to know where my blind child was, where he was being hidden. Not that the problem is limited to the Lighthouse for the Blind. Sometimes it seems like charitable organizations are vast money-raising and party-throwing institutions which, incidentally, anecdotally, and somewhere far away, in places unseen and unreachable, also help individuals unknown and unknowable.

So with $1,000 that I couldn't keep, I invited readers to send in letters beginning "My name is Mr. So-and-So and I want you to give your $1,000 to this charity because of what it did for me." The idea worked. We received hundreds of letters, moving and sincere tales of the genuine good that philanthropic groups can do—a camp for families with HIV, a refuge for the homeless, money to pay medical bills for the uninsured—so many that I decided not just to honor one charity, but to also print the top ten runners-up, plus photos. We ran a picture of a girl gazing at a horse, a letter from a child in Lithuania brought to Chicago for life-altering surgery at Shriner's Hospital. I got the Sun-Times Charitable Trust to kick in another thousand dollars so we could give $100 to each runner-up, while of course inviting readers to send their own contributions, then gave the thousand bucks to the Joliet Area Community Hospice, which I found most worthy simply because of the vital mercy it provides, comforting people, rich or poor, at their time of death.

Just before this package ran, I had lunch with David Radler, the publisher of the *Sun-Times*. Sports columnist Jay Mariotti had gotten himself fired during one of his periodic fits of ego and temper, but had gone crawling to Radler and begged for his job back, or so the story went. I thought: that might be a helpful path for me to blaze for myself, ahead of time, just in case I ever get canned and need to appeal to a higher power. So I asked Radler to lunch.

Now we're sitting in Shaw's Crab House, just Radler—a short, bald, deeply tanned older man with a pendulous nose and wild, unkempt gray hair at the sides of his head—and me. As with all columnists, I'm puffing myself, touting my upcoming column, which happens to be about giving away this Bassmaster money. I tell him all about the bass boat, the $1,000, and the heartwarming three-page spread in his newspaper that came out of it—the nuzzled horses! The sick Lithuanian children! I am in midtale when he interrupts me, eyebrows raised.

"You gave the money *away*?" he inquires, awestruck and indignant.

That takes me by surprise. I explain how the tournament isn't a one-time story—the Pro-Am was just a preliminary, the tournament came back a month later and I had to cover that too. Taking $1,000 from a group you're in the midst of writing about seems, I tell the publisher, a little morally dubious.

Radler sweeps his arm out, gesturing to the well-dressed lawyers and bankers slurping up their chow in the elegant seafood restaurant. "You think these people care about that?" says Radler, dismissively, shaking his head broadly as he answers his own question. "They don't care."

I point out that the *Tribune* had a photographer there. "They took a picture of me, accepting the check," I say. It could end up in their gossip column.

A look of revulsion contorts Radler's face. "Now you're letting the *Tribune* decide what you do?" he says, scowling with disgust. I walk away from lunch, smiling, or trying to, while marveling: Only at the *Sun-Times* could you get in trouble with your boss for doing the right thing and giving money to charity.

But that was the bright spin. To be honest, I felt stupid, felt I should have just kept the thousand bucks—though that feeling passed, particularly a few years later, after Radler went to prison for stealing from his own company. The crime is complex, but basically he and his boss, Conrad Black, the Canadian-born British lord and newspaper magnate, plucked away parts of the vast Hollinger newspaper empire and sold the divisions to themselves for far below their actual value, convincing themselves, apparently, that it wasn't stealing, since it was their own company. The Hollinger stockholders—whose company it actually was—disagreed, and investor inquiries turned into criminal charges.

A reminder that cronyism has its dark side. The newspaper chain's board of directors, including former Gov. Jim Thompson, were rolling on their backs, having their tummies scratched, and never bothered to look closely at the documents they were signing, cataloging the fraud and folly.

Radler at least had the decency, after he got out of prison, to disappear from the public eye, whereas Black can still occasionally be seen, twirling in the limelight like the inmate of a lunatic asylum who thinks he's a prima ballerina at the Bolshoi Ballet, wearing a shred of rag tied around his waist as a tutu, swaying in a shaft of sunlight in the dayroom, believing it a spotlight, eyes closed to how repellent he looks, tunelessly humming a ditty about being the greatest man in the world, a blend of Napoleon and Jesus, a misunderstood giant brought down by a conspiracy of fleas.

* * *

Cozying up to people you despise, or who despise you, or both, is part of the art. Radler and I were having lunch because I wanted him on my side, supporting me, refusing if somebody demanded that I be fired, tossing a fat, wriggling raise into my wide-open yapping baby bird mouth from time to time. That's why I suggested going to lunch—why he went is a mystery, perhaps nobody at the paper had ever asked him to lunch before. He struck me as a lonely man.

I had no trouble bobbing my head and acting polite, even though I considered him what I call "BFJ"—Bad For Jews, a conniving, grasping, charmless crook who fit every negative stereotype of my tribe. "He's like a Jew off the cover of *Der Stürmer*," I'd say, referring to Streicher's notorious anti-Semitic magazine. "Put a top hat on him and a money bag in each hand, set him astride a globe sprouting snakes and he'd be perfect."

I didn't tell him that. Candor is for children, amateurs, and artists. Chicago was built by enemies working together, at least in part. The professionals do it so smoothly that you can know exactly what's going on and still not mind.

The *Sun-Times* had a political columnist, Steve Neal. Everybody liked Steve. He was a large, loping man with ginger hair who wore sweaters and held glorious, booze-soaked luncheons in the upstairs room at Gene & Georgetti. It was a great way to get to know a politician, to sit at a crowded table in the middle of the afternoon in an otherwise empty room at Gene's, pounding back red wine while Dan Rostenkowski, once the most powerful man in Congress, chairman of the House Ways and Means Committee, tells some well-polished story about negotiating toe to toe with Lyndon Johnson, clamping his massive hand emphatically on your forearm as if he were passing along a legacy of insider clout, the squeeze moving from LBJ to Mr. Chairman to you. It was an illusion, of course, but for a moment you felt like you were part of something.

If Steve liked you, he was a tremendous friend; his buddies revered him. I wasn't his friend—too far down the pecking order for that—but a young colleague he knew well enough to ask to lunch and generously allow to poach books from his wonderful library, his office jammed floor to ceiling with rare political volumes from over the past half century.

Steve at first supported Dick Durbin, the senior senator from Illinois, but then took a dislike to him and would lambast him at every opportunity. "A bit player," he wrote. "A born minor leaguer." Neal found him "inept" and "outmaneuvered" and "sneaky," and a "silly chatterbox." And that was in just one column.

Then in 2003 Steve Neal killed himself. People were puzzled as to why. There were theories—I certainly have my own—but nobody knew for sure. The unexpectedness of it threw people—he seemed a man on top of the world, an influential columnist, two lovely daughters in college, another meticulously researched and crafted book about to be published—even more than such a tragedy normally would.

After Steve died, I felt obligated to pick up the cudgel and carry on his work bashing Durbin. This wasn't mere tribute. As if trying to reprise the shortsightedness of the Chicago business community resisting railroads in the late 1840s by clinging to the farmer-in-town trade, local opposition was now holding up the expansion of O'Hare over noise concerns and reluctance to relocate a small cemetery. Durbin promised he would ram something through the Senate. But he didn't. In my eyes, this was a life-or-death moment for Chicago, a city whose greatness was built on its being a hub for transportation and depended upon it still. The airport had become outmoded and sclerotic; delays were mounting. Great economic forces don't care which city benefits—without an Ogden, who knows what Chicago might have become? If O'Hare stumbles, and suddenly Denver or Dallas or—horror—St. Louis becomes the major airport hub, what then? Galena had been a big deal too, before the canals went dry.

So partly out of conviction, partly out of respect for Steve, I picked up where he left off and began delivering kicks to Durbin in print. Almost immediately, I got a phone call from Durbin's communications director. The senator, she said, wanted to have breakfast with me. That took me aback. "You do realize who you've phoned?" I said, instantly seeing the dilemma. If I went, I'd be coopted. It would put a face on Durbin—well, I had met him many times, at the editorial board, but that was always a different, adversarial setting. It wasn't eating pancakes together. Steve Neal always refused—he wouldn't even attend editorial board meetings with Durbin. I remember Durbin arriving for a meeting, outraged, sputtering, demanding that Neal be brought to him immediately. As the youngest guy in the room, I was sent trotting back to Neal's office to get him. He wasn't there.

But if I didn't meet Durbin—well, I'd be turning down breakfast with the senator. I always thought Mike Royko was wrong to leave George H. W. Bush sitting in the Billy Goat Tavern, that he was wrong to refuse to go down to the bar when the president of the United States was asking to see him. It was ego, hubris, showing off on Royko's part by snubbing Bush. You're a reporter—you're supposed to go places, talk to people. God knows Royko had no trouble haunting the Billy Goat when the president *wasn't* there, talking to his band of softball buddies, friends, and toadies, or whatever daring tourist or worshipful novice had the misfortune to approach him. I would say, err on the side of talking to the president. You never know what you may learn. If you stay in your office, well, you're already vastly familiar with the person there.

So I went to breakfast. Durbin was niceness itself. He waved off our earlier misunderstandings and fed me some choice dirt on Vicente Fox, then the president of Mexico, that I could promptly slip into my column. The next thing I knew, Durbin was reading my books aloud on the floor of the Senate and I was getting fan letters from Ted Kennedy, saying that Durbin had introduced him to my work. So now Durbin and I were pals.

I didn't castigate him the way I once did—but then again, the O'Hare expansion got approved, eventually. Reflexive hostility is a bias too—somehow, we've decided that it represents being neutral, when it doesn't. Opposition has become the default value in our society. As it turned out, Durbin became the second-most powerful man in the senate, bringing home the bacon for Illinois, year in and year out, and while he might lack the color of a great national figure, he was smart enough to quietly push for Barack Obama from the very beginning and to be an active, energetic legislator. Nobody works harder than Dick Durbin. We've had regular lunches and breakfasts since then, and I always ask myself if we have a genuine relationship, or if he secretly loathes me but is too much of a pro to show it, not while there is still another election to win. But it can't be that—I'm not important enough to curry favor with.

* * *

I tried to learn from Durbin's example. Save feuds for junior high school. When people complain to me after being roughly handled in the column, I always try to soothe them. Remember *The Godfather*? I say. It's nothing personal; it's just business. You did something stupid and I made fun of you—next time you'll do something smart and I'll praise you. That's how the media works. We hold a mirror to the world—don't blame us if you don't like what you see.

Human nature doesn't work that way, of course—the insults burn, the praise tickles, and depending on which comes first and which is most recent, people divide into friends and enemies. They can, sometimes, be gently nudged from the latter to the former camp, with effort. But I find that, as a rule, humans are quick to take offense and slow to forgive. That's how I am.

In 2008, Cook County got a new medical examiner—its third—and the thought crossed my mind that I should go back to the morgue for a visit. Patrick Donahue, the outgoing ME, had refused when I asked him; I think he was reacting to the open circus that Dr. Stein's administration always flirted with becoming. Stein took what some considered an unseemly pride in his work, in having handled the Gacy killings and the American Airways DC-10 crash at O'Hare. He always spoke dreamily about opening a public museum in the basement of the morgue, an idea that made some people squirm.

But Dr. Nancy Jones was new, so I thought I should call her up and suggest we get to know each other. I almost didn't, because I had done the medical examiner's office story before, and I don't like to repeat myself. Then the thought bubbled up: That was seventeen years ago. Nobody is going to open the paper and think, "The MORGUE!? Weren't we just there in 1991?"

So I got Dr. Jones on the phone. She wasn't enthusiastic, but she didn't completely refuse either. "Todd Stroger hired me," she said. "You'll have to get permission from him. If he says it's okay, I don't have a problem with it."

Todd Stroger was the president of the Cook County Board. Not only had I been castigating him for years as a weakling and an idiot, but I had denounced his father before him—John Stroger, the previous president—as the same. Under the Strogers, Cook County had worsened as a sinkhole of nepotism, waste, and incompetence, but for me to say so in the column was immediately tarred as racism by his band of stooges and hirelings. I don't probe for corruption, but have no trouble pointing it out when it ends up on my shoe. Just before his last election, John Stroger had a stroke, and I wrote a harsh column—at first I thought he was faking to garner the sympathy vote—saying, basically, don't feel sorry and vote for him because he's sick, or feel solidarity and vote for him because he's black. Feel sorry for yourselves, because you live in Cook County, and show solidarity with your own interests, and vote against him. A coalition of ten black pastors came to the paper, demanding that I apologize to Stroger, threatening a boycott, and my bosses, terrified of provoking the Great Racial Beast, bowed to them and forced me to kneel on a rail and confess my sins. Securing permission from Stroger's son for a field trip to the morgue seemed like a deal-breaker—I wouldn't demean myself by asking, and even if I did, he would never say yes.

But I really wanted to go back to the medical examiner's office; the place was interesting; it would make a good column. It had to—a reporter who can't find a good story at the county morgue is in the wrong business. And the Todd Stroger requirement was a challenge to my ingenuity. There is always a way, if you push hard enough and look for it. As Lyndon Johnson used to say, if you do everything, *everything* you can do, you will succeed.

The most rational and approachable member of Stroger's staff was Gene Mullins, a former cop then serving as communications adviser, and I asked him to breakfast—he seemed to have acquired the charmed notion that I was going to write a column about him, the cop turned presidential staffer, and I didn't dissuade him from that. Yes, I said, I've written some harsh things about President Stroger, but that's just business, and to be honest, I'm not a political columnist. I like to describe processes, such as the performance of autopsies. The medical examiner is willing to let me write a column, but she insists that Stroger has to personally say it's okay. I know we've had our differences in the past, but there's the future to think about, and if he lets me do this, then I'll try to include something positive about him in the column. Who knows? It could be the start of a whole new beginning.

He bought it. Stroger gave the nod. I spent the morning with Jones, who turned out to be very quotable. "It is difficult to take fingerprints of the dead," she said, as she did just that, a line that could be the title of a mystery. "They really are not that cooperative."

There was also one of those details that I love: a down-to-earth woman who grew up in a small town in Pennsylvania, Dr. Jones used carpet needles and a regular pair of pliers instead of an expensive medical dura stripper that cost four times as much. And, the crowning detail: the primary tool she used to cut up bodies was not a scalpel, but a ten-inch Henckels kitchen knife, the kind of fancy German cutlery sold in the housewares section at Macy's. "They hold their edge, and they're a lot less expensive," she said. As if autopsies weren't creepy enough, autopsies with a kitchen knife.

There is a coda to the story. A few years later, when Dr. Jones made a medical ruling that Mayor Daley didn't like, he accused her of grandstanding, of doing hurried, shoddy work so she could get some attention. As much as loyalty was stressed in the old machine, Daley the Younger was willing to throw any friend or cringing underling beneath the bus if it scratched his itch at the moment. I'm sure the entirety of his thinking was: *She works for the county—screw her.* At his press conference, Daley didn't even seem certain whether the medical examiner was a man or a woman. As the one reporter who had bothered to get to know Dr. Jones, I was in position to point out that she was the exact opposite of the person that the mayor, in his flailing, blame-shifting fashion, was trying to portray—that she had never convened a press conference before in her career at Cook County, not one; that she didn't want attention on an ordinary day, never mind over a controversial high-profile suicide case; that she wouldn't clear her throat without permission from her boss; and that the mayor, as usual, was just lashing out at anybody who said anything he didn't like. I went to her defense because I knew she wouldn't defend herself—first, because nobody wanted to clash with Daley, and second, a person chooses to work among the dead for many reasons, including the possibility that they are more comfortable there than among the living.

12

A visit from the Angel Nacht

DEATH WEARS A BROWN SUIT. Not traditionally—traditionally it's neither brown nor a suit, but a black hooded gown, accessorized with a scythe and, often, a large hourglass.

I mean today, at this moment, in this instance, Death, in the form of me, is wearing a brown suit—not even a dark brown suit, but a sort of rich chocolaty brown. A thick fabric; you could make a passable bear costume out of it.

Not that I think of myself as "Death"—too grandiose a conceit, even for me. I think of myself as the "Angel Nacht." The *g* is hard—"Ahn-gull nachhht," the *hhh* being that harsh, dragging, back-of-the-throat sound that not all Americans can make. I thought it was German for "The Angel of the Night" or, as I believed, "The Dark Angel." Also known as Death. In all seriousness. Okay, not quite in all seriousness—there's a kind of grim lunge at bemusement to it. Any job that requires you to occasionally visit the grief-stricken relatives of the newly dead and pepper them with questions about the tragedy that has just destroyed their lives demands a certain ironic distance.

I'm sitting in a heavy wooden chair, legs crossed, hands draped limply over the armrests, in the anteroom of a lawyer's office in the Chicago Temple—an office building with a Gothic spire and a Methodist church on the ground floor, unexpectedly located in the heart of the Loop, just south of Daley Plaza. An eccentric structure with a tiny "Chapel in the Sky" twenty-five floors up, whose altarpiece is a wood carving of Jesus weeping over the skyline of Chicago circa 1952. For years the reverend living in its parsonage, twenty-two floors up, was said to have the only residential telephone in the Loop.

It's an old-fashioned law office, with glass-fronted oak bookcases, big wooden tables, and a waist-high mahogany rail with a spring-hinged gate leading to the secretarial area and the doors to the private offices of various lawyers.

Leon Despres bustles by, says he'll be right with me, and hurries to finish some business. I watch him go, a small, spry, white-haired, big-eared elderly man in eyeglasses, fussing about with papers, looking for something.

Take your time, I think. Death is patient.

I've got papers of my own, folded into thirds and tucked into my jacket pocket, and I touch them to make sure they're there—Despres's obituary, the summation of his life which will run in the newspaper the day after he dies. It begins, "Few things are sadder or more haunting than to imagine what Chicago might have been like had anyone listened to Leon Despres."

I consider that a particularly fine opening, and have buffed it for years. You could argue over one word: "anyone." Certainly he had supporters. There were like-minded individuals. Despres was alderman of Hyde Park's Fifth Ward for twenty years, from 1955 to 1975. But "more people" thuds when I try it—"had more people listened to Leon Despres"—so "anyone" it is, underscoring the image I paint of Despres as Chicago's Cassandra, rising in the city council chambers to continually denounce the official bigotry and folly of his day, all for naught.

(Though now that I read it again, "had more people listened" might indeed have been better—it indicts the reader a little, suggesting that if only you, personally, had gotten behind Despres, then things might have been different. "Anyone" lets you off the hook.)

I'm not planning to show Despres his obit—what elderly man would react well to that? But I have brought it nevertheless, for complex reasons, reasons I'm probably not the right person to try to sort out. I *may* show it to him—the need might arise. That, I tell myself, is why I brought it.

Most people think it's strange to routinely look at others and realize they're going to die and begin to act on that realization. Morbid. Friends are often surprised when they discover that I write advance obituaries—cheerfully, willingly, without being asked. It isn't my job; I just do it for fun. The subject usually come up when I casually mention some tidbit learned while writing the obituary of someone, and whoever I'm talking to says, "Oh, I didn't realize he's dead," and I breezily reply, "He's not."

It strikes them as ghoulish, the singling out of someone, such as the poor gentleman I'm waiting for now, the positing of his death, and then acting—it's almost like planning his murder—so as not to be inconvenienced later on, so as not to have to rush.

That isn't how I see it.

"Who would you rather write your obituary," I drawl, eyes dancing, enjoying their discomfort, "Some intern who's never heard of you, slapping your life story together in two hours on a Saturday night—or me, working on it for years?"

That isn't an exaggeration. I wrote Despres's obit for more than a decade. Meeting him wasn't necessary; I had enough information for three obituaries. It was more of a perk, one that I just couldn't deny myself. One of many side benefits of being the Angel Nacht—which I would discover, years later, is practically gibberish in German, and certainly doesn't mean anything close to "Angel of Death," which is how I thought of it—"Engel der Nacht" means "angel of the night," but that has a sexy ring to it, like an incubus. (A big drawback of trying to impress yourself in a language you don't understand is that your error comes to light if your subterranean fantasy life emerges into the brightly lit world of the actual.)

* * *

My first taste of the pleasures of obit writing came through a routine assignment. It was the day before Thanksgiving 1988—exactly one year after mayor Harold Washington died—when Al Raby passed away unexpectedly. It was early evening when we got the news, and I was just beginning my shift at the *Sun-Times*.

Raby had been an important, if little-remembered civil rights leader in Chicago. (Almost everyone is little remembered, sooner or later, fame being the brief period before a person is utterly forgotten. Writing obituaries teaches you that, big-time.) It was Raby who sued the Chicago Public Schools to deny them federal funds until they integrated, Raby who invited Martin Luther King Jr. to bring his open-occupancy campaign to Chicago. I can still see Dick Mitchell, our city editor, stand up—tall, ramrod straight, the dignity of a Masai prince, his deep black skin set off by a crisp white shirt and gold cufflinks—pointing at various reporters, calling to them across the newsroom, sending this one to the hospital to talk to the family, that one to Operation PUSH to track down Rev. Jesse Jackson. Me, he sent to the *Sun-Times* library to pull the clips. That I was pleased to receive this assignment should tell you much about what kind of reporter I am.

We all had to hustle because it was a few hours before deadline, and nobody, of course, had bothered to prepare an obituary for Al Raby. The *Sun-Times* doesn't have the staff to routinely do that kind of long-term planning. We have a newspaper to put out every day. And to be honest, none of us except for Dick knew who Al Raby had been before we started writing his obituary, an echo of the famous line, attributed to Lord Chesterton, that much of professional journalism consists of saying "Lord Such-and-Such Dead" to people who didn't know Lord Such-and-Such was ever alive.

A newspaper clip file is a unique collection of information, the product of decades of diligent, long-gone librarians cutting apart newspapers and squirreling away relevant stories by subject. Not only articles, but candidate biography forms, personal letters, anonymous telephone tips—typed light-blue carbon copies, or rough, crumbling beige newsprint, scribbled over with blunt lead pencils and red china markers. Nothing online can match it—a search engine buries you in generic, repetitive information, obscuring the telling details you are looking for, assuming they are there in the first place, which often they're not. Not everything is online, yet we're so tickled about all the information we can get on the Internet that we never seem to notice all the material that isn't there. The newspaper stopped gathering the clips in the late 1970s when computers moved to the fore, and the obituaries of people whose fruitful years came later invariably are less interesting, not because people live more constricted, less colorful lives nowadays—though it's always tempting to conclude that—but simply because it's harder to find the full scope of finely detailed information about them. With the Internet, you get the identical bland description echoed a thousand times.

Without a computer culling for you, it required a special kind of vision to run your eyes over all those stories, to rip through that clump of newsprint and recognize the relevant stuff, the parts that matter, and I was particularly pleased that a quote I dragged out of a block of verbiage from Richard J. Daley—"Who is this man, Raby?"—was used as the headline of the obituary. It is a pleasure to reach into a batch of yellowed clippings and extract somebody's story, to take a pile of dry, dead, brittle slips of crumbling newsprint—a handful of dust—mold them into a person, then breath life into your creation, if only for one day, if only for tomorrow.

* * *

After Abraham Lincoln Marovitz came to our apartment to marry Sam and Yuri, I naturally became interested in the judge and his long stroll across Chicago's stage.

Being on the night shift, I had plenty of time sitting around, passing the hours. It was easy to pull the clips and read them. It was educational. Marovitz had a complicated career—yes, he defended mobsters, but Marovitz had also enlisted in the marines in 1943, at age thirty-eight. The middle-aged private was assigned to desk duty, but Marovitz pulled strings so that he saw action in the Pacific ("Abe, your mother's never going to forgive me for this," said Adlai Stevenson, then special assistant to the secretary of the navy, arranging the transfer to send Marovitz into combat, where he was wounded.) There were mysteries. Marovitz went into law practice with his brothers Harold and Sydney. Then he wasn't in practice with Harold and Sydney anymore—what happened? And why didn't Marovitz ever run for governor? It seemed for a moment that he would; then he didn't. At the time he said that he vowed to his mother he'd stay a judge because dispensing justice was the highest calling a Jew could aspire to. But that has to just be a glib line, right? Who ignores a possible political career in deference to his mother? He sure didn't let her stop him from going to fight in the Philippines.

Then there was the question of marriage. Marovitz was what they used to call "a confirmed bachelor." What was that about? Could he be gay? I began piecing the facts together, what I could from the clips, and started writing his obituary—it seemed a waste not to. Marovitz was in his eighties. He wouldn't live forever. No point in doing this research twice.

But Marovitz held onto the ghost and, having finished his obituary, I branched out to others—broadcasters Harry Caray and Jack Brickhouse, ministers Billy Graham and Louis Farrakhan, writers Studs Terkel, Ann Landers, and Irv Kupcinet, entertainers Milton Berle, Frank Sinatra, and Bob Hope. Politicians Dan Rostenkowski, Jane Byrne, Ronald Reagan, and Chuck Percy. Anyone famous, old, and with a connection to Chicago.

Not only did the clips offer richer lives, but the subjects I wrote about were big in a way that is very rare nowadays, a certain omnipresence that the specialization of modern life usually thwarts—Brickhouse broadcast the Cubs, White Sox, Bulls, and Bears games all in the same season. He would bolt from one contest to another, his partners covering for him if the games overlapped. Irv Kupcinet wasn't just the main gossip columnist at the *Sun-Times*, but he had a TV talk show, *At Random*, and provided commentary for Bears games, alongside Brickhouse, for nearly a quarter century, when he wasn't acting in Hollywood movies or writing books or popping up as a linesman holding the chains during the Chicago Bears 73 to 0 demolition of the Washington Redskins in the 1940 National Football League championship game.

And they had longevity. They were not only big, but big for decades. Brickhouse was the first face seen on Chicago TV when WGN fired up its television station in 1948—and in 1983 he was master of ceremonies at the contest picking which Chicagoan would place the first cellular telephone call from a member of the general public, a PR stunt that involved a footrace in the parking lot of Soldier Field.

Kupcinet—everyone called him "Kup"—began as a sports writer at the *Chicago Times* in 1935, started his column in 1943, and was a major Chicago media presence through the 1940s and 1950s and 1960s (and 1970s and 1980s and 1990s). For his last thirty-four years at the paper, he had a tall, brassy secretary named Stella Foster—a moniker out of a *Superman* comic—and an office filled with photographs of himself with Harry Truman, with Sinatra, with Louis Armstrong. Before transcontinental jets became the way to cross the country, movie stars going from coast to coast would change trains in Chicago and pay an obligatory visit to Kup—the twentieth-century celebrity version of the portage. Kup had lunch with Humphrey Bogart and Lauren Bacall the day after they were married. Truman would phone him and ask him to keep an eye on his daughter Margaret when she was in town. While Kup was showing movie stars Gary Cooper and Veronica Lake around Chicago, selling war bonds, the blonde bombshell gazed at the cowboy actor and asked, "Do you want to fuck me?" Kup put that moment in his autobiography. On page two.

Kup's TV show ran on Saturdays for twenty-seven years, a late night talkfest that literally had no finish time—they would talk until they got tired and decided to stop. His guests ranged from Richard Nixon to Linda Lovelace, the porn star, from Alger Hiss to Malcolm X, Yul Brynner to Robert F. Kennedy. Carl Sandburg once wandered off stage in the middle of the program, saying he had to go "wee-wee." Abbie Hoffman lit up a joint, on air, and Kup threw him off the show.

The barrier between journalists and entertainers wasn't as high as it is now. When Kup went on vacation, he might stay at comedian Jack Benny's house, and crooner Bing Crosby once stepped in to write his column while he was away. The *Sun-Times* held a party for the twenty-fifth anniversary of Kup's column: Bob Hope was the master of ceremonies.

My twenty-fifth anniversary at the newspaper was in 2012. Let's just say I didn't expect a party and wasn't disappointed. I couldn't dream of living a life like Jack Brickhouse or Irv Kupcinet did—nowhere close. The times have changed, the media has fractured into a million pieces, I never had my own show on television—but at least I could be the guy who knew about these people, and just knowing about them was something. Most everyone my age had no idea about what these lives had been like.

Maybe it was also my way of immersing myself into the city, of trying to become a Chicagoan. I wasn't here when Frank Pape was famous for being the toughest cop in Chicago, with a hidden suede-lined pocket his wife sewed into his suit coat for his nickel-plated .38 Special, which must have worked, because he killed nine bad guys—though some he waited for in ambush and mowed down with a Tommy gun. But I could make up for lost time by learning about him, by giving him a proper send-off, along with all the other outsized, distinctive characters who made Chicago what it is.

Kup's credentials for coolness were off the charts. He got in a notorious brawl with Dizzy Dean and most of the St. Louis Cardinals' starting lineup in the lobby of a Tampa hotel in 1937. Lenny Bruce did a scathing routine about Kup; Saul Bellow based a character on him in *Humboldt's Gift* ("He looked haughty, creased and sleepy, like certain oil-rich American Indians from Oklahoma," Bellow writes). Kup's friend Otto Preminger gave him bit parts in two of his movies, *Advise and Consent* and *Anatomy of a Murder*. A. J. Liebling discusses Kup's column in *Second City*. Publicists would drive him places just to get his undivided attention. After the infamous Lincoln Park Towing hooked Kup's Cadillac in front of the Lyric Opera, they took the car—which a dealer lent to him, in return for occasional plugs in his column—to their lot, ran the plates, and realizing whose car they had towed, returned the vehicle to where they found it. Now *that's* clout.

And yet. Time had thundered by Kup and his contemporaries when I met them. When I started writing Kup's obit, he was in his eighties;

his fame was on the wane; the celebrity gossip he specialized in was now available everywhere. Having Nat King Cole's private number didn't mean anything anymore. The paper's editor ordered Kup to stop accepting his free cars; it looks bad. Nigel Wade had retired to a cottage in the South of France—the benefit, he said, of living his entire professional career on an expense account. A pair of Canadians came in to run the paper, and paying attention to Kup, honoring his various anniversaries and traditions—every year he chartered a boat and took Purple Heart vets on a Lake Michigan cruise—began to seem an annoyance. I was constantly explaining Kup to people: "Don't you understand? This is the guy who crashed Queen Elizabeth II's coronation rehearsal by flashing his Chicago police press card. When he met Marilyn Monroe, she was still a brunette." Fine, they said, *you* go cover Kup's last Purple Heart cruise. I did; Tony Bennett showed up, unannounced and unpaid, to sing for the wounded vets.

I began to feel like the keeper of the flame, the official mourner. It was my responsibility; if I didn't write their obituaries, we wouldn't have one ready, and some intern would hurriedly scrape it together, or more likely, we would use the Associated Press obit, which might overlook the fact that Ronald Reagan was the only president born in Illinois and that as an infant he lived in an apartment over a storefront on the South Side of Chicago.

Yes, there were a few delicate moments. We had a secretary named Shirlee DeSanti, an elderly lady who, when I met her, was the paper's grandmotherly receptionist, sitting at a desk at the front door, a twinkly white-haired gal who liked to set out plates of cookies. But she had a long editorial career before that, working on *Panorama* with Herman Kogan, a revered Chicago journalist and historian (as is his son, Rick). She was his liaison with writers like John Steinbeck and Nelson Algren. In 1963, Kogan sent Shirlee down to a comedy club to ask Woody Allen to write something, resulting in the comedian's first published story, for which he received twenty dollars. When John Belushi was filming *Continental Divide* at the Sun-Times Building, DeSanti approached the comic and tried to persuade him to let her tap-dance in the film. I found this out chatting with her at the reception desk, nibbling a cookie, listening carefully, asking polite questions before trotting back to my desk to update her obituary. That could be seen as being a trifle cold, I suppose, but how to get the stories otherwise? When she was dead it would be too late.

Someone had to write them; someone had to push for them. The closest I ever came to a fistfight in the newsroom was the night in 2003 when Bill

Mauldin died. While they were dimly aware that he was a cartoonist of some sort, nobody on the desk knew Mauldin had changed not just editorial cartooning, but how the American public views war, with his slouching, exhausted, dirt-covered Willie and Joe characters in *Stars and Stripes* during World War II. They did not know that he had won two Pulitzer Prizes, had worked at the *Sun-Times* for twenty-five years—we were his own goddamn newspaper—where he had penned the famous drawing of a weeping Lincoln statue the day Kennedy was killed. Nor did the editor I informed of the fact particularly *care*—it was late. He initially wanted to give the obit thirty-five lines, which is the length we'd run for the obituary of a popular florist.

* * *

I was among the few people at the paper who had spoken with Mauldin, first phoning him when the US Postal Service put Willie and Joe on a stamp. Having dug up his number, I kept it, and would call every year on his birthday to check up on him, the way that Snoopy would visit Mauldin in *Peanuts* on Veteran's Day for a root beer. Readers remembered Maudlin fondly, and I figured they'd like an update about him. I sure did.

One year a woman answered the phone and identified herself as "Norma Jean." "Norma Jean?" I said, without thinking. "He divorced you in 1946. What are you doing there?" Because I had written his obit, I knew who she was, and because I knew her, she answered my question, pouring out her heart about the problems she was having with Bill and his struggle with alcoholism, as if we were old friends. I guess she needed to talk to someone. That root beer of Snoopy's, it turns out, was Charles Schulz's sly finger wag in Mauldin's direction.

That is the drawback—or benefit, or both—of doing obituaries. You know so much about a person, and while decorum insists you keep the information to yourself, knowledge, like water, has a way of dribbling out. Mauldin's first wife asked me not to write anything about his drinking problem. "It would kill him," she said. So I held onto the notes for five years, until he died, then wrote a column about his battle.

In that instance, I was restrained. But the urge to show off sometimes became irresistible. I was doing an interview with Leonard Solomon, who ran a big wine and cheese importing business. Did I know, he asked me, that he was related to someone at the *Sun* . . . ?

"Essee Kupcinet is your sister," I said, interrupting. Kup's wife was born Esther Solomon, and I wrote her obit too, while I was writing Kup's. She was a wisecracking, chain-smoking dame, and her life held too many piquant details not to—she produced Kup's TV show, and once, while he was on camera talking about his "audition" with the pope, Essee could be heard off-camera, hissing "It's *audience*, you idiot!" During the 1940s, she went out on the town wearing a blouse stenciled with his column logo. "She was a firecracker . . ." the obit began. Essee was buried with a pack of Pall Mall cigarettes.

At the time of my visit with Solomon, Kup and Essee were still alive. "I know more about her than you do," I told her brother. Leonard Solomon eyed me dubiously, so I decided to show him. "Her middle name is Joan but it used to be Janice," I said. He nodded, slowly. "Do you know why she changed it?" I asked. Solomon shook his head no. I smiled, paused, then leaned in, as if sharing a confidence. "Mad for Joan Crawford," I whispered.

But having such in-depth knowledge was good for more than showing off. Because I wrote Marovitz's obit, I knew that his secretary, Mickey Curtin, was not just a loyal gal Friday for half a century. They were lovers, a hidden *Abie's Irish Rose* romance. He was Jewish, she was Catholic, and in the 1920s that meant they couldn't easily wed, particularly not given his bond with his mother. So they kept it secret, and their relationship survived into the 1990s, when Curtin was in a nursing home with Alzheimer's.

And then she died. I suppose I could have written the "Longtime secretary, 93, dies" obit and ignored the risqué backstory. But at this point, it seemed to me, the years had wiped away any need for discretion. The romance was the most interesting part of her life—why keep hiding it? Or as poet Robert Lowell wrote, "Yet why not say what happened?" The 1920s were a long time ago. The woman was dead. So I wrote her obituary, about this nearly seventy-year-long love affair, without the benefit of a marriage certificate, where the judge paid for her nursing-home care and remained faithful to the end, visiting her regularly, despite the emotional toll it took on him. Why go through it? Why visit someone who doesn't recognize him? "I have to," Marovitz said. "I love her."

Sun-Times editorial guidelines require that every obituary be read to the next of kin before being published. Pleased with the sweet story that I had unearthed, I dutifully phoned Curtin's brother, an elderly priest, and began to read him her obituary.

To my surprise, Rev. Curtin was not nearly as pleased with my work as I was. In fact, he asked that I not print it at all. "You know, I should have called the judge instead," I said, trying to extract myself from the conversation. "As far as I'm concerned, *he's* the next of kin."

My worries were not on the impact that revealing this secret might have—everyone in the judge's life, his friends and family, of course had long known about the couple—but on losing a good story. In my view, the priest was ashamed of something he should have been proud of. But by the time I got Marovitz on the phone, Curtin's brother had already talked to him.

"I've respected their wishes for seventy years," Marovitz said. Sure, I could have printed the obit anyway, but with both the priest and the judge against it, it was asking for trouble over a story that, from a straight news perspective, need never be told. Besides, it stank of ingratitude. The only reason I knew about Marovitz in the first place was that he had agreed to come to my house to marry my brother. Defying him over this seemed cold thanks.

Thinking hard, I came up with a solution. "Your honor," I said, "what if I wrote it, not as an obituary, but as a column? I won't mention any names, so anybody who doesn't know won't be told. And those who already know, already know." The priest would have no basis to complain. Marovitz said that was fine with him.

So I began the column "A man and a woman met in Chicago seventy years ago and fell in love" and told their story, never identifying either one. Marovitz not only wasn't angry, but kept the column folded in his wallet and would take it out at parties and show it off—I would hear back from people who had seen him do this. And for the rest of his life, the few years he had left, he would take me to lunch at the Standard Club around the anniversary of her death. I think it made him feel better, perhaps somehow closer to her; I know for me it was strange and wonderful, to lunch with a man born in 1905, a man who grew up in the West Side Jewish ghetto around Maxwell Street, a lightweight boxer in the early 1920s, to have him link his arm in mine as we walked out of the Federal Building, as old people will do, quietly talking, as if the history of the city had come alive, and was telling me about itself.

I don't go to many funerals, but I went to Judge Marovitz's. Much of old-time Chicago turned out—Mayor Daley gave the eulogy with rare eloquence. As I scanned the crowd, a familiar face, beneath a stylish black hat, popped out. A very famous face. Sitting in the crowd by herself, just another mourner. I slid over, apologized for bothering her. But what was she doing here?

"I love him," she said. "Beyond wonderful. He was one of my inspirations. He was a dear friend to me when I most needed him."

And what, exactly, had Judge Marovitz done for her?

She smiled, sphinxlike, and replied: "I'm not saying."

I believe that every man would like a mystery woman to show up at his funeral. But for the mystery woman to be Oprah Winfrey, well that should give you a hint of just how special Abe Marovitz truly was.

* * *

It didn't always work out well.

When Joe Colucci was dying, I sat down with his son Jimmy in the social room at the Division Street Russian Baths. We talked about his father and I took notes. This isn't something I'd do with a stranger—"Hi, I'm Neil Steinberg from the *Sun-Times*—I hear your dad is about to die; mind talking about him a bit now so we won't have to go to the trouble when the moment comes?"

But I knew Joe and I knew Jimmy, from my years at the baths. We talked about the baths, about what kind of guy Joe was—he had been a newsboy, and always supported newsboy organizations. Jimmy said his father lived in River Forest.

"So he's a mobster," I remarked, thoughtlessly, scribbling in my long, thin notebook, not looking up.

"No, no, no," Jimmy said, darkening. "What makes you think that?"

"Everybody who lives in River Forest is a mobster," I replied. I'm not the Jedi Council, and can be swayed by stereotypes just like the next guy. There were whispers that the baths were a mob hangout. Maybe I was channeling Art Petacque.

We left it at that. I pulled the clip file for Joe, but didn't look inside—just shoved the battered beige envelope into my briefcase and carried it around for two weeks. Then Joe died and I finally read them. Colucci hadn't just been "an alleged crime syndicate hoodlum," and a known West Side bookie. He was also one of the names on the infamous chart of Chicago organized crime "top hoods" that the head of the Chicago police intelligence unit displayed before the Senate organized crime hearings in 1963; toward the bottom, yes, but on the same list as mob bosses Tony Accardo and Sam Giancana.

I phoned Jimmy and told him what was in the clips.

"Why do you have to put that in?" he said. "Can't you leave that out?"

"Jimmy, the *Tribune* has the same clip file," I said. "They're certainly going to print it. If I leave it out, they'll wonder why, and realize that I belong to the Russian Baths—I've written about being a member. I could lose my job."

"Well, take out the stuff that I told you then," he said. "I don't want to be involved."

He didn't want to be quoted in his own dad's obit.

"Jimmy," I said, "your quotes are the only parts that *aren't* about him being a mobster."

He said he didn't care, and I agreed. Leaving out the mob connection would have been corrupt—the bill for all those free backrubs come due. Leaving out the son saying what a swell guy his dad was, well, if that's what Jimmy wanted, it was a favor I could manage.

The obituary I wrote focused on the baths, but mentioned the bookmaking allegations—the man was never convicted of anything, and maybe I was overcompensating by putting it in. The *Tribune*, it turned out, had different clips—they ignored the bookmaking charges altogether and focused on Colucci being subpoenaed to testify regarding mob drug sales and on how a deputy superintendent on the police force got busted to captain just for being caught playing cards with Colucci. It also quoted a Russian Baths patron calling him "the last of the true Chicagoans."

Still, I felt bad about the whole thing, and I didn't go back to the baths for a year.

* * *

I first noticed Leon Despres's name in December 1996, the twentieth anniversary of Richard J. Daley's death. The paper printed a page of reminiscences from significant figures of the Daley era under the headline "Pals, foes remember 'The Mayor.'"

The last word was given to Despres, then eighty-eight. Not that what he said was so unusual—it wasn't. He credited Daley for being elected mayor for six terms and having flexibility on all matters "except the racial issue." "Who would think he would ever tolerate a Picasso in front of the Civic Center?" he said. "I'm sure in Daley's eyes the statue must have looked crazy."

Nothing profound. But eighty-eight? That's getting up there. The downside of writing obits is you have to wait for years to see your work in print. Computer systems change. They tend to get lost. Eighty-eight! Why not stack the deck a little?

So I pulled Despres' clips—a pile of fat envelopes, three inches thick—and began to read.

He became the alderman of Hyde Park's Fifth Ward in the mid-1950s. Many consider that time a halcyon age of social certainty and family values. Maybe so. But it also was an era of nightmarish repression, of puppet aldermen jostling each other to praise Richard J. Daley, a mayor so concerned with the possibility of unruly citizens denouncing him from the gallery that he filled the public section in the council chambers with "rulies"—city workers on the clock whose job was to sit there all day and not be unruly.

Despres had been the sole opposition to Daley, the lone voice of dissent, the solitary "no" in 49-to-1 votes, and he took the heat for it. "Despres has been told to shut up—in one form or another—more than any grown man in Chicago," Mike Royko wrote in the *Daily News* in 1972.

Nevertheless, Despres spoke his mind, ceaselessly, eloquently. "The Board of Education is short-changing the children of Chicago," he said on January 17, 1963, calling on the city council to "electrify the world" and "vote for the greatness of our city" by withholding tax funds to the schools until the board ended segregation. "It is educating nearly all children in damaging racial isolation. Separate education is never equal education.... The board is providing inferior facilities and teaching staffs for most Negro children."

This was the quote that got under my skin, that got me thinking about what might have happened if people had listened to Despres, the heartbreaking loss and damage to generations of Chicagoans that might have been avoided, the problems that might have been addressed then, when they were smaller and more manageable, that instead were allowed to grow and deepen and fester and create the havoc we see today.

But people did not listen. Not even black aldermen, who denounced Despres, just as they would later denounce Martin Luther King Jr. as a meddlesome outsider, so eager were they to be blessed with a smile and a pat on the head from Daley. (The deal was, Daley permitted them authority within their own wards, to be kings of their own little fiefdoms, rolling in patronage and power, and in return they sold out their own people and supported him blindly in everything else. The true sin of corruption: ignoring the wider public good for narrow personal gain.) Meanwhile Despres, who, though white, was still sometimes referred to as "the lone Negro on the city council," didn't just march at Selma himself: he chartered two planes to take marchers with him down to King's epic civil rights protest (joined by Charles Chew, a flashy Rolls-Royce-driving, African American maverick who served six years as alderman of the Seventeenth Ward, giving Despres an occasional ally in the council, before being elected to the state senate). Roll that around in your mind one more time: *Despres chartered two planes to take marchers down to Selma.*

Then there was his private life. His mother had decided that the University of Chicago Laboratory Schools—a progressive academy founded by John Dewey—was not challenging enough for her son, so she sent him to France to study in 1922, when he was fourteen. Despres arrived in Paris less than a year after Hemingway did, and was wandering its streets while the writer was still scribbling poems in cafes. Despres saw James Joyce's newly published *Ulysses* in the window of Sylvia Beach's Shakespeare & Co. bookshop on the rue de L'Odeon. He returned to Chicago, got his undergraduate and law degrees from the University of Chicago, went to work for the National Labor Relations Board, became a socialist. In the summer of 1937, Despres went to Mexico on a three-week vacation, and at the request of a lawyer friend, brought a letter and a suitcase of clothing to Leon Trotsky. The exiled Russian revolutionary was staying in a Mexico City suburb, at the "Blue House" belonging to painter Diego Rivera. During the visit, Despres commissioned Rivera to do a pastel of his wife, Marian. While she was sitting for the portrait, Despres took Rivera's wife, the feminist art icon Frida Kahlo, to the movies, to see a French film, *La kermesse heroica.*

Given the reputation of the artist couple for open-mindedness in personal matters—Kahlo was already having an affair with Trotsky the summer that Despres visited—you had to wonder, was it just that? A trip to the movies?

"She was very attractive, very pretty," Despres said. "We had a good time."

Most Chicagoans don't know who Frida Kahlo is, and here was a man who went on a date with her.

But that wasn't why I asked him to lunch. My burning question wasn't "What was Frida Kahlo like?" or "Did Diego Rivera screw your wife?" Rather, I had been struck—awestruck really—by his words, his positions, his prescience. It was Despres who stopped the Chicago Theological Seminary from tearing down Frank Lloyd Wright's Robie House to make room for a dorm, creating the city's first architectural preservation group to do it; who spoke out against public-housing high-rises, not from the vantage point of hindsight, like everybody else, but while they were being built; who fought lead paint before its hazards were commonly known. Despres was like a man of today transported back in time, challenging the accepted bigotries and habitual mistakes of the past with a blast of contemporary outrage. He was right about almost everything. "He has been in the forefront of just about every decent, worthwhile effort made to improve life in this city," cheered Royko, who didn't cheer many people.

I wanted to meet Despres, wanted to know: How did you do it? How did you stand alone in the city council for twenty years, introducing resolutions you knew wouldn't pass, that you knew would receive one vote—yours—making speeches people would ignore or ridicule, knowing you'd lose every time but fighting anyway? Why did you never compromise, never do your best but then give in and get what you could for yourself?

Despres finally was ready, and we headed downstairs and to a nearby office building that has a restaurant in its atrium. We settled ourselves at a small table. He ordered a glass of white wine. "It was really very rewarding to be alderman, because it was an entry into political and governmental life," he began, diplomatically. Despres talked about community, about how being alderman allowed him to see things he would have missed—he viewed being an alderman rather in the same way I viewed being a reporter, as an interesting job. The things he believed in, he said, he knew were true, then, and over time became accepted by everyone, for the most part. His rabid foes—aldermen like Tom Keane, one of several who threatened to punch Despres unless he stopped talking, or Vito Marzullo, who once called Despres "a nitwit, a vicious person, and a menace to the city council and the public at large," and other Daley henchmen—ultimately didn't matter. Despres was always looking beyond them. "I would really have to laugh at these fellows, sometimes, they would get up and attack me so virulently," he said. "I would really laugh inside myself because I knew they were just building support for me. That was very helpful."

Of course I wrote a column about our lunch—why sit on the fascinating facts of his life? They'd be fresh again when the time came, which in Despres's case had to wait until 2009, when he was 101. "Despres is still laughing," I concluded, in the column. "I realized, then, that he didn't need my sympathy, because he hadn't lost at all. He had won. First, he's still here. Thomas Keane is gone. Vito Marzullo is gone. Daley and his machine are gone. But Despres is sipping his white wine, savoring life around him."

* * *

It is not always easy, figuring out somebody's story. That's another reason I enjoy writing obituaries—where else do you get the chance to look at a person's life, beginning to end, up close, to feel the weave of the fabric, study the contours, and render some kind of judgment?

John F. Kennedy Jr. crashed his plane in 1999 and they called me in on a Saturday to write the obit—I had become the go-to obit guy, having taken a realm previously ignored and made it into something the paper thought was valuable. Or maybe they just needed a body to do the chore and they knew that I, deluded enough to believe it was important, would drop everything and come in. I pulled the clips and became lost in Kennedy's infancy—he was born November 25, 1960, between the time his father was elected president and his inauguration, the only child ever born to a US president-elect. I hadn't realized that. Every coo, gurgle, and tottering first step that Kennedy took was publicized. I began his obituary, "He came into the world already famous."

The art is to compress an entire life into that opening sentence, to sheer away the passing crises and distractions and reach for what it all *means*. That's good for an obituary, but it can be an unsettling thing when examining your own life.

About the time I took Leon Despres to lunch, my brother Sam took a hard look at his own life and came to a troubling realization: he was a limo guy. Approaching thirty-five, with a wife and two kids and a house in the suburbs, he worried that, as enjoyable as the day-to-day might be, with a Lincoln Town Car in the driveway, rubbing elbows with NBA players and rock stars and top executives, and plenty of time to hit the Division Street Russian Baths with his brother, he was still spending his life driving other people where they wanted to go. Not a bad life, running a limo company, but not the life he thought he signed up for either. That's not why he'd gone through four years at Washington University. He was plagued by the idea:

there's got to be more than this. He is my brother, after all. Contentment is fleeting with Steinbergs. We're always wondering what's over the next hill. So Sam quit the limo company and went back to school—DePaul—to get his master's degree in finance.

That took guts. I could relate to being driven forward by the scourge of unfocused ambition. But I tend to hedge my bets, to reach for the future with one hand while clinging to the security of the present with the other. I'll slip away from the paper for a year to raise my kid and write a book, but only while clutching the tether of paternity leave, so I know I can find my way back at the end. I'm not a leaper.

Not so with Sam. He closes his eyes, lets go, folds his arms over his chest and does a trust drop backward into the hands of Fate. He did that both moving to Japan and again coming back to live with me. Though five years younger than I am, he got married before I did, had children before I did, and bought a condo before Edie and I did. A house too. Me, I would have stayed with the limo company as a base while going to school at night. Not Sam. He quit the company cold—done. He walked away from the sliver of equity the owner was forever dangling in front of him and went to DePaul. Pay the check, grab your hat, and walk out the door.

Part of it is due to his ability to make decisions. I've always admired that. When Sam arrived in Chicago from Japan, he needed a bed, so I took him to a mattress store. I'll never forget the transaction. He walked into the store, saw a promising mattress, went over to it, lay down, closed his eyes for a moment, then got up and said, "This one's fine," and headed toward the counter to pay for it.

"Wait a minute!" I cried. Wasn't he going to try out the other mattresses? To compare and contrast? To see how much better the more expensive mattress/box spring combinations felt and how much worse the lesser sets felt, and perform the complicated cost-benefit analysis before making his decision? That's what I'd do. Try every mattress, agonize, leave the store, think about it, come back the next day, do it again, flip a coin, eventually draw Edie in for consultation, and then, finally, reach some sort of tortured decision.

In a word, No. This mattress is fine. The price is acceptable. End of story. That's Sam.

Still, having made the decision to quit his job and go back to school didn't mean the consequences were easy to bear. Now he found himself a college student, again, this time in his mid-thirties with a wife and two kids and a house in the suburbs and no income, which felt even worse than being a limo guy had felt. Your job is your status, and without a job, you're nobody.

"You did the right thing," I kept telling him. "You're like Tom Hanks in *Castaway*. You had to try to get off the island or you were going to die there. So now you're on the raft, waiting for that tanker to show up. Hang on. The tanker's coming."

He graduated from DePaul, went to work for Morgan Stanley, the investment firm, a grueling entry-level job that involved luring potential investors to seminars and pressuring them to give him their money to manage for them. A miserable *Glengarry Glen Ross* existence of cold calls and tip sheets, of setting up easels at the front of windowless hotel conference rooms, of wheedling wary seniors and distant acquaintances, a life I wouldn't wish on a dog, but one that Sam assaulted with his usual enthusiasm and hard work. It was unpleasant to even listen to what his routine was like; I couldn't imagine living it.

Wasted effort anyway. Sam scrabbled up the greasy pole at Morgan Stanley for three years and was laid off one day along with a thousand other employees. "At least you know it's nothing personal," I told him.

Casting around for some kind of job with a future, he signed up for a spot in an Enterprise Rent-A-Car management-training program. But then he blew out something in his lower intestine. He needed minor surgery, and was in so much pain he couldn't make it through the program, and was unemployed, uninsured, at home in pain. The months rolled up. We'd meet for lunch, I'd buck him up, or try to. What can I do? Be there, take him out, listen carefully, offer money if he needed it—he didn't; Yuri's family was helping—spoon out advice, which he didn't need either, and pick up the check. "You can take me out to lunch after you're rich," I'd say. I couldn't think of anything else to do. What else could there possibly be? I pressed Metra tickets on him. He was obviously struggling, but I had faith in Sam, faith that he would see himself through. He was smart—he would figure it out, identify the path to take, find a solution, and eventually he did.

"Neil," Sam said. "Can't you help me?"

13

"A lot of broken hearts"

"HOW OLD DO YOU think I am?" she asked, turning her face under the streetlight; a worn, freckled face, under crinkly red hair, a face spotted with open sores. She looked about forty-five. Trying to be kind, I suggested she might be thirty-five.

"I'm thirty-one," she said. Her real name was Pamela Bolton, but everybody called her "Cotton" for the drawl in her voice that harked back to her youth in St. Louis. "I come from good family," she said. "If you had told me when I was ten years old that I would be out here doing this, I would have laughed."

"Out here" was Cicero Avenue and "doing this" was being a prostitute. I had spent the evening with Cook County Sheriff's police, picking up hookers and arresting them, a spinning revolving door that found the prostitutes back on the street before the cops finished filling out the paperwork for their arrest. I had my story. We were about to call it a night. But I wanted a sidebar—a photo of a streetwalker and a secondary article, a profile of who a hooker was, what her life was like. I wanted to talk to one we weren't in the process of arresting, since being busted made the women surly and silent.

We saw Bolton on the street and pulled over. She didn't flinch at the approach of three men—a cop, a reporter, and a photographer—and was not at all concerned with being arrested herself. "Oh baby," she said. "I walk Cicero Avenue like it's legal."

We only talked for about five minutes—about her kids, her family. "My daddy is a police," she said. About how she could leave the life at any time she likes, and sometimes does, but always comes back. It baffled me that men would pick up somebody like this and have sex with her—I was uncomfortable standing on the same street she was standing on, breathing the same air.

The story included a line that I would later regret—it wasn't said by Bolton, but by one of the county cops who had arrested her hundreds of times. "We know she has hepatitis," a vice investigator told me. "We believe she has AIDS, but she won't admit it."

That was a sharp detail, and I didn't hesitate to put it in my story. Three weeks later someone picked up Pamela Bolton, put a gun in her mouth and pulled the trigger, then dumped her body on the side of the road in West Garfield Park. Three weeks is a long time, and maybe the killing was completely unconnected with my story suggesting she had AIDS. I like to think the two were unconnected, that it was a coincidence. The cops never found the killer, so it's not like I can ask him. But she had been a street hooker for a dozen years and nobody ever murdered her before. I wouldn't have put that quote in, had I thought it might get her killed. But I didn't think about it until it was too late.

* * *

Her death shook me. Not tremendously. I don't want to exaggerate. I wasn't crushed. Rather, I was taken aback, made a little less cavalier, a little more skittish. It made me pause. Partly because I hadn't even bothered myself about whether it was indeed true—I just printed what the cop said. After Pam Bolton, I'm not sure I would have put Delores Dorsett and her cocaine baby into the paper as blithely as I did ten years earlier, at least not without giving what I came to call "The Speech," a little preliminary warning I deliver to people who might not be fully cognizant, who might not be factoring in all the consequences of publicity.

"You understand that I write for a newspaper," I tell them. "That I'm talking to you because I'm going to put what you say into an article, which will appear in the newspaper, which people will then read."

Part of that is selfish, a desire not to waste my time. You can talk to a person for half an hour, and only when you say "And you spell your name . . . ?" will their features cloud as the terrible realization dawns upon them that you have been jotting down their words for an ulterior motive. "Hey," they say, alarmed, drawing back, "you're not going to put this in the *newspaper* are you?"

I once ran into a guy I knew at college, Andy Hess. He had wanted to be a writer, just like I did. Now he worked at Custom Medical Stock Photo, on Irving Park Road, the nation's largest supplier of medical images. Andy catalogued slides of bubonic plague and horse intestines spilling out tapeworm. I bumped into him in Friar Tuck's, an East Lake View bar, learned what he did for a living, and invited myself to visit his workplace, to look at the horrendous photos of limbs that had been mangled by farm machinery and exotic African diseases left to do their devastation unchecked. I remember looking through a magnifying loop and shooting my hand out to steady myself against the light table, so I didn't pitch forward onto it in a swoon. His niche business was a perfect subject for a column—a strange, unexpected, and disturbing corner of the city that the reader heretofore never imagined existed.

After that column ran, I got a phone call from Michael Mages, whose hardware store was directly across the street from Custom Medical Stock Photo. If I could write about a photo business, he said, his tone implying that it was a questionable thing to do, why not write about his hardware store? It was, he said, a fascinating place and historic too. I was dubious. A hardware store? But he was on the line, so I asked questions. How old is the store? Eighty years old—this year. *Anniversary stories*, I thought, *bleh*. And eighty years, not even a hundred. The hardware store had been started by his grandfather. "In the same spot?" I wondered. Yes, the same spot, he said. The same store fixtures. That helped.

"How many employees do you have?" I asked, idly casting about, still hoping to thank him and ring off the line, saving myself a trip back to Irving Park Road. None, he said. He was the only employee. His mother used to do the books, but he had to let her go.

I told him I'd be there.

A few days later I walked into the narrow store, only twenty feet across, with floors worn to bare gray wood and oak display cabinets with curved glass—the place was built as a bakery about 1910.

"This is a treasure," said Mages, forty-five, by way of greeting. The inventory was old—he carried white rubber sink stoppers, wooden clothespins. The nails were in bins, not boxes. The shelves were dusty. Purchases were wrapped in brown paper and twine.

He had posted a sheet of paper behind the cash register with the names of all the relatives who had ever worked there, along with the locations of their grave markers, which he frequently visited. Mages was at the store nine hours a day, from 8:30 to 5:30 p.m., six days a week. As a hobby he bowled. His average was 125.

"I'm going to write about this," I cautioned him, "but people are going to feel sorry for you. I want you to understand that."

He didn't care. He wanted the store publicized. He wanted to attract business—the big chain hardware stores were killing him. Heck, he had asked the Irving Park Historical Society to include his store on its house walk. They turned him down.

The column touched upon his relationship with his brother, a corporate big shot, and his father, who had been a demanding boss. Mages showed me a golden-plated claw hammer on a plaque he had arranged for Stanley Hand Tools to send his father for the store's anniversary five years earlier. "At the seventy-fifth anniversary he was pretty sick," said Mages. "He was in seventh heaven with this thing. He brought it to show people at the synagogue. He did everything but take it to bed with him. It was the one thing I did in my life for him that he really appreciated." That last sentence hung in the air of the empty store.

The column didn't change anything, of course, and two years later Michael Mages was dead, at forty-seven—I only found out because his brother called, hoping I would publicize the sale of the hardware store's fittings. Again, not my fault—he had troubles when I found him. And the cause was cancer, the family said, though in my view it was clearly loneliness and disappointment.

Andy Hess—and I'd never put the two together before—the guy across the street at the medical image bank, also died suddenly and young, a few years after the column ran. Maybe the whole *Angel Nacht* routine hits closer to home than I realize. But it wasn't me—life can be very hard, fraught with tragedy and failure, and sometimes people are ground down before their time. Sometimes they can't take it anymore and give up. You want to err on the side of human kindness. My job requires that I tramp through the lives of a lot of people, and while that doesn't then make me responsible for what happens to them forever after, it also makes me reluctant to add to their woes, if I can avoid it.

* * *

The city herds countless people past you in a steady, striding stream. Most you ignore and they in turn ignore you. But a few come into your world, for one reason or another, for a second or an hour or a week or a decade. You could treat them harshly—a lot of people are reflexively mean, the armor they use to deflect life. But to be a decent person, you need what they call in Yiddish *rachmanis*—pity, compassion. When I worked the night shift, the city desk would get calls from the lonely, the elderly, the drunk, the baffled—in the years before the Internet, if you didn't know something, if you had a wager in a bar, and wanted an authoritative answer, you'd phone a newspaper and ask.

One regular we called "Dictionary Dick"—an elderly man who wanted to know the definitions of words. Some on the desk got annoyed with Dictionary Dick, or said they were busy and hung up, but I would trot off to the dictionary and check for him, if I didn't know the word off the top of my head. Why not? We had time on our hands. A drunk lady who said she was Jane Byrne sometimes phoned. Maybe she was the former mayor, maybe she wasn't, but I believed her. She *sounded* like Jane Byrne. So I would listen to the slurred opinions of the erstwhile mayor. Byrne was out of office for more than thirty years. A lot of time to fill.

One night, a guy calling himself Roger Rhenium phoned. He had, he told the editorial assistant who took his call, developed a motor to power flying saucers. He left his phone number so a reporter could call back. I phoned him, and we began a dance common to those who claim to have discovered wonders—machines of perpetual motion, bleeding statues, cold fusion. They always say: the wonder is real but you can't see it, not quite yet. It's here, just beyond this curtain. It isn't finished; you can take a quick peek, but I can't let you look at it directly, or at length, because you'd steal it. Look, but not too closely.

My theory is they want the pleasure of attention, the status of recognition, without the letdown that actual scrutiny would bring. Rhenium knew the motor would work, he said, but it wasn't ready to be shown to the world. He just thought the press should be informed of this historic breakthrough bearing down on us.

That's what he said when I phoned him. So I kept his phone number. And that was perverse of me. Kindness only goes so far in this business. We are not, as I said, a social service. Every six months or so, I would call him—how is the flying saucer engine going, Roger? Could we come by and look at it? Could we take a picture? Always the same answer—almost ready, thanks for asking, but not quite yet.

Part of it was my bristling at the inherent offensiveness of the deluded—they've fooled themselves, a task accomplished with breathtaking ease, and now they assume that everybody else can be fooled too. Not that this is conscious—they seem to be sincere, and seem to believe they're spreading the truth. They think they're savvy. They think they're geniuses. But they're actually naïve, stunted, ignorant, walling themselves off from the knowledge and protective incredulity that intelligent people use to evaluate the world.

I want to put Roger's engine on a table in a well-lit room and look at it, want to make him show it to me. Here is a man who phones a newspaper to say he has invented something fantastic; there should be consequences for that. A price to pay. He awakened the beast and stuck his arm in the cage; now the beast gets to chew on him a little.

Eventually I grind him down, win him over—he won't let us visit his lab, but he will bring his device into the paper. I can talk to him and we can take his photo.

That startles me. I didn't expect him to actually agree to appear. To be honest, I am nervous, excited, and I brief the photo desk. A man coming in today is bringing in his flying saucer motor. We are going to handle him gently. We are going to be respectful and polite. I badgered him out of vindictiveness, but now that he is actually coming . . .

A slight fellow in a coat and tie, Roger Rhenium—a pseudonym, of course (his doing, not mine; "rhenium" is an element, maybe he assumed nobody else would know that)—arrives at the *Sun-Times* offices carrying an assemblage of white PVC pipe, about a foot in diameter. A few ball bearings rattle around inside. The bearings would be made to spin around the circuit of pipe, he explains, providing power to the craft to operate in three dimensions. The heart breaks. Looking at this man and his contraption, I resolve to somehow write a column that will please him while everybody else will understand. The solution seems to lie in finding the right tone. I begin:

> Chicago is home to big inventions. The first nuclear reactor, as many know, was built [inside the stands of] a University of Chicago squash court. Less known is Elisha Gray, the Highland Park electrical whiz who invented the telephone, only to have it swiped by Alexander Graham Bell.

In that light, I welcomed Roger Rhenium to the office. Mr. Rhenium is building a flying saucer engine in his North Side basement. He's kept me informed of his progress over the years, but I never dared hope to actually meet him, never mind hold his Rhenium Reactor in my hands.

The device involves a pair of D-shaped tubes through which ball bearings flow. Turning the tubes as the balls race through them builds up torque—I'm not able to explain exactly how, but Mr. Rhenium assures me it could be not only used to power flying saucers, but also cars and boats.

Mr. Rhenium, 59, is a professional house painter and amateur scientist. He has been working on his reactor, sporadically, for 40 years. He has also said he created "a very important energy device," too revolutionary to reveal to the media at this time. . . .

You get the picture. He later called to thank me for the publicity. I was glad of that, relieved that he didn't feel ill-used or ridiculed. We never spoke again.

* * *

As the years go by, I try to move softly through people's lives, not to just barge in and start poking around. Leanna Dorsett, for instance, the jittery cocaine baby whose frantic, wide eyes bored into me at the Northwestern Perinatal Dependency Clinic.

Every now and then I'd think about how old she'd be and imagine what she might be doing—she'd be five years old now, I'd think, kindergarten. Ten years old, elementary school. I'd wonder, at what point could I pop up, announce that I had held her as a baby, and ask if I could write about how she fared after her rocky start, how she rebounded from being beaten up in the womb by her mother's drug habit.

My naïve optimism tells me that everything will be all right. I will wait a decent interval of years—and those years just snap by—until she is eighteen, or maybe even twenty-one. And then I will swoop back into her life and find out.

I truly expect—or hope anyway—that she will be a college senior somewhere. I imagine her bright, vivacious, pretty, her hair in a ponytail, the missing fingers the only hint that she had to battle her way into this unhappy world. Her story will be inspirational.

Would it be fair of me, I occasionally wonder, to present myself at all?

This unexpected person, the uninvited observer, dropping out of the sky into her life to tell her that her mother was a drug addict, that she had to be swaddled tightly to give her the sense of security that most babies possess naturally but cocaine babies have lost, a balm to her shattered nerves? Is that an ethical thing to do? Maybe she will appreciate learning the truth. To have mysteries finally illuminated. Maybe she will resent it. Who can tell? I always believe that the truth helps. That sunlight is a disinfectant. But what if your truth is an awful truth?

I never got the chance to decide.

One day I am sitting on the sofa with Edie, watching the local TV news, and they report that a thirteen-year-old girl collapsed and died while standing at the chalkboard in front of her seventh-grade class at the Garrett Morgan Elementary School. The girl's name is Leanna Dorsett.

"That's my cocaine baby!" I exclaim.

So I do write the follow-up column, prematurely, but instead of talking to her, I talk to her foster mother—her real mother, Delores, the drug addict, exited the scene long ago. I inform her foster mother that Leanna had been a cocaine baby; she hadn't known, the Department of Children and Family Services never told her. It's odd, to know things about someone that her own mother doesn't know. Though she is also able to tell me things about Leanna that I didn't know.

"She was a beautiful young lady," says Claudette Winters, who took Leanna in when she was six. "She liked to dance. She liked music. She liked all her classes."

Her principal, talking about what a joyous child Leanna was, weeps.

"There's a lot of broken hearts at the school," says public schools CEO Paul Vallas.

Life is not fair—that is utterly clear. But life is far more unfair to some than to others.

* * *

Of course I can help Sam. To be honest, the thought of leaping to help him never crossed my mind—had it, I would have suspected that he'd be insulted if big brother barged in and tried to solve his life for him. He has his pride. I always assume Sam has a handle on any situation he might be in; he's perhaps the most in-control guy I know.

But help him how? It isn't who you know, remember, but who you know knows. Who do I know who can help Sam? I start by trying to take care of that minor surgery. I had gone to Lithuania the year before to meet up with a group of American orthopedic surgeons from Shriner's Hospital—a direct result of giving that Lithuanian group $100 of the bass fishing money. They had been so pleased to be in the paper, the group invited me to come to Lithuania with the doctors. If these doctors could fly five-thousand miles to operate for free on kids they had never met, maybe they could also operate on my brother right here.

Surgeons are not quick to call back. Waiting, impatient, the process now begun, I phone the publicist for Cook County Hospital—that's where uninsured poor people go. So . . . if you need surgery you do . . . what? Just walk in, give your name, and wait? Take a number? Present your driver's license and say "Hello, I'm here for some minor surgery—anybody free?"

It feels odd, almost wrong, to be calling Cook County Hospital on a personal matter. My brother lives in Cook County, true, but he isn't their target demographic. I know that Cook County can barely serve the population it is supposed to serve—poor inner-city minorities. Now I am adding a straw to the system's sagging back. Well why not? He is an unemployed person in need of medical care, is he not? He is in pain. But it still seems strange. An editor smitten with the movie *Gremlins* once sent me to Chinatown to find a store like the cluttered herbologist's shop in the opening scene of the movie. There were places dispensing Chinese folk cures off Cermak Road all right, but they were not dispensing them to tradition-bound Chinese immigrants, nor to wayward American tourists, but to obese black women tired of waiting for Cook County Hospital to treat what ailed them. You can sit in the ER all day at County and get nothing for your trouble or you can spend ten dollars on a bottle of Chinese herbs that won't do anything either but you can pretend might help. At least in a Chinatown shop someone will pay attention to you.

Sam doesn't belong at County. I've been there—I once almost got arrested sneaking up to the room of a gunshot victim. It's galling to think my brother would go there; it's beneath us, like taking the bus had once been.

Imagining walking Sam into the grim, gritty, crowded florescent-lit waiting room at Cook County Hospital expands my mind. He's not traveling steerage. Sam doesn't just need surgery. He needs health insurance to pay for surgery. He needs an employer to give him health insurance to pay for surgery. Getting medical care is a half measure. What he really needs is a job. "Neil, can't you help me?" The question echoes. Well yeah, I could, sure . . .

The medical problem gets me moving—there are no ethical conflicts to trying to find medical treatment for a jobless, uninsured person who needs minor surgery, even if that person happens to be your brother. But a job?

* * *

Here's how I make my decision. I consider the fact that it might be seen as wrong, for a newspaper columnist, a member of the editorial board, to phone somebody up looking for a job for his brother. Forget "seen as wrong." It might be wrong. I could get in trouble. I could lose my own job.

Heck, forget "might be wrong." It *is* wrong. The kind of back-scratching we expose every day. Influence. Corruption. The easy, familiar, your-guy-builds-an-addition-on-my-house-I-support-your-legislation graft that poisons Chicago, Cook County, Springfield, and almost everyplace big enough to support government more complex than a solitary postmaster. Every week, almost every day, we put politicians on a spit and roast them like rotisserie chickens for slipping their relatives onto the public payroll. That I don't make a habit of denouncing this practice helps. I am far more interested in potato chip factories. Many lapses can be forgiven by readers, but hypocrisy is fatal. I'm not a politician, I'm newspaper columnist, and not just a columnist, but one who likes to baldly admit being biased, influenced, lunching with pals, and swapping secrets. A humorist, someone who originally aspired to be a fez-wearing Robert Benchley sort of writer, holding up the bar at "21" and coining quips, rather than someone who ever saw himself as a rumpled Bob Woodward type, pulling at the threads and unraveling the scandal. Nor do I make my enjoyment of the perks of the profession a secret. I once began a column, "One great thing about working for a newspaper is free stuff and lots of it."

Still, I can see it becoming a problem if I start working my contacts to get my brother a job. All that has to happen is for me to write something negative, years later, about someone I once asked to interview Sam. "Is this how it works?" they'll complain. "If I don't hire your brother, you go after me in the paper?" I can see that happening. Easily.

But if I don't help Sam . . . I imagine him quietly going down to the basement of his neat split-level home in Arlington Heights, tossing a rope over a pipe and . . .

Guys actually do that. Particularly guys without jobs, guys without medical care. Life serves up one trouble too many, and the only answer they can find is to sit in the driver's seat with the car running and the garage door closed. A permanent solution to a temporary problem, as the cliché goes. It's hard enough when it's someone you sorta know. But Sam? My brother? How could I live with myself then? How could I live with myself if I let something like that happen to him?

Not that Sam ever would—he's a more calm, Zen, centered, solid person than I am. But I imagine it, and once I have that vision in mind it settles the matter for me. And, frankly, not doing anything seems like cowardice, like putting my own needs and my own security above my brother's. Protecting my own job while my brother doesn't even have a job to protect. Gosh, I would love to help you, Sam, but then I might get into *trouble*.... There's a profile in courage for you.

Before I even make the call, I think through what I will say if the matter ever comes up. No apologizing, no equivocating. I hate when people do that. If anybody asks, I'll say: "Yes, I knew it was wrong and I did it anyway." Own the sin.

I start with Gloria Majewski, a commissioner of the Metropolitan Water Reclamation District of Greater Chicago, one of the numerous governmental shells encasing the city, an entity people hardly know is there, despite its $1 billion budget and two thousand employees.

Why her? Majewski and I met because commissioners are elected, and she hired Ed McElroy, who in addition to doing publicity for the Water Reclamation District and the Fraternal Order of Police, also helps a gaggle of judges and commissioners with their election campaigns. I had just gone to a cocktail party, courtesy of Ed, for Majewski at O'Brien's steak house on Wells Street. Politicians such as her need to constantly fund-raise so they can afford to attend all the fund-raisers thrown by their fellow politicians. *Manus manum lavat.*

So there is a comfort level. I attended her fund-raiser—not that I gave her money, but I was there, lending whatever sequin's worth of twinkle my presence conveys. Because of that, I know her, now. I'm already familiar with the Water Reclamation District, one of the more flush and forgotten areas of government, even though its opulent headquarters is steps away from the Gold Coast heart of North Michigan Avenue. Given the ongoing carnival of favoritism that the Water Reclamation District represents, asking Majewski to meet with my brother doesn't seem out-of-bounds.

Heck, it's like walking up to the buffet at a wedding reception. Nobody says, "Hey, can I have some of these Swedish meatballs? Can I have some of this cheese?" You've been around, you grasp what's going on, you know what you're supposed to do because everybody else is doing it already. Grab a plate and dig in.

Majewski, it turns out, is happy to meet Sam. Delighted. But one contact may not be enough to do the trick. Onward! Flush with success, my second call is to Maria Pappas, the Cook County treasurer. Has not the woman fixed me dinner? Are we not coffee buddies? Heck, she already offered me a job—that makes it almost seem like she's doling them out. Besides, Sam isn't some clod relative who needs a paycheck and a dry place out of the rain. He is the holder of a masters in finance from DePaul University, a Washington University graduate who lived in Japan, speaks fluent Japanese, worked as a headhunter for a Swiss firm, ran a limousine company for ten years, worked at Morgan Stanley for three. He has skills.

If he were a stranger, I might pass his name along—I've done that plenty of times. I've helped get jobs for vets through the column, a job for my niece, a job for my nephew, jobs for my nieces' friends whom I've never met. I've written letters of recommendation lauding borderline-competent interns just because fate has to cut you a break at some point in your life. It sure did for me; I feel obligated to return the favor. When Phyllis Smith, the bartender at the Billy Goat Tavern on Washington, had a fight with Sam Sianis and quit, I introduced her to Grant DePorter, who gave her a job behind the bar at the Harry Caray's restaurant in Lombard. Is that abuse of power? I view it as kindness. The key fact is: she's a good bartender, which is why Grant hired her, not as a favor to me—heck, he thought of it as *me* helping *him*. He was *grateful*. She's worked there for *years*.

Did Abe Peck do something wrong by connecting me to a job instead of telling Drew Davis to conduct a general outreach to all journalists everywhere and then form an independent Norwegian committee to select his new Mr. Weekend? Hell no. So why punish Sam because he's my brother? I can recommend him more wholeheartedly than anybody I've ever met.

* * *

Nobody lives in Chicago alone. It is all a web of relationships and interactions, loyalties and grudges. Before you step off the bus, coming to the city for the first time, you've probably already started the process, getting to know the person sitting next to you. Maybe he'll give you a lift to where you're going. Caroline Meeber is still on the train to Chicago, taking the first step to escape her Wisconsin girlhood farm, when she encounters the smooth benefactor who will boost her toward stardom in *Sister Carrie*.

You cannot have your hand against the world—you need friends, colleagues, people you trust, people you look out for and who in turn trust and look out for you. Often in Chicago it would be people you grew up with, who you went to school with, or your fellow church members or neighbors. Why? You know them, you like them, you trust them. Or your coworkers. Police officers look out for each other, so much so that if one commits a crime, almost any crime, the others will not turn him in. It isn't just rare; it never happens, or at least I can't think of an instance when it ever happened. Cops dislike crime, but they despise a squealer. Supporting each other is a stronger value than upholding the law—the implication of course being: it might be *you* next time—and anyone who bucks that reality can't be a good cop because he won't last in the department. No one will have his back.

Indeed, the idea that it should be otherwise—that everybody should suffer the consequences of their actions, should rise and fall on their worth, their resumes, without nebulous personal considerations getting in the way—is the rarity, the impossible standard that people pay lip service to and then ignore. Like communism, it's a lofty idea that deflates on the thorns of how human beings actually are. Those who take pride in being impartial tend to be, upon closer examination, merely blind to their own biases.

The network of people who support you—your family, your friends, your neighbors, your customers, your bosses, your colleagues, your associates, the guy you met on the bus—quickly grows so complicated it almost defies words. There's too much history, too many connections and intersections: you would need a chart to show it. Heck, it's hard enough to figure out the true situation between yourself and somebody else, between you and one single individual picked nearly at random from everyone you know.

14

Driving with Ed McElroy

"THIS IS VISITATION Parish," says Ed McElroy, clear of eye, sound of mind, and eighty-three years of age, as he guides his black Cadillac down Halsted Street.

It is sunny, summer, Chicago, and the South Side neighborhood is quiet, as befits the former epicenter of lace curtain Irish-Catholic gentility. The generations of politicians and businessmen who grew up and lived here have all died or moved elsewhere. But they left their mansions and graystone three-flats behind. Those grand shells radiate a certain calm and security, even now, when the current inhabitants lead vastly different lives from those who dwelled there in years past.

Ed is doing what he has always done—driving around big shots, introducing people, smoothing the grease of his charm and his connections over the clanking machinery of the city. He has given lifts to cardinals, judges, police captains, and baseball commissioners. Ed picked up John F. Kennedy at the airport on several occasions, back when JFK was a senator, but he also squired around Barack Obama when he was coming up in the world, and he has the photos to prove it.

Most publicists nowadays email press releases to a thousand people and consider their work done. A few follow up with a telephone call, robotically suggesting a story, seemingly indifferent to whether it is of interest or not, unprepared to even discuss the idea, as if they are secretly eager to be rejected so they can move on to the next number on their list. Ed, old-school, shows up himself and takes you where he wants you to go and then treats you to lunch afterward.

That makes it easy to say yes, at least for me. Some reporters never accept a free lunch; I never turn one down. I don't know where Ed's taking me now—some kind of school. I don't know why we're going, only that we've taken an unannounced detour so he can show me the neighborhood where he grew up in the 1930s. I don't know when I met Ed—it seems I have always known him. I do know that when I'd gotten in trouble with the law a few years earlier, it was Ed who phoned first. Ed who, alone among everyone I know, took it upon himself to find a lawyer and have him call me.

"See that vacant lot?" says Ed, as we cruise down Garfield Boulevard, a broad avenue with mature honey locust and American elm trees gracing the wide strip of green running down the middle. "I must have played ten thousand hours of football there. I was playing football there when Gabby Hartnett hit his home run."

That would be "The Homer in the Gloamin'," September 28, 1938, when the Cubs slugger sent a game-winning home run into the Wrigley Field stands as darkness fell.

Ed seems to have complete recall, an instant grasp of every name, face, and fact he has encountered in his lifetime. It almost goes without saying he has never had a sip of alcohol, never smoked a cigarette. Nor has he tasted coffee, he says, or bet on a horse. His beverage of choice is milk, or if he's feeling festive, 7 Up. "Your waistline is your lifeline," Ed has told me more times than I'd care to hear it, since my lifeline is greater than his.

I don't know who Ed works for, at least not all of his clients. I am certain he is in the employ of the Metropolitan Water Reclamation District of Greater Chicago—the entity that handles all the water that goes down a drain or through a sewer grate in Chicago and most of Cook County. I know this because twice he took me down the Deep Tunnel, the district's pharaonic, multibillion-dollar, decades-long public works project. When Ed brings the Water Reclamation District's president, Terry O'Brien, into the newspaper for an editorial board meeting, and O'Brien thanks us for seeing him, I reply, "Don't thank me; thank Ed. I have to do whatever he says." It's a joke, sort of.

And I'm fairly certain he works for the Fraternal Order of Police; he has taken me to meet the FOP president, Mark Donahue, and invited me to FOP functions: plaque dedications, memorial services for slain cops, speeches, including one by Obama where, afterward, Ed made sure

Obama and I were photographed together, the FOP banner prominent in the background, the shot snapped by a photographer Ed had conveniently brought along. The resulting 8 × 10 photo showed up in the mail shortly thereafter, in duplicate, and is framed in my office. I'm glad to have it.

Given his affinity for the force, I sometimes suspect Ed might not actually work for the cops, that he might be volunteering. When he got married in 1955, Ed's best man was Timothy J. O'Connor, Chicago's police commissioner at the time. Also there was Ed's close friend Frank Pape, the toughest cop in Chicago, who always insisted that the nine men he killed in gunfights all had guns, or at least might have had them. Pape sent another five crooks he didn't get the chance to kill to the electric chair. "They were all rape guys, stick-up guys, all bad actors," Ed tells me, from time to time. "Every one of them had it coming."

Ed's tales of his adventures with Pape—incidents he describes, but doesn't want printed, even fifty years later ("I'm a Catholic," he explains; "I'm supposed to set a good example")—jar a bit with the Ed I see before me, a lean, white-haired gentleman, not as tall as he was a few years ago, with an enameled flag pin on his lapel and a golden jeweled cross that shows he is a past national commander of the Catholic War Veterans of the United States of America.

Ed's way is the old way—gifts for the reporters, bottles of bourbon at Christmas, cases of the product you are pushing, and gewgaws with a publicist's name on them. Ed prefers the latter; every year, he sends out a small, tasteful present: a clock, a business card holder, a letter opener. The gifts feature three decorative elements—his name, his phone number, and an image of the American flag. Ed loves the flag. He not only wears one, and has an American flag flying from a fifteen-foot flagpole in his front yard, but he displays another flag, with a gold fringe, in a corner of his living room.

Then there are the Fraternal Order of Police Chicago Lodge No. 7 ballpoint pens and blue Chicago police business card wallets he's always giving to me. And the die-cast replica of a Chicago police squad car, a foot long, with doors that open and everything, still sitting on my older son's dresser, a present for his fifth birthday. Ed must work for the Fraternal Order of Police.

I used to introduce Ed as the father I never had, until an acquaintance's face fell and he said, "Oh, I'm sorry—I didn't realize you didn't know your father," and I had to explain to him that no, I know my father all too well, he is very much alive, thank you, doing fine, painting watercolors in Boulder, Colorado. It's just that my father never comes around in a new Cadillac to buy me lunch the way Ed does.

* * *

It takes a long time for us to drive from my newspaper office at Wolf Point— where the Chicago River splits into its North and South Branches—to wherever it is we're going. I slump in the cool black leather seat of the Cadillac and tell Ed how tired and out of sorts I've been lately—breathing problems at night, apparently. Sleep apnea. He says he has a dentist who could help me with that. After nearly an hour of driving and sightseeing in Visitation Parish I say, hoping to move things along, "So this school, Ed—why are we going there?"

"Ed Carik; do you know who he is?" he replies. I shake my head no. "Ed Carik used to work for Mike Sheehan"—the former Cook County sheriff. "Now he runs security for Daley Plaza. Ed Carik was a tremendous football player at Marist High School. Ed Carik's wife, Mary, is a teacher at the school."

That answer satisfies me completely, and only later, writing this, do I realize that Ed said nothing about the school itself or what particular merits it may or may not possess. Why should he? Ed is doing a favor for a friend and so am I. Ed McElroy is my friend. At least I think he is. No, I'm certain. Fairly certain. For a long time I didn't think so. I assumed he was merely another publicist, one of an ever-dwindling band of aging gentlemen who visit the paper to tout the glories of this or that.

They used to arrive every day in platoons, guys like Nate "What'll You Have?" Perlstein, who made his name ballyhooing Pabst Blue Ribbon beer at the 1933 Century of Progress fair, and who once told me that if I wrote about a certain plastic surgeon client of his, I could be a guest aboard his yacht and maybe get some free facial work. The offer seemed crass and I ignored him—you had to know how to handle these guys. They made the rounds, they bought the drinks, they pressed the flesh and passed along their bits of information. Nate lived in the Ambassador West hotel for seventeen years and used to visit Paul Harvey, the hugely popular syndicated radio broadcaster, every day. Once, while I was tagging along with Nate, observing his routine, I saw Harvey do something to Nate that I never saw one man do to another before or since. While Nate was talking, Harvey reached into his pocket, took out a comb, and wordlessly straightened Nate's unruly hair. That isn't the usual reporter/publicist relationship.

The years passed, the media world shattered and fragmented, stretched and diluted. The platoons of shoe leather publicity agents turned to squads, then solitary individuals. And now it's pretty much Ed. The idea that we were actually friends was slow in dawning on me—he's thirty-five years older than me, so the age difference threw me.

And I am not a man who makes friends easily. Something about me must be off-putting. I'm slow to warm to others, and those I do like have a habit of drifting away, no matter how I try to reel them back.

My view of Ed changed after his eightieth birthday. His friends held a birthday luncheon for Ed at the Walnut Room of the old Marshall Field's department store on State Street. Maybe twenty people were there. A number of judges—Ed has handled many judicial campaigns. His wife was there, a trim, smiling, upbeat woman with twinkling eyes whom Ed often introduces lyrically as "Rita Marie, mother of three." I was surprised to discover that I was the only reporter, surprised to see that his son Eddie was seated at his right hand and I was seated on his left. That means something. As did his coming up with that lawyer. It was a humiliating drunken episode that made the local TV news. The *Tribune* bannered it across a page in its Metro section as if it were an elementary school fire. Not all my friends stuck with me. The sky darkened, the wind gusted, and they took wing and never came back. But Ed stuck around and tried to help.

That's friendship. Still, it is a Chicago kind of friendship. A delicate interplay of favors given and received, of information offered and withheld. Ed is a friend who expects me to write about his clients in the newspaper, and I am a friend who expects him to pick up the lunch check (indeed, one of the signs that made me suspect we might really be friends was when I started occasionally paying for a meal, to apologize for neglecting to write about something that Ed really wanted me to write about, or to celebrate his birthday). Though I may turn him down, once or twice or even three times, eventually the chit becomes due and I have to cough up some publicity or our friendship would begin to sour. He doesn't say this, but I sense it. If I fail to return a phone call or don't take one of Ed's suggestions, if I ignore a judge running for election or pass on an opportunity to write about Terry

O'Brien—a nice enough man but not a font of fascination—Ed will be mystified, even hurt. A tone of bafflement will enter into his voice, an edge of irritation. He will repeat the merits of whomever he is boosting, as if explaining something simple to a stubborn child. I had to go with Ed to this school today—no choice—even though I was busy and didn't want to go, because I'd already canceled on him once for this visit, and thus used up my allotment; once is acceptable; twice would be an affront.

Ed goes to mass almost every day and never neglects—as he often reminds me—to offer up a prayer for my immortal soul. On Sundays he gives communion, and if someone noteworthy kneels before him—say our mutual friend Illinois Supreme Court justice Anne Burke or her husband, Chicago City Council powerhouse alderman Ed Burke—Ed McElroy is not shy about sharing that fact. He carries a few spare communion wafers in a round gold box in his pocket because he visits shut-ins and the infirm so they can perform their sacred duty. Ed used to drive around cardinal John Cody after his eminence, in a fit of public poverty, renounced his car and driver. Ed stepped up at a party to offer his services, and an informal relationship began, though Ed's motivation was piety leavened with more worldly concerns. "I represented Blake-Lamb for eighteen years," he says, referring to one of the city's premier funeral homes. "I got the cardinal to commit to Blake-Lamb."

Burying the cardinal is good for business. It also happened thirty-five years ago. There is an intermingling of the past and present in Ed—with his sharp memory, clear eye, and vivid language, it sometimes seems as if the past is ongoing still, perhaps a few minutes ago and just around the corner. Visitation Parish is almost entirely inner-city black now—a mile east down Garfield Boulevard is the second-most dangerous neighborhood in America. But as Ed drives down the street, it seems like his mother, his pals on the block, the five priests serving twelve masses every Sunday, the seventy Dominican sisters who lived at the Visitation nunnery, have just stepped away for a moment and will be right back. He parks next to a weedy lot and reminisces about the newsstand he ran there as a boy. A pair of large men, in new baseball caps turned sideways and enormous oversize t-shirts, amble in our direction.

"What's up guys?" Ed calls to them, before they reach us, in a completely confident tone that suggests he might leap out of the car and toss them against the hood. They mumble something and move off.

Ed McElroy swings his Cadillac the wrong way down 63rd Place, a one-way street. Typically that would cause some kind of alarm or at least consternation in a driver. But Ed does this coolly, intentionally, without so much as a flutter. The same way, a few minutes earlier, he had sat at a red light for a respectful period then, glancing to the left and right, accelerated the car through it. His license plate is not the typical jumble of letters and numbers, but "185." He leaves his car in front of the school, in a buses-only tow zone. This is his town.

Inside the Blair Early Childhood Center, Ed doesn't so much as say hello as he compares roots.

"I'm South Side Irish Visitation Parish," he announces in the school office.

"I was in St. Dorothy's in Chatham, then I went to St. Cajetan's," replies the principal, Karen Bryar. "I went to Longwood School."

Ed takes a step back, eyes wide, as if thunderstruck. "The girls from Longwood School!" he exclaims, his hand on his heart.

Blair Early Childhood Center is a school for children with disabilities—Down syndrome, autism, birth defects. The halls are lined with a sobering train of special wheelchairs, complex seating devices, and heavily padded restraint boards. Principal Bryar takes us to each classroom, introducing us to every teacher and teacher's aide and to many of the 103 students. We see them eating, singing, being read to. Ed quizzes the teachers about who they are, where they're from, even gym instructor Kathleen Houtsma, whose Dutch last name would seem to put her well beyond the charmed circle.

"A good Irish name," Ed ventures. "You didn't go to St. Leo High School . . ."

"No," she says, "But my grandfather, Cornelius Houtsma did."

Ed brightens. "He was a judge . . ." he says.

Yes, she says.

"His son was a football player . . ."

"My dad, Mark," she says.

Rosemary Cavanaugh doesn't need to wait for Ed to excavate her past. She recognizes him as soon as he walks into her first-grade classroom. "I'm Paul Lawler's sister," she says, hurrying up to him.

"I can see the Lawler right here," Ed says, framing her mouth and chin with his hands. "Your mother just died this summer," Ed continues, as if informing her of the fact. He turns to me. "Her mother was beautiful. A beautiful woman." Of course Ed was at the funeral—attending wakes and funerals is a duty. "Before they closed the casket, my son Eddie kissed her," he adds.

"My mother loved your son," she replies, moving on to lighter topics—a perennially wayward Lawler brother, Ed's driving habits. "We would laugh, because you used to park in our driveway to go to church," she says, brightly.

Occasionally a teacher's attention strays over to me, and I have to admit that I am nobody, an *auslander*. I was born in Cleveland, went to Berea High School, and came to Chicago to go to college in 1978, which in other communities might earn me some kind of status as an honorary resident. But not here, not in Chicago, at least not in the places that matter. Here, if you aren't from the old neighborhood you might as well be from Mars. Nobody knows my parents, nobody has heard of the high school I went to, I'm obviously a Jew, and while I am in the newspaper four days a week, that is little more than a sporadic significance, a quasi fame that allows me to get reservations at certain booked restaurants. Nearly three hundred thousand people buy the *Sun-Times* every day, true, but Chicago has almost three million residents, and I seldom meet anyone who knows me or cares what I do.

Nor is Ed particularly important. He is, as I said, a publicist, a driver, not an alderman, or a big campaign contributor, or a friend of Richard M. Daley, whom he calls "Richie" and has known since Daley was a child, but whom he is not close to and hasn't gotten wealthy from, two qualities that go together naturally: bread and butter, rod and reel, knowing the mayor and making money.

Perhaps it is our common marginality that allows Ed and me to become friends, to form this symbiosis, this partnership, a single strand of connection, one bond among a vast, constantly shifting network of associations, loyalties, debts, and mutual dependencies that have built Chicago and allowed it to grow and prosper, to escape the rusty decline that wrecked other midwestern cities, Detroit and Cleveland, Milwaukee and St. Louis, and instead continue building skyscrapers even as periodic recessions hamstring America, to remain a "world-class city," to use the buzz phrase that so swells the hearts of Chicago boosters.

Yet these bonds also undercut Chicago; these chains of obligation also weigh it down, distorting the efficient operation of the city and helping to sink it into corruption and endless scandal. How does new construction get city approval? A developer performs $40,000 worth of home remodeling work for an alderman, then the alderman signs off on the developer's project in his ward. Is the project good for the ward? Who cares?

That isn't an imaginary example; it's what alderman Isaac Carothers was charged with doing by the US Justice Department the month before Ed and I go for our drive. Ed of course knows Carothers and knew his dad, Willie Carothers—sometimes it seems as if Ed knows everybody's dad. Willie Carothers was also an alderman, and went to jail for nearly the identical remodeling fraud his son later pleaded guilty to committing, following his father's footsteps into prison.

A Chicago alderman is convicted of federal corruption or other criminal abuses almost every year—thirty aldermen between 1973 and 2009, or nearly a third of those who served on the city council during that period. At one point in the mid-1990s there were four Chicago aldermen confined in the federal prison at Oxford, Wisconsin—quite an accomplishment for a legislative body that only has fifty members.

In our own small way, Ed and I are part of that. At least I am. Ed is just doing his job, promoting his clients. But what about me? Am I doing my job? Does Ed provide my readers with a fascinating glimpse into a hidden world of Chicago cops and storm water drainage projects, a view they might never otherwise get if I didn't keep his company? Not one Chicagoan in ten thousand has been down the Deep Tunnel. Or is this stuff pallid, public relations pap that I occasionally spice up best I can and spoon-feed to my tolerant audience as payment for a car ride and a steak lunch? Or is it both? Is the entire friendship—I sometimes worry—an elaborate self-deception? And if so, who's fooling whom?

Corruption is a lot easier to see in others. Four of the past eight Illinois governors have gone to prison. One—George Ryan—is behind bars as Ed and I tool around Visitation, for pocketing envelopes filled with cash, kickbacks from developer pals, among other crimes. Ryan would soon be joined by his successor, Rod Blagojevich, making two governors in a row and two incarcerated at the same time. Though in pure brazenness Blago tops them all—he is the first Illinois governor to be arrested while still in office, handcuffed early one morning in his home by the FBI, taken away for trying to sell the Senate seat left vacant by Barack Obama. And he did so after he knew the feds were investigating him.

"I want to make money," Blagojevich said on tape. Just a few years earlier he had run as a reformer, a man dedicated to fixing education in Illinois. People were shocked in a town that does not shock easily. Blagojevich is an oily, two-bit operator, deranged by self-regard, who never should have been governor in the first place. He got there, and quickly too, for only one reason: he married the daughter of Dick Mell, a powerful Chicago alderman who gave Blago his political career as a wedding gift, the way other fathers-in-law will give their new sons-in-law a job in the family construction business.

And Illinois politics is without question a family business. Richard M. Daley, our all-powerful mayor of twenty-plus years, at that point, is the son of Richard J. Daley, the previous all-powerful mayor of twenty-plus years. Todd Stroger, then president of the Cook County Board, is the son of the previous president, John Stroger, who contrived to hand over governance to the next generation with a minimum of inconvenience from the electoral process by retiring after he had already won the primary—the true test in a predominantly Democratic county—and pressuring party leaders to slate his son as his replacement.

It goes on. Lisa Madigan, the Illinois attorney general and governor-in-waiting, is the daughter of Michael Madigan, the mighty Speaker of the Illinois House of Representatives and chairman of the Illinois Democratic Party. ("Mighty" is actually an understatement. Madigan *is* the state legislature; the other members, mere puppets doing his bidding.) Republican Rep. Dan Lipinski was an obscure academic in Tennessee when he received his Chicago congressional seat from his father, Bill, who not only, like Stroger, used a carefully timed retirement to spare his son a primary battle, but further hedged his bets by recruiting a sham Republican opponent to be handily defeated in the general election, thus avoiding the risk that his boy Danny—obviously not the sharpest knife in the drawer—might face an actual opponent mounting an earnest campaign. Daley's wife Maggie sat on a number of corporate boards showering her with six-figure salaries, but it was considered bad form—insulting the mayor's wife!—to even point out that this was without question influence peddling, if not outright graft. Nor are the Carothers the only parent/child pair in city council history— there are the Sawyers, Eugene and Roderick; the Beaverses, William and Darcel; and others further in the past.

Nor is it limited to politicians. TV news anchors ease their children into slots at their stations, and the occasional newspaper columnist uses connections to slide a son or a brother into a job. Maybe the problem isn't that it's done, but that when it comes to government, people somehow expect that it *shouldn't* be done. It sure doesn't work that way in business. Nobody says, "Henry Ford III? What the heck is *he* doing as a regional manager at a car company!?"

We Don't Want Nobody Nobody Sent, the evocative title of Milton Rakove's oral history of the Richard J. Daley years, refers to something a ward boss told Abner Mikva in 1948 when the future federal judge and White House counsel, then a twenty-two-year-old from the University of Chicago, tried to volunteer at the Eighth Ward Regular Democratic Organization. He had answered the classic question "Who sent you?" with the naïve reply, "Nobody."

"Nobody" got him nowhere. "We don't want nobody nobody sent," the pol snarled.

That basic connection—the favor done for a relative, a friend, a classmate—is the building block of power in the city. *Manus manum lavat.* One hand washes the other. Flip open the 1960 yearbook for De La Salle Academy, the high school where Richard M. Daley graduated, and look at the faces—they became the movers and shakers, the attorneys and investors, of Chicago for the next half century.

Daley relatives pop up in the news with regularity. Robert Vanecko received $68 million in city pension funds to invest in risky real estate schemes. The fact that Mayor Daley is his uncle had nothing to do with it, Vanecko insisted. For his part the mayor said he was shocked, shocked, to find his nephew doing business with the city. Just as he was surprised when Vanecko's brother Richard killed a man outside a Rush Street bar and the police shrugged and decided that the case wasn't worth pursuing.

Daley said the same thing about his twenty-nine-year-old son Patrick, when the boy was found to be an investor in a sewer company suddenly awash in city cash. The mayor—by all accounts a doting and attentive father—knew nothing of his son's investments, an evasion that Daley's father would have felt was both unnecessary and beneath him. "If I can't help my sons, then they can kiss my ass," Richard J. Daley said, famously, in 1973, when it was revealed that Democratic judges were steering receivership cases to young Richie Daley and his brother Michael. "I make no apologies to anyone. If a man can't put his arms around his sons, then what kind of world are we living in?"

Can anybody rise by merit? Of course. It does happen, maybe even in the majority of cases. It's just that the fix, the inside deal, the cut to the front of the line, stands out so much—violates some inner sense of fairness—that a little seems like a lot. It feels like the norm, even if it isn't. Ed McElroy's father was a dentist who died in 1930, when Ed was four, so Ed had to live by his wits and his boundless capacity for work and his ease at meeting people. He is a sober, church-going, Irish-Catholic man who can be trusted, and who proved himself useful to powerful people.

He also grew up in Visitation Parish. Two Chicago mayors were at Ed's wedding in 1955—the outgoing reformer, Martin Kennelly, and the man who replaced him, Richard J. Daley, who had taken office the month before. Or rather, Kennelly attended the wedding ceremony itself, and Daley went to the reception afterward, a bit of sly political maneuvering to keep the rivals apart. Why were they there? Kennelly lived on Poplar Avenue, around the corner from Elizabeth Alice Grogan, Ed's mother. They knew each other all their lives.

And Daley? Ed had put out campaign signs for Daley's unsuccessful 1948 campaign for Cook County sheriff and was a loyal supporter. Daley—for all the criticism he received over the years—was a detail-focused politician who knew enough to take care of his people. If you wanted Daley at your wedding, Daley went to your wedding, with the unspoken understanding that someday he would want something from you in return.

We are in Bridgeport now, historic home to the Daleys. Prim streets completely devoid of people. Neat blond brick bungalows and four-flats, their only concession to the past half century being clusters of satellite dishes perched under the eaves like nesting birds, like flowers tracking the sun.

"Holy Jeez, these places look good," says Ed. "Imagine how happy people would be if blacks moved in here?"

Ed is no racist—at the school he joyously high-fived and fist-bumped kids of all races, he held their hands and danced with them. But there are facts to contend with. Race is the major consideration in Chicago—well, race and money—the twin electrical charges that hold our universe together, and Ed moves through a range of highly polarized worlds. The police department, where the number of African American officers would need to increase 50 percent to match the black share of the city's population. The fire department, where white firefighters not long ago insisted that blacks don't belong because they're afraid of water and afraid of heights. Where, when firehouses were first haltingly integrated—a process that lurches and stumbles and creeps forward today—white firemen would shatter the communal coffee mugs used by new black colleagues rather than drink from them. Ed didn't invent any of this, but he has to live with it, as do we all.

Ed is no racist, but he is of a generation that notices differences and remarks upon them with almost childlike candor. If a judge is Jewish, Ed will invariably point out to me that he is of my tribe. The idea being, I suppose, that I'll appreciate him more. Signing off the phone, he'll often say, "Shalom," which I initially found offensive and patronizing. It isn't as if he says goodbye to everybody that way. I tried to get him to stop, but that was futile, and now I just accept it as how Ed is.

For lunch today, Ed takes me to Schaller's Pump. From the outside, the place seems unremarkable—a modest two-story brick building, a large welcome to White Sox fans painted across the wall. In the gravel parking lot, I mention that I was last here with Mary Mitchell, a black *Sun-Times* columnist who was hesitant to walk into Schaller's because of its reputation, unsure of how she would be received, though the regulars warmly welcomed her once she did muster the courage to go in.

"The only black you'll see here is the cook," says Ed.

On the inside, Schaller's Pump is also unremarkable—your standard small, dim neighborhood tavern, with an elbow-worn wooden bar and a dozen tables. Patrons are older, all white, and Ed knows most of them. We sit down and are joined by Jackie Schaller, a tiny man in a blue cardigan, not two years older than Ed but looking far more elderly, shrunken, pale—his face seems like soft stone worn away by a river. His grandfather started the bar in 1881, and it has operated continuously since then—all through Prohibition, which merely required installation of the peephole that's still in the side door. Schaller calls Ed "Eddie" and they reminisce.

"Who took you to your first World Series?" Ed says, and they both laugh. To St. Louis in 1946 to see the Cardinals beat the Red Sox. "I drove down in my car," says Ed. "The Chase Hotel. A guy I knew took care of us."

Schaller is cooler toward me. Though in Ed's company, I'm still a stranger and a newspaperman at that.

Did Schaller know his grandfather, I ask. Did he know the man who started the tavern?

"Yes," Schaller replies.

Silence.

What was he like?

A pause. "Five foot one," Schaller says, without a trace of warmth. Nothing more.

An older black couple arrives and is shown to a table nearby, where they quietly eat. Times have changed, in some ways, and not in others. I ask Schaller how old he is.

"My birthday is Jan. 15," says Schaller. "Do you know what day that is?"

I shrug—nothing comes to mind.

"Martin Luther King Day," Schaller says, with a quick flick of the thumb toward the black couple. There doesn't seem to be malice in the gesture—those days are gone—but maybe the memory of malice. It inspires Ed to tell a story.

"Martin Luther King was always good to me," he says. Ed was a radio announcer and on-air newsman in the 1950s and 1960s and attended King's marches both in Chicago and down South. Being good to Ed meant that King would always pause to be interviewed. Ed was probably the only marcher at Montgomery who after the demonstration dined at the governor's mansion with George Wallace, whom he had befriended at the 1964 Democratic National Convention in Atlantic City, where Ed was assistant sergeant at arms. "After dinner, Wallace had his car drive me to the airport," says Ed. "But I had them pull over and let me out before we got there—I didn't want King and his people to see me drive up in the governor's car."

Ed orders a hamburger and a glass of milk. I order a steak sandwich and a cup of coffee, with only the briefest glance of instinctive longing at the men having Budweisers at the bar. Jackie moves off, to see after a big group of tourists arriving in the back room. Ed tells me a little about him. "World War II guy. I think he got hit," Ed says, describing how Schaller went from an eighteen-year-old playing on the St. Leo Light Basketball Squad and mouthing off to the priests to a soldier fighting in the jungles of the Pacific. A common path for the boys of Ed's generation. They played ball, they went overseas, they fought, they got hit, they came home.

"All those guys. Overseas. Bronze stars. You couldn't get a better bunch of people," says Ed. "All out of Visitation Parish. In Chicago, you know, we go by parish. Especially South Side. Visitation—it's like the pope lived there." Ed holds up his hands in amazement. "Unbelievable, Visitation. So many priests came out of there. So many policeman. Commanders. Firemen. It was so friendly."

Friendly, of course, if you belonged. Blacks strayed south of the railroad bridge into Visitation at their peril. When a rumor ignited in 1949 that a certain homeowner in Visitation was considering selling his house to a black family, thousands of people—one estimate put the mob at ten thousand—surrounded the house for days on end. That story doesn't get told much at Schaller's Pump.

A big man with prominent ears, in khakis and a striped polo shirt, balding, sixtyish, wearing glasses, walks over to say hello. Ed introduces me to the man, Bob Degnan. "He's in the paper today," Ed whispers, in an aside to me. Is he ever. The brother of Tim Degnan, one of the mayor's closest friends, Bob Degnan just retired from a $116,000 a year Chicago Transit Authority job, a position created especially for him, taking advantage of an early retirement legal loophole that allows him to receive two government pensions at the same time, something, the article notes, "particularly galling at a time when under-funded city pensions threaten to saddle future generations of Chicagoans with a debt they cannot handle."

The newspapers create a momentary fuss, but tradition endures. Cronyism, nepotism, partisanship—they almost sound like religions, like they should be capitalized. "I used to be a Baptist, now I practice Favoritism." They continue because they are inherent in human nature, in a society that has been based on the family unit for a hundred thousand years and which developed democratic government just a couple hundred years ago and civil service a century after that.

Consider all the forms of government lining up to drink from Schaller's Pump. There is the ward—the Eleventh Ward Democratic Headquarters is directly across the street. There is the city itself. The sprawling bulk of Cook County—with a population of 5.2 million, were Cook County a state, it would rank between Minnesota and Colorado. And other, less well-considered entities—the Chicago Park District, the tollway authority, our old friend the Water Reclamation District, an autonomous body covering 883 square miles. Illinois has more special-purpose governmental districts, thousands of them, than any other state in the nation. A government agency can represent a kind of graft merely by existing—the Suburban Cook County Tuberculosis Sanitarium District rolled onward for decades after the last TB sanitarium closed and the disease ceased to be a significant problem in greater Chicago. The sanitarium district was absorbed into the Cook County Department of Public Health only in 2007, and while its last officers insisted that vanquishing tuberculosis was their doing, as opposed to, say, the work of antibiotics, you could also argue that they were contributing to corruption and waste just by showing up at their offices every morning.

There's more—don't forget the state government, which, headquartered down in Springfield, exerts less control on Chicago than do the smaller, closer entities, but still has to be considered. And of course, finally, the federal government, whose dual main purposes are as a provider of cash and a dispenser of justice. The most important federal representative in Chicago is whoever is the US Attorney for the Northern District of the State of Illinois. It is that office—the Justice Department—along with the FBI and the Bureau of Alcohol, Tobacco, and Firearms, which, coupled with the Internet-ravaged media, have kept Chicago honest, to the degree that it is honest, to the degree which people are actually upset about insider influence. It can't bother them too much; they're certainly used to it. A University of Illinois at Chicago study found 1,531 elected officials and government employees were convicted of corruption in the Northern District since 1976, making the Chicago district the most corrupt in the nation.

And that is just illegal corruption. Consider what goes on that doesn't constitute a crime. All this government, all those jobs. And every job that needs to be filled is power that can be used—to help a friend, repay a debt, cement a relationship—or an opportunity to be squandered, picking a resume blindly off a pile, with no guarantee that the guy best qualified on paper is any better than your wife's second cousin. I was against Lisa Madigan when she ran for Illinois attorney general—too young, obvious nepotism. The paper's endorsement of her was the only editorial that I ever refused to write, citing moral principles. But you know what? She's done a good job. Her performance gets high marks.

And we have lunch—I should probably mention that. Do I have lunch with Madigan because she's turned out to be an able attorney general, or do I think she's an able attorney general because I have lunch with her? That's a toughie, though in my defense I would observe that lots of people who *don't* have lunch with Lisa Madigan, who don't happily hug her at events or swap enjoyable books with her, also think she's doing a good job. At least I assume they like her and don't do those things. Maybe they're just quieter about it.

Either way, I'll support her when she runs for governor—she couldn't do worse than our recent crop, and the familiar always has a foot up on the competition.

"You want to hire some *stranger*?" Ed asks, after Degnan leaves, draping the final word with revulsion. "You hire somebody you know. You come from a neighborhood. How do you say no to people? People you played ball with?"

Another kind of system—a pure meritocracy where knowing the guy in charge or not knowing him has no bearing on the outcome—is almost unimaginable in Chicago. Here reformers are sneered at as the failures they frequently turn out to be. They are "goo-goos"—short for "good-government" types, but also a name that sounds evocative of the nursery where they belong. Rod Blagojevich was a reformer—at least he styled himself as a reformer—and everybody knows how well that turned out. Some sharp-eyed observers view reformers as a central if unknowing part of the corruption process—they're the ones who rush in every once in a while and provide the comforting illusion that the system isn't utterly rigged, the sorbet between courses of scandal who cool the public's inflamed sensibilities, setting the table so the next plate of boodle can be served up and hungrily set upon by the crooked.

Friends get friends jobs. They get their children jobs. You know someone, you go to the front of line, the top of the pile. To suggest it could be otherwise, to suggest that your nephew shouldn't get $68 million in city investments, seems almost a form of communism—a failed system that indeed did try fairness, briefly, from each according to his ability, to each according to his need. That philosophy, simple and humane, almost beautiful, in theory, promptly falls apart and turns into a form of fascism, in practice, because no philosophy is so strong that it keeps the guy unloading the truck from reaching into a crate and finding something for himself. The rest flows from there, and you end up with Stalin.

Again, nothing new. Fresh from law school, Richard M. Daley flunked the bar exam, twice, before getting his law license. By all accounts, he was not the brightest bulb in the box. No matter. As a young attorney in private practice with his brother Michael he did extraordinarily well, right away—judges fell over themselves to assign him estate cases, which generated six-figure fees for almost no work. Nobody quibbled about his grades. Nor, it should be pointed out, did his father need to personally phone the judges and wheedle or threaten them to direct cases to his sons. It was not necessary. Everybody understood and played his part. That's just how things worked then, and how they work today.

* * *

Is Ed sincere? Of course. Am I? Again of course. Both of us sacrifice for our friendship. Ed has to take ribbing from cops who ask him why he's hanging out with that drunk from the newspaper who's always writing nasty stuff about the department, how police officers should obey the laws and such. He has to accept the occasional overly candid column, difficult for a man who summed up my memoir about going through rehab this way: "You're telling on yourself." And I spend time with him that I don't always have, and find myself skewed toward subjects I would otherwise ignore, in addition to being forced to confront the guilty secret of corruption—it gets things done.

A dull topic proffered by Ed McElroy gleams more brightly than one nestled in the hand of a stranger. Altruism sleeps late while self-interest sets the alarm clock. That isn't always the case. Reformers occasionally get power. Look at the man who replaced Blagojevich, Pat Quinn. He was a longtime goo-goo loose cannon who lucked into the lieutenant governor's office solely because of its complete marginality—the lieutenant governor goes to pancake breakfasts and ribbon cuttings. If anyone cared about being lieutenant governor, then Pat Quinn could never have been elected. But no one wanted the job. Then Blagojevich was dragged away and Quinn, Cinderella-like, became governor.

What happened next? Quinn, his heart pure, his soul unstained, wanted to do the right thing. But his initial call for a tax increase—the rejection of which would cause deep cuts to social services, including slashing health care for poor children—was immediately batted away by a yawning legislature. Having never compromised himself, Quinn had no friends to help him. Ditto for his attempts at ethics legislation. If ever there were a time when tough ethics guidelines would pass, having one governor in prison and another on the way would seem to be the moment. The ethics reforms went nowhere. The legislators didn't even bother with a symbolic gesture. Jane Byrne is an even better example. Elected as a maverick, once in office she discovered that, despite being mayor, she couldn't get anything done. Not without running into the arms of foes like alderman Ed Vrdolyak and developer Charlie Swibel. She had no choice. A newcomer can take over the controls, but you need someone who knows what they're doing to operate the thing.

Being in Schaller's Pump buoys Ed—he is almost beaming. "This is Chicago here," he says. "No place like it. These are neighborhood people. It's like going to church."

I hint that I'm ready to go back downtown. "But I'm not done with you yet," says Ed. We instead stop by his neat, spacious home in Beverly, where he and Rita Marie have lived for exactly forty years. In Ed's paneled basement office, I feel the heft of his collection of honorary Chicago police billy clubs. I admire photographs of Ed taken with every president from Truman to George W. Bush—he has one with Obama, too, but hasn't framed it yet. I meet a pair of grandsons, handsome boys, helping Rita Marie with her gardening.

When Ed returns me to the paper, it is nearly 4 p.m. A long lunch. He is elegiac, almost as if sensing his extended hour on the Chicago stage is drawing to a close. "At the funeral," he says, referring to the recent burial of a slain police officer, "I didn't know 99 percent of the people. Captains, commanders. I used to know them all." He says this almost with an uncharacteristic trace of weariness.

"Times change," I say, my stab at being comforting. We are in front of the newspaper now, with its stunning view south, of the bend Wacker Drive makes, following the river. I thank Ed, wish him well, promise that I will see him soon.

As always, he leaves me with parting advice, as I step out of the car. "Stay sober," he says. "Anyone who wants you to get tight with them is not your friend."

"Thank you for that, Ed," I say, with less than complete sincerity. Later in the day Dr. James Hogg—Ed's dentist—calls on the phone. Ed has told him I have some medical questions about breathing problems at night, and he wants to be of help to me.

15

"Gee, ya think?"

THE CITY OFTEN LOOKS empty. We usually don't even realize it. Streets without people, expanses of tarpaper rooftops, sagging garages, vacant graveled lots. The train pulls into the station, you gaze out at the block around it, the mute signs, the front steps with their black iron railings, the sides of closed-up brick buildings, the junked cars, the commercial yards, the chain-link fencing, the weedy scrubland, and there's no one there. A lonely park, a still swing set and deserted basketball court. Then the train moves on.

It shouldn't come as a surprise. First, because most people spend most of their time indoors, out of sight. It's too cold in Chicago to linger outside for half the year. Plus television mortally wounded the evening stroll; then computers came along and finished the job. Whenever I see highrise apartments with those little balconies, I always scan the side of the building, searching for someone who's actually sitting out on one, enjoying the view. Chairs, tables, grills, bikes, satellite dishes, but almost never a person, even in the nicest weather. Second, because there are fewer people in Chicago—the city lost a quarter of its population between 1950 and 2010—from 3.6 million to 2.8 million.

Emptiness might be the norm, but Chicago can assemble a crowd. The festivals that decorate the city summers. People listening to blues or eating ethnic food or dancing salsa on a warm July evening under strings of party lights. Or something big happens and a substantial chunk of the population pours into the street. The enormous throng who turned out to cheer the Blackhawks after they won the Stanley Cup in 2010. The joyous celebrations of six Bulls championships—generally joyous, though in a city of this size there is always some corner where it seems not a celebration but a riot or a frenzy. The rule of law seems suspended, and even white suburbanites on Rush Street will turn over a taxicab if it suddenly seems okay to do so.

It might be the rarity, the monumental achievement being celebrated, or some bit of ancient human brain wiring that associates urgency and history with crowds, but the city seems most alive when its residents gather together in one spot.

The mass of people at Grant Park the night Obama was elected—I almost didn't go downtown to be part of that. My tendency is to shy away from crowds and, besides, the paper had it covered. There was also a concern—what would happen if he lost? It might get ugly.

But Ross wanted to be there on the historic election night, and I understand that impulse. A kid doesn't want to miss anything. So we drove downtown, left the car by the Sun-Times Building and walked over to Grant Park. A calm, pleasant night in early November. I've never seen the park so crowded. Big searchlights threw shafts of white light into the night sky. We had passes to a crowded press area. Barack Obama was across the park, on a distant stage—most people were watching him on giant TVs, but I figured we were here, we should see him, not just on a screen, but directly, at least once, with our own eyes, his image reflected against our retinas.

All the vantage points were taken, so I went up to a group crowding around a gap in the fencing, pushed Ross ahead, and said, to no one in particular, "Could this boy take a look, just for a moment?" A large black woman turned, regarded him, and then commanded those in front of her, "Let the baby through!" and they parted, affording Ross and me a momentary glimpse of the future president, a tiny figure, far away. I thought of that famous photo of Lincoln delivering the Gettysburg Address, a distant, barely recognizable speck in a multitude.

But that wasn't the moment that lodged in my heart. That came afterward, when a quarter of a million people flowed from the park onto Michigan Avenue, buoyant with victory, intoxicated with promise and possibility and hope, filling the street from curb to curb, from Roosevelt Road to the Wrigley Building. They were in their new Obama t-shirts and in church clothes, whole families, including wide-eyed toddlers, some cheering, some walking in quiet, careful formality.

It seemed so strange, so fantastical—this famous street, empty of cars but crowded with Chicagoans, waving flags in the brightly lit midnight.

"Take a good look around," I said to Ross, then thirteen, as we walked up the middle of Michigan Avenue. "Because you are never going to see this again." People whooped and hugged, beat cowbells, and chanted.

We were walking north, toward the brightly lit Wrigley Building in the distance. We passed in front of the Hilton and I stopped, actually bending down to pat my hand against the asphalt. "This was the Conrad Hilton," I told my boy, in my pedantic dad fashion, choking up a little. "This was the spot where the protesters sat down and were beaten by the cops in 1968. It was right here."

The contrast was stunning, between the long-ago violent night, so seared in public memory for so many years, and now this harmonious scene, not to replace it but to soothe it, finally, another cool layer of dirt spread atop the burning memory, adding to the 1996 Democratic Convention another strata of forgetfulness, the police this time watching from the medians, some steely-eyed, some scowling, some beaming, some bemused. Maybe it was finally time to put the 1960s away. Maybe the party was happening right now and we were in the middle of it.

I usually never smoke a cigar in front of the boys—I have an example to set—but this was a special night, and I pulled out a celebratory stogie, brushed off Ross's protests, and fired it up as we walked, taking in the commotion around us.

Did they dance in the street? Yes, they danced in the street. Were people really singing? Yes, I can report on good authority, that at least one prematurely cynical teenage boy, a born skeptic, by genetics and by upbringing, who earlier that evening compared Chicago to a wormy apple, "addled with corruption," spontaneously broke into song as he walked up Michigan Avenue at midnight.

"O beautiful, for spacious skies . . ." he began.

"For amber waves of grain," his father, no small cynic himself, joined in.

"For purple mountains majesty . . ." they continued together, loudly and off-key, really murdering the high notes, linked arm in arm. "Above the fruited plain. America, America, God shed His grace on thee, and crown thy good, with brotherhood, from sea to shining sea!"

Maria Pappas hired Sam. The Cook County treasurer met him, liked him, and took him on as a bank compliance officer. His job was to ride herd over the county's relationship with local financial institutions. Twelve billion dollars a year of taxpayer money flow through the treasurer's office. They don't keep it in a vault; they park it in various banks, and thus, as a huge honking depositor, they have a certain leverage with those institutions.

Or should. Cook County government is not a marvel of efficiency, even those departments under Maria Pappas's sweeping cameras and cracking bullwhip. Part of Sam's job was to pick over the bank fees and find places where money could be saved. To go to LaSalle Bank and say, "Hey, I see here you're charging the county a $10,000 monthly 'safekeeping' fee. Here's a thought—why don't you drop that fee, and we won't transfer the $900 million we have deposited with you over to the Harris Bank?"

Invariably, LaSalle Bank would grasp the beauty of Sam's logic. It was refreshing to see that kind of thing. Private business usually gets all the sharpies, because that's where the money is, and I liked watching my brother going through the pockets of these rather surprised local financial institutions, getting taxpayer money back.

Trying to get Sam a job felt wrong, but having helped him find one felt like the best thing I had ever done. Our parents were delighted. Big brother to the rescue. He got his health insurance, got the surgery he needed. Plus he worked in the County Building now, only a few blocks from the newspaper. We'd meet for lunch, or a drink after work. It beat the hell out of sending microcassettes to Japan.

And pulling that string made me feel that, in a real and tangible way, I had finally arrived. I was in the action, playing the Chicago game. I was the somebody who sent somebody.

Yes, from time to time one of Sam's subordinates—he rose through the ranks, quickly, and eventually had thirty people working under him—would want to get back at him. Occasionally, some disgruntled employee in the treasurer's office would call one of our investigative reporters and drop a dime on him—did we know that Neil Steinberg's brother is working here? I'm not sure what they expected—the newspaper to do an exposé, I suppose. Which they could have done, as far as I was concerned, perhaps in a general story blowing the lid off the secret relationship between

Richard and Maggie Daley, or the mysterious link between Mike and Lisa Madigan.

Perhaps because of this, because of the occasional suggestion that something was unseemly here, I made a point of putting Sam in my column, a process I think of as "homeopathic truth:" a dollop of revelation meant to prevent the disease of scandal from breaking out later.

Cook County commissioner Larry Suffredin had begun to draft legislation requiring that property tax be paid quarterly instead of twice a year—smaller payments, easier on the beleaguered consumer. Simple logic, in Larry's mousetrap mind. He did this without consulting the treasurer's office, which sends out the tax bills, a process that Sam was supervising by then, an ordeal he conveyed to me in excruciating detail. If you think it's a challenge to figure out your own tax bill and mail in your tax payment in a timely fashion, imagine the difficulty of figuring out the tax obligations of everybody in Cook County and then mailing them their bills on a strict schedule set by law. Endless hassles with formatting, printing, postage, plus legal requirements dictating what needs to go into the envelopes and what instructions must be given to baby-step the easily confused taxpayer through the process.

When this new quarterly payment law was proposed, Pappas let out a howl, which amazed Suffredin, who expressed the baffled innocence of do-gooders across the ages. Who could complain when we're so sincere? Is there a problem? What could possibly be the problem?

Knowing what I knew, I had to wade in. Bear in mind this was at the end of September. I wrote:

> Perhaps I can use my secret insider knowledge to explain it to the commissioner, who suffers from extraordinarily bad timing.
>
> Cook County has just finished printing 1.7 million property tax bills, a mammoth logistical challenge. My brother, Sam, supervises the task, switching his crisp suits for jeans and settling in on the 7th floor of the County Building to watch a room filled with high-speed printers belch this stuff out. It is a process fraught with possibilities for expensive and embarrassing screw-ups, so it has to be done exactly right. No piece of mail ever gets the scrutiny that a property tax bill does, and if it's wrong, not only do taxpayers complain, but the flow of money into the government stops.
>
> Suffredin choosing this moment to float his new law is like a husband, popping his head into the bespattered kitchen where his wife has just slipped

six German chocolate cakes into the oven, waving a recipe card and suggesting, "Honey, maybe the guests would like angel food cake instead."

Besides bad timing, Suffredin reveals an alarmingly loose grasp of the machinery of government he is jamming his fingers into.

"We probably can't do anything for this November," he told me.

Gee, ya think? Given that the tax bills are all printed up and being readied to mail, yeah, I suppose that changing the payment structure of the tax system before they get posted is probably a stretch.

There are two ways to view that column. You could say that I was shilling for Pappas, scratching her back because my brother works there. That's one perspective. Or you could take a completely opposite view: because my brother works there, I was in a unique position to cast light on a dumb grandstanding proposal—which, I must add, went nowhere.

Either way, my link to Sam is there for all to see, the wires of my decision-making process visible. Well, not entirely visible. I printed that he works there—no big secret—though left out the part of how he got connected to the job. Was that germane? Do I have to include a few agate lines at the bottom of anything I write about Northwestern, explaining that I went to school there and how Abe Peck got me my first job? I don't think so, because bias is on the page. You can be the most impartial reporter in the world and still turn out something skewed, through ignorance or accident. Or you can be completely partial and yet still be fair in your treatment of a subject. I wrote Ronald Reagan's obituary and I *despised* Reagan. Yet people were pleased with it, because I didn't allow my portrayal of him to be colored by the contempt I held, at least when I was a young man, but treated Reagan in a balanced, respectful way, as befits the passing of a president.

Frankly, my declining to trumpet my role in getting Sam hired was simple modesty. Given my druthers, I'd have advertised it: Neil Steinberg, powerful columnist, pulling the strings of elected officials, dispensing perks and favors with a generous hand. That's not an embarrassment to hide, that's an image to ballyhoo.

But you do something for a person, you ruin it by bragging. Bragging destroys any accomplishment. If, walking by a burning building, you hear a baby's cry from the upper floor and run inside, defying the flames, and reappear on the street with the rescued tot in your arms, a dramatic smudge of soot on her nose, and they stick a camera in your face, and you run a hand through your tousled hair and say, "Hey, did you see that? I just saved this baby! I'm the biggest hero in the goddamn world!"—at that point you might as well turn around and go put the baby back inside the burning building, because your name is mud. People will laugh at you and hate you forever, just for stating an obvious truth that puffs yourself up. Because people are looking for someone to hold in contempt—it's a basic human requirement, like the need for food and shelter—and changing societal values keep plucking away objects of comfortable scorn. Queers and cripples and colored folk might be off the table for most, but it's still open season on oblivious braggarts and always will be. That's why sports heroes are always aw-shucksing after every victory. They're trained to do that—they have to—and though reflexive it-was-a-team-effort mumbling sounds stupid at times, it doesn't destroy you the way self-congratulation would.

Which leaves me with the problem that some will say I'm bragging now, by recounting the tale here instead of leaving it buried. I hope it's not that simple. In my view, I'm telling a story about Chicago, about myself and my brother and our lives in the city. Whether it is a story worth telling or not is for other people to decide. Of course *I* find it interesting, but then again, I'm biased. I know the participants.

* * *

There is a statue of Irv Kupcinet on Wacker Drive, just south of Trump Tower, where the Sun-Times Building once was. He looks very much as he did in life, confident and calm, with a *Sun-Times* folded under his right arm, casually gesturing to the city with his left, as if giving it to you as a present. Although in life he wasn't ten feet tall.

It's odd, to know a man rendered into bronze. Actually, I've met six guys who ended up as statues on the streets of Chicago—Kup, Michael Jordan, Harry Caray, Jack Brickhouse, Ernie Banks, and Billy Williams. Quite a lot, really. Of the six, I only knew Kup and Brickhouse well, and I'll add that, despite knowing them, I believe only Jordan really deserves a statue, for his epic greatness. Statues honoring the others were erected by grieving friends and relatives or overzealous fans.

That's understandable, but also unwise, in my view—the city has warehouses filled with unwanted statuary, bronzes of forgotten figures. The statue of someone you never heard of doesn't keep the spark of his memory alive so much as it serves as a mockery, a monument to the all-encompassing vanity of human beings. As if bronze can thwart the obliterating hand of time. I'd rather have a phrase of mine live on than be cast in bronze. Kup, God bless him, was a nice man who knew a lot of celebrities. But if he wrote one memorable sentence in his sixty-year career, I missed it.

* * *

Up until 2010, I would never go downtown on the Sunday of the Chicago Marathon if it could possibly be avoided. This reluctance is due to the years that I worked on Sundays and would have to navigate the maze of marathoners and road closures and enormous crowds, trying to get to the newspaper the morning of the big race. One year I just abandoned the car and walked for half an hour to get to work.

But in 2010, Sam decided to run the marathon, and of course I came downtown to cheer him on, or try to. Kent and I grabbed a Metra train in the morning and took up a position at the corner of Halsted and Monroe, in Greektown. An endless stream of runners—some forty-five thousand—ran clopping forward, their faces slack with exhaustion. A crowd thirty times that size, holding encouraging signs, cheered their support. It's extraordinary to see the downtown so populated, not to celebrate some civic triumph or general holiday, but for forty-five thousand individual achievements. We stood for an hour, watching the runners stream by. None of them were Sam.

It occurred to me, scanning all these unfamiliar faces, hoping to see the one I knew—as if I didn't see him all the time—that the key to belonging to a city is not found in the years you rack up in a particular location, not in the Chicago history you may know, but rather in the familiarity, the bond you build with people in it. Otherwise, any city, even a city as grand and glorious as Chicago, is just an agglomeration of structures and strangers and chaotic disorder. A place you might want to visit for a week, look around, and then leave to go back home. You have to know people to be able to make sense of what is going on. Knowing people is the difference between being here and belonging here.

We eventually caught up with Sam—at the Palmer House, with his wife Yuri and his kids Rina and Ryan, now almost adults. Rina is in college, Ryan about to go. Kent and I shook Sam's hand and congratulated him, patted him on the back then left him to rest and headed back to our home in the suburbs.

16

The city in fog

WHEN THE PLANE carrying Kelly Cassidy made its approach to Chicago's Midway Airport, the young woman turned to peer out the window for the first glimpse of her new home. She had grown up on a beautiful little island off the west coast of Florida called Anna Maria, and as the plane came in to land, she looked down and wondered, *Why are there sand dunes at the airport?*

She had never seen snow before and had no context for it. It seemed to her like dazzling white sand. Nor had she ever worn a scarf for warmth, and puzzled over the winter scarf she had received as a going-away present. *What is this tiny piece of fabric supposed to do to help me? Don't I need some kind of head-to-toe polar suit?*

Cassidy almost immediately realized her mistake, and smiled at herself. But she never forgot that little burst of astonishment, when for one second she thought the beach had followed her from Florida and gathered around the airport runway to welcome her.

When I meet her for the first time, she is standing with her supporters within a jumble of metal barricades on Halsted Street, just north of Barry, an hour before the start of the forty-second annual Gay Pride Parade, a trim woman wearing almond-shaped eyeglasses in the dazzling sunlight of a bright, hot day late in June.

I haven't been back to the parade in eleven years, not since the day before we moved out of Chicago. Walking out of your condo and strolling over a block is an entirely different proposition from getting into your car and driving in from the suburbs, then maneuvering into the congested-on-an-ordinary-day Lake View neighborhood and trying to find a place to park. Then there were the kids to think about. "Hey boys, let's all go to the Gay Pride parade!"—that's not an activity most parents float past their grade-schoolers. Or their middle-schoolers for that matter. Some years I thought of going, but never acted on that thought.

Which would have been the case this year, too. But activist Rick Garcia has invited me to ride on a float with him, the float for the Civil Rights Agenda, a new organization. We'll be accompanying a dozen couples recently joined in civil union. Governor Quinn, who despite his political limitations, is a man of strong ethical principle, signed a law that went into effect a few weeks earlier affording gays and lesbians the protections of marriage, though still withholding the dignity of the word "marriage." I figure that whatever happens at the parade will be more interesting than reading the Sunday papers in my kitchen would be.

I do invite the family to the Gay Pride Parade. Edie wouldn't mind going, but she has already promised to help out her elderly mother. Ross, my older boy, declines. "Is not pride a sin, father?" he asks. He actually utters those exact words; he's fifteen, and greets the world with a puritan's stern, judgmental formality.

So I go alone, driving downtown, parking at the newspaper and taking the Brown Line—the el car is packed with people when it stops at the Merchandise Mart, just room enough for me to tuck in beside a pair of young guys with shaved heads and neat beards.

At Belmont Avenue, the train empties. We all pound down the stairs, into the festive commotion, past a line of transit workers in orange vests who are eyeballing the throng, then maneuver by vendors clustering around the station entrance, selling rainbow flags and strings of beads.

"Happy Pride! Happy Pride!" cries out Nick Kamboj, wearing a rainbow-colored Mohawk wig—a "Pride fauxhawk" he calls it—standing in front of the Standard India Restaurant, "the gayest little Indian restaurant in the world," he declares, selling cans of soda for a dollar apiece from a square tub filled with ice. "We've got mango lassi coming up," says Kamboj, a second-generation restaurateur, following his father, Pardip, who came to this country from New Delhi after seeing *Hollywood or Bust*, a Dean Martin/Jerry Lewis comedy that impressed him with the glittering bounty that is America. The senior Kamboj started a pen pal correspondence with a couple in Appleton, Wisconsin, who helped him immigrate, arriving in Chicago in 1974.

My float is supposed to be at Halsted and Barry. There are floats there, long, wheeled platforms covered with enigmatic white arches, but none display anything connected to the Civil Rights Agenda. I stop by a group of young people wearing identical t-shirts touting some politician to ask if anybody knows where float 20 is. Kelly Cassidy walks over.

The float I'm looking for is directly across the street, she tells me. They haven't gotten the signs on it yet because it was late in arriving—a lot of floats were vandalized last night in a warehouse in Bridgeport. Her float isn't even here yet.

Sometimes, it's better to be lucky than good. Out of the six hundred thousand people at the parade, I ask directions from a person who not only knows that fifty-one floats had their tires slashed the night before, but knows the name of the warehouse where the crime occurred, its location, and the owner's name and phone number. I call the news in to the city desk.

Like most people, Cassidy initially frames her reasons for coming to Chicago in grand, general terms. "I wanted to be in a bigger city," she says. "I wanted to live in a more open and accepting environment, being gay, and being a feminist, being a Democrat, all of those things."

That is the polite, ex post facto take. What got her on the plane at age twenty-two was not the social and political environment of Chicago, however, but the fact that she was in love with her girlfriend, an older woman who was ready to quit the confines of Florida and see the wider world. The girlfriend worked at Arthur Andersen. The accounting firm is now defunct, but at the time it was so far-flung that working for the company was in one sense like being in the military: you could put in for a transfer to another post. She requested three cities, Chicago among them because her parents lived in Indiana. Cassidy, who had never been outside Florida, went along to be with her, though it was Arthur Andersen that decided the couple would be together in Chicago rather than Atlanta or Boston.

Once in Chicago, with her girlfriend working, Cassidy needed to do something, so she went to the Chicago chapter of the National Organization for Women and volunteered. "That led to this," she says, gesturing to her t-shirt, which announces that Kelly Cassidy is a state representative to the Illinois legislature from the Fourteenth District. "I was the original nobody nobody sent."

So why did she remain? The relationship with her girlfriend that brought her across the country fizzled. Why not go back to Florida then? It's pretty there too. Why stay in Chicago?

"It's been home, from the minute I figured out how to use a scarf," she says. "I love the collection of neighborhoods. It is a big city full of small neighborhoods, and neighbors and community and friendliness. It's beautiful. I love being close to the lake. What I love is that you can go out and meet people from all over, find yourself in a conversation with a person from a different part of the world who had the same experience of landing here and finding their home. It's great."

* * *

Being on a parade float elevates you, so you can see the sweep of the crowd, not only lining the street, but up ahead, filling both sides, and the line of marchers nearly bridging the gap between them, melding into one enormous field of humanity, waving rainbow flags, hoisting signs, spanning the horizon. Nor can you tell that the people packing the sidewalks are waving enthusiastically at the passing parade in general—from the float, it seems as if they are waving at *you*, specifically, cheering ecstatically for *you*, and the only thing to do is smile and wave back, vigorously, arm raised and extended straight out, twisting your hand at the wrist as if you were polishing the sun.

A bouncy pop song—Lady Gaga's "Born This Way"—pumps from the float. A deeply tanned guy next to me—buzz cut, Castro Street mustache, sweat-soaked muscle t-shirt—holds a rainbow flag in both fists high over his head and shimmies ecstatically. I do the only thing a person can do under those circumstances: dance, bopping in place, grinning broadly, with nowhere to be but here, nothing to do but this, my own personality, my own hopes and worries, winking out of existence for a few glorious moments, replaced with an egoless joy, a communal happiness, and I have no other thought but the big blue summer sky, the enormous mass of people, their welcoming faces and outstretched hands, the whoops of enthusiasm, the dazzling sun, and the throbbing music.

* * *

Ed McElroy, a youthful eighty-three just a few summers earlier, turns an older eighty-six. The Cook County judges decide to have another publicist represent them for the next election. They don't officially fire Ed, but rather give his job to someone else—someone younger, someone connected, someone black. Ed takes the news hard—won't I call Tim Evans, chief judge of the Circuit Court of Cook County, he asks me, and see what I can do? Maybe he'll listen to me.

I try to back out—why would Evans listen to me, Ed? I'm nobody. But Ed has faith in me—I can do it. I can get him his job back.

I set the suggestion in front of me and examine it on all sides. At first glance, it seems like a bad idea. You stick your arm into the cage of the legal system, you never know what you draw back out. A bloody stump. The chief judge could resent me calling him, if he takes my call at all. He could feel threatened, intimidated. What kind of idiot calls a judge—the chief judge—to ask for special favors? And what can he do for Ed? Nothing. The judges group has already given the job to someone else.

But I have a nagging suspicion—that after all the years, after a wedding attended by two mayors, with the chief of police as his best man, after looking over in the passenger seat and seeing famous profiles from John F. Kennedy to Barack Obama, Ed's clout, his Chicago insider world, has boiled down to me, or me and a handful of marginal figures like me. Maybe I can't help Ed, but I have to try.

First, I have to decide what's possible. They aren't going to hire Ed back; they're just not. The decision has been made. So calling Tim Evans and asking him to do that would be wasting the one shot I've got for Ed. But maybe . . . maybe they can sit down and talk to him. Maybe somebody can buy him lunch, gently explain what they're doing. Put a good spin on it for Ed. Make him feel better. That's doable. That isn't asking the impossible. Nobody can put me in jail for suggesting that—I'm not asking anything for myself. This is for Ed. There's no reason loyal service should be summarily cut off. Ed has his pride.

I phone Evans, leave a message, and he calls me back immediately. That startles me. I give him a little spiel worked out ahead of time—this is a personal call, I tell him; this has nothing to do with the newspaper or coverage of his office. I'm phoning unofficially, on behalf of my friend, Ed McElroy, who performed so much good work for judges at election time over the years.

The chief judge is sympathy itself—of course Ed should be treated with respect. He and a few fellow judges have been meaning to take him to lunch, to talk to him. He promises they will call, right away. And Evans does, but Ed rebuffs him. I hadn't expected that. I misread the situation. Ed wants work, not sympathy. Shortly afterward, the Fraternal Order of Police lets Ed go, too, and I perform the same ritual with the president of the FOP, with the same nonresult. Ed doesn't seem to mind—he seems glad that I tried. As am I. We still go to lunch, huddling at a small square table at Gene & Georgetti, greeting the other old-timers as they pass by. Ed talks about the way it used to be while I listen, and we are both happy for each other's company.

* * *

Sometimes at the end of the day, after working at the newspaper downtown, in the spring and summer and early fall, if the weather is nice, I'll fire up a cigar on the walk to the train, and pause at the plaza between the old Daily News Building and the Chicago River to finish it. The plaza has square benches set around planters, each holding flowers and a tree, and it is pleasant to sit on a bench in the shade and read a newspaper or watch the people go by, to gaze across the river at the Civic Opera Building, shaped like a chair—the throne of Sam Insull, they used to say, the electricity king who built the opera house in the late 1920s. It's home to the Lyric Opera to this day, a reminder of the way the past can perpetuate anachronistic wonder into the present. Nobody would do it now; nobody would dare say, "Okay, let's put up a theater at Wacker and Madison. Let's have it seat 3,500 people, so there's plenty of room, and have the grand foyer be, oh, forty feet tall, all marble and bronze and gilt, with a deco stenciled ceiling—that'll impress 'em when they come in. And we'll put on shows, but let's have the shows be sung—no talking, that's low-class—with a full live orchestra. So let's have the orchestra and the singing, but not in English, not generally. Too easy. Let's have the shows sung in Italian and French . . . and *German*. . . . That's the ticket! Let's have the shows sung, with a live orchestra, in German, and five hours long, as a challenge to the audience . . ."

Nobody would do that now. Never. But there it is, today, nonetheless, a gift from the past.

As the time approaches for my train, I relocate to a spot just south and west of the Madison Street Bridge overlooking the water and the commuters streaming across the river. It is calming, reflective, a foot on the railing, to puff and watch and know the day is in the bag, only a train ride away from home and family and dinner and rest. A very content feeling, to gaze at the sun-dappled waters, a complex shade of undulating olive green and brown, a chance to remember how lucky I am, to be able to do something I love, to write about things I am interested in, to set my own routine, how precious, to be in this city, to go home to my family, to live this life of mine for these years. It might end any time—no one's future is certain, particularly not in newspapering, which seems to teeter and tremble at the precipice. At times it feels like I'm calmly spooning tomato soup at an outdoor restaurant on a cliff side that's crumbling into the sea. Every now and then another table or a few chairs clatter over the edge and I look up at the sound, startled, then sigh and go back to my soup. Sure, I could get up and leave the restaurant. I should. I must. But the truth is, I've been here for so long that I don't know where else to go—there might not be anyplace for me to go—and the soup is still right there, in front of me, for the moment. And it's good soup.

Eventually, when I really need to be getting to the train, I take a last puff of the cigar. Once I'd hesitate and linger until the very last second, until the glowing orange end approached my fingers, but eventually I've learned the concept of the last puff. There is always a last puff, an end, and rather than drag it out, rather than agonize, delay, and regret, it is better to take your last puff abruptly, flick your cigar butt into the river, and move on. Nothing to be sad about—with all cigars, as with all endeavors, all professions, all lives, there is always an end. There is always a last puff.

That last puff is coming, though we try not to think about it, busy with our lives. We have good days, bad days, good years, bad years; we chug along for so long it almost seems like forever. Then we peak, we age, the end of the roller coaster suddenly lurches into view, our energies wane, yet we plow forward, relying upon our momentum, our knowledge, our connections, to keep us in the fun a little longer, as gravity claws at the trajectory of our lives. Then at some point, usually very suddenly, it's all over, the ride jerks to a halt, and it's time for us to unbuckle and depart.

That's how it is for us. For the city, however, there is no end, no grand conclusion, no possibility of summation—any discussion of Chicago is by necessity a partial reckoning, a snapshot, a gloss of a topic of bottomless detail and complexity. Any stab at thoroughness overlooks whole chapters of wonder, long streets teeming with life, with shops and traffic and pedestrians in colorful clothing; any attempt to peer ahead immediately dissolves in a the-future-remains-to-be-seen cliché. You have to at some point just end. Take a final puff, flip it away, admire the ripple you made and be done.

* * *

The morning after the parade, I'm supposed to meet Joey Colucci to tour the Division Street Russian Baths. The grandson of Joe, son of Jimmy, Joey called me about three months earlier to say that he had bought the baths and would be reopening them. "I know how special the baths were to you," he says. I tell him I'd love to be the first to report their revival, and also want to see them—I haven't been inside for nearly five years. We arrange to meet there. Several times. Because every time we have an appointment to walk through the place so I can see what he's doing to it, he backs out at the last minute with some excuse. There are papers to sign. Meetings with banks. Trouble with the key.

My theory is, he is trying to help a pal who's promoting a new online business. Shortly after he first called me, the pal starts calling, dropping Colucci's name. He seems to think that would be enough to get me to write about his business and, at times, Colucci sounds more concerned with getting his pal in the newspaper than with publicizing the baths. The pal's business is nothing special, and my reaction is: first let's see the baths, then we'll worry about your friend.

This time we're set, Colucci assures me. Today we'll do it. We're meeting in front of the baths at 10 a.m. sharp. Still I have my doubts. "Joey Colucci isn't going to show," I tell my wife that morning. "But I'm going anyway." I get there twenty minutes early, buy a cup of coffee from the Milk & Honey Café next door—Wicker Park long ago went from blue collar to cargo shorts, from heavily working-class Polish to the international world of the comfortable young. Division Street is given over to cute little businesses, art galleries, and trendy bars: Real Naked Food, the Greenheart Shop. Nelson Algren would vomit.

I walk up the steps to the front door of the Russian Baths and peer through the plaster-smeared glass. It is utterly empty inside, the entire room gutted wall to wall, floor to ceiling—no barred window dispensing rough towels and Ajax Unbreakable Pocket Combs, no narrow hallway lined with *Herald-American* front pages, no sleeping room. Sheetrock and debris and an unhinged door are piled against the walls; there are a few metal chairs and a two round yellow coolers.

Hammering. The muffled sound of hammering. A good sign. Something is going on inside. I peer through the smudged glass door, see two workers. I rap a knuckle against the glass. Nod my head hopefully, pull at the door handle. Locked. One worker pauses, as if he hears, but he doesn't walk over. I knock again. Nothing.

Ten a.m. passes. 10:10. I see them moving around inside and start knocking and keep knocking this time. The workers disappear. Finally a man with close-cropped hair walks out from around the back of the building and challenges me in halting English. What do I want? I tell him I'm here to meet Joey Colucci. He looks at me blankly. Who? "You don't know who Joey Colucci is?" I ask. No, he doesn't. "Are you remodeling the baths?" He says no. They're doing work on the stairs.

I phone Colucci. He doesn't explain. He isn't apologetic. Says he'll be there in ten minutes. "The workers don't know who you are," I say.

"I told them to say that," he says.

"You'll meet me in front of the baths in ten minutes?" I say.

"Ten minutes," he says.

"You'll be out front in ten minutes?"

"I will."

He isn't coming—I'm certain of that—but I wait anyway. Two women with a stroller and a toddler walk by. "It's messy inside," the older woman tells the toddler, referring to her car. I check my watch: 10:15. I figure I'll give him until 10:30. I stand there, calmly, looking up at an elm tree and at the overcast morning sky to see if the rain will return, listening to the sound the cars make on the wet Division Street, a steady ripping noise, like long strips of tape being pulled away. I check my watch: 10:20 a.m.

For some reason, I'm not upset, I'm not annoyed, I'm not impatient. I'm not mad at Joey Colucci for standing me up. This all makes sense. Colucci is not reopening the Russian Baths—he's just another jamoke with a dream, trying to pull a scam that didn't work, trying to help a friend and too embarrassed to admit it. Or something else. Who knows why he called? Maybe he thought I'd announce he was reopening the baths without first establishing that he indeed owns them, and that my doing so would make it somehow magically happen. Maybe I shocked him by insisting he take me through the place. Or maybe he does own them; maybe he really is reopening the baths and this is all just miscommunication. People do strange, mysterious things. There's a lot of crazy in the world.

Ten twenty-five. It's all clear to me. He's never reopening the baths, but even if he does, it wouldn't be the old Russian Baths anyway; it would be something else, something different.

Nor would I be the same—I am not thirty and about to get married, living on Logan Boulevard. I'm fifty-one, married more than twenty years, living up in Northbrook with two teenagers. Nor is Sam a kid in Edie's old place on Melrose Avenue. We've changed. Sam wouldn't be able to pull himself away from the treasurer's office to sit and take the heat; he wouldn't want to hurry over from Arlington Heights for a massage. And who knows if dumping a bucket of cold water over your head would feel the same to a man in his fifties as it did for a man in his thirties. Even if the Russian Baths opened, which it won't—though you never know, the place still stands so anything is possible—we wouldn't end up coming here much. Two or three times, until the hard fact of the change and disappointment set in, and that would be it. Better to leave it in the past.

I peer through the glass again. The past isn't here; it's not a place. The past doesn't really exist. Only in our heads, in our hearts, and in books and movies. The past is a thought, a blurred photograph, a scratchy song, a memory no more substantial than the charge on a battery. The past is a big empty room where something once happened. A gutted building where something you loved used to be. You can't go back—you can remember it, read about it, cherish it. But the past isn't actually there, not anymore, and any attempt to find it, to hold it in your hands, to return to it in the living world must inevitably be thwarted.

At 10:29 a.m. a car pulls over to the curb in front of the baths. I take a step forward, hope dawning. But there is a couple in the car—it's not here for me. The car drives off again. At exactly 10:30, I turn and briskly walk half a block down Division to the van, never looking back, then get in and drive off. A quick left, down through the neighborhood of modest brick two-flats to Chicago Avenue, then another left.

Downtown Chicago is shrouded in fog, the top third of the John Hancock Building visible but the base obscured. It is an eerie, marvelous sight, this city of mystery and beauty, half seen, half hidden, distant yet right there.

The fog-wrapped city is so lovely, I pull over on Chicago Avenue and just sit and look at it for a moment. The Hancock Building. Nine Hundred North Michigan. The Montgomery Ward Building with Augustus Saint-Gaudens's *Spirit of Progress*—a woman holding a torch—atop it. I have my camera from the parade the day before, and try to take a picture, but the soft gray skyline doesn't register the way I see it. Too subtle, obscured by mist. I can look at it in front of me and savor it, but not capture or keep it. This moment now is all I have, all anybody ever has. One last glance, then I pull into traffic again, heading toward the newspaper, toward those enigmatic towers.

ACKNOWLEDGMENTS

This book exists because John Freeman, editor of *Granta*, the excellent British literary quarterly, invited me to contribute to their fall 2009 special issue about Chicago. Robert Devens, an editor at the University of Chicago Press, read "Driving with Ed McElroy" and wondered what kind of book I might write about the city. This is it.

Thanks to Robert, for his skillful oversight, and to his colleague Bill Savage—Northwestern University literature professor, baseball expert, and this book's thoughtful, knowledgeable editor, whose keen understanding and passionate love of the city was a tremendous asset, and whose steady, patient, good-humored guidance made writing this book a pleasure. Carol Saller, at the University of Chicago Press, was a meticulous and sensitive manuscript editor. Thanks as well to my friend and agent of twenty years, Susan Raihofer at the David Black Literary Agency, who stepped away from the big-money rainforest of commercial publishing and into the more modest linden grove of academia to help shepherd this book along.

Were it not for the kindness, energy, wit, and enthusiasm of Ed McElroy, that grand gentleman of Chicago, none of this would have happened, and I treasure my friendship with him, with a nod of course to the secret of his success, Rita Marie, mother of three.

This book was researched at the Northbrook Public Library, the Northwestern University Library and the Newberry Library—thanks to their helpful staffs.

Cook County treasurer Maria Pappas generously shared her memories with me. Thanks to her, as well as to Dr. Eva Dreikurs, Prof. Abe Peck, Illinois Rep. Kelly Cassidy, former State Sen. Rickey Hendon and George C. Schneider.

I can't list all the figures on the Chicago scene who make me feel at home here, but I have to mention a few, such as Rich Melman, who gave many of my books a hearty send-off. Thanks to Illinois Supreme Court justice Anne Burke, Roe Conn, Art Danz, Grant DePorter, Dominic Di Frisco, Jay Doherty, Sen. Dick Durbin, Tony Durpetti, Justine Fedak, Rick Garcia, Chris and Sheila Kennedy, Magda Krance, Kelly McGrath, Kasey Madden, Illinois attorney general Lisa Madigan, Ken Price, special agent Ross Rice, Rich Varnes, and Eric Zorn.

The *Chicago Sun-Times* has been my home for twenty-five years, and I must express my gratitude for the extra forbearance required by this volume to publisher Tim Knight, editor in chief Jim Kirk, and managing editor Craig Newman. Were Jim Tyree alive I'd thank him too, for saving the newspaper at its moment of crisis, but since his tragic passing, I'll have to be satisfied to honor his memory: a good, decent man who loved Chicago. And a warm welcome to our new chairman, Michael Ferro Jr., who believes that a city needs a newspaper, whatever form it takes.

Thanks also to Mark Brown, Chris De Luca, Albert Dickens, Roger Ebert, Zach Finken, Scott Fornek, Tom Frisbie, Andrew Herrmann, Jack Higgins, Rummana Hussein, Mark Konkol, Tom McNamee, Frank Main, Carol Marin, Mary Mitchell, Maureen O'Donnell, Abdon Pallasch, Richard Roeper, Terry Savage, James Smith, Polly Smith, Shamus Toomey, Brian Washington, Bill Zwecker, and all my other friends at the *Sun-Times*.

Particular thanks to my pal at the *Tribune*, Rick Kogan, the dean of Chicago journalism, who gave the manuscript a careful read, as well as to Colleen Kelly. And to Rick and Judy Telander and the members of the Lake Superior Philosophical Society. Plus a fond good-bye to my friend Jeff Zaslow, who was always so supportive, and who read the first hundred pages of this book, but never got the chance to finish the rest.

My brother Samuel Steinberg courageously allowed me to tell his story, with only one caveat—"Just don't get me fired"—and I've tried to avoid that. Thanks to him, as well to his lovely wife, Yuri, and their kids, Rina and Ryan. Thanks to my parents, June and Robert Steinberg, for indulging the occasional barbs that show up in my writing; to my sister, Debbie; and to my cousin, Harry Roberts and his wife Yi. Thanks to the entire Goldberg clan—Alan, Cookie, and Don Goldberg, and Jay and Janice Sackett, as well as my lovely, smart nieces Julia, Esther, Rachel, Sarah, and Beth.

I'm a man blessed with old, true, good friends—Robert and Val Leighton, Cate Plys and Ron Garzotto, Jim and Laura Sayler, Kier Strejcek and Cathleen Creiger, Larry and Ilene Lubell, Sandi and Lise Schleicher—plus some wonderful neighbors: Michael and Shelly Frame, Bill and Carla Martens. Thanks as well to the indefatigable Michael Cooke, the older brother I never had.

Finally, bottomless gratitude to my own family, my sons Ross and Kent, whose curiosity helps me to appreciate the city anew, and finally, as always, a kiss-laden thanks to my wife, Edie. This book is dedicated to you, my city girl, because I never would have made it in Chicago without you.